SHE

of the

SEA

LUCY H. PEARCE

WOMANCRAFT PUBLISHING

The information provided in this book is intended to complement, not replace, the advice of your own doctor or other healthcare professional, whom you should always consult about your individual needs and any symptoms that may require diagnosis or medical attention and before starting or stopping any medication or starting any new course of treatment.

Published by Womancraft Publishing, 2021
www.womancraftpublishing.com

ISBN 978-1-910559-71-0
She of the Sea is also available in ebook format: ISBN 978-1-910559-70-3

Design and typesetting: Patrick Treacy, lucentword.com
Cover image © Lucy H. Pearce
Illustrations: Bodor Tividar, S.N.Ph, AlinArt, chronicler
(all Shutterstock.com)

Womancraft Publishing is committed to sharing powerful new women's voices, through a collaborative publishing process. We are proud to midwife this work, however the story, the experiences and the words are the author's alone. A percentage of Womancraft Publishing profits are invested back into the environment reforesting the tropics (via TreeSisters) and forward into the community.

Other Books by Lucy H. Pearce

Creatrix: she who makes
Medicine Woman: reclaiming the soul of healing
Burning Woman
Full Circle Health: integrated health charting for women.
Full Circle Health: 3-month charting journal
Moods of Motherhood: the inner journey of mothering
Reaching for the Moon: a girl's guide to her cycles
Moon Time: harness the ever-changing energy of your menstrual cycle
The Rainbow Way: cultivating creativity in the midst of motherhood

5% of the royalties from this book will be shared between the following charities to support those working tirelessly on the issues raised in this book:

> Ballycotton RNLI, our local lifeboat charity.
> Clean Coasts Ballynamona, a local environmental charity which is dedicated to this part of the East Cork coast.
> Greenpeace, an international charity dedicated to protecting our oceans.
> As I Am, an Irish charity supporting autistic people and their families.
> Mermaids, a UK charity supporting gender-diverse children and their families.

For Patrick,
with deepest gratitude and love.

This is my love song. To the ocean. To becoming. To magic.
To freedom. To me. To you.
And to our future as a species.

Contents

OPENING

I am wind on sea,
I am ocean wave,
I am roar of sea.

The first words spoken on the island of Ireland
by chief poet and druid, Amergin

The Road to the Sea

The sea makes itself felt, even when it is not seen. It is there in the low-hanging mist trapped in the valley, in the browning boglands dotted with migrant birds, in the salt wind that buffets the rooks.

The thorn trees lean inland, after a lifetime of salt winds sculpting them, silent ciphers of the sea beyond the skyline where the fields end and the cliffs drop away. The statue of Mary, Star of the Sea, looks out from her rocky grotto, arms open towards the ocean. A lone pink thrift flower bobs in the breeze at her feet, white gulls wheeling over the golden stubble of the newly harvested wheat fields behind her. Mackerel clouds swim against a powder blue sky, the last swifts darting.

I pass the graveyard, which stands on a blind bend, mossy weather-worn stones leaning at strange angles. Around the corner, the mountains appear as if by magic, purple and hazy in the distance, and then the grand reveal that takes my breath away every day, as the bay sweeps into sight, startling in its turquoise majesty. Expansive and wild, it calls the adventurous spirit to follow it to freedom.

I cannot resist. I take the winding boreen down to meet it: a road only wide enough for one car, and unused enough that there is grass growing up the middle. The hedges hug the sides of the car: fat red fuchsia buds dangle like Christmas baubles against the green bushes. The last of the montbretias' fiery flowers are fading. I park and walk to the silver sands.

I am called by four friendly voices – their faces obscured by the low-hanging September sun. Every day, all year, these women gather, to swim, to talk, to escape from the challenges of lives that sometimes seem insurmountable, emerging from their daily baptism in hope for a better day.

The waves crash, the birds wheel.

I breathe it in.

1

THE CALL OF THE SEA

The sea that calls all things unto her calls me,
and I must embark.

Kahlil Gibran, *The Prophet*

Sea Shell

ome, join me. I've been waiting for you. Slip off your shoes. Feel your toes sink into the sand. Stand with me here on the beach and look out at the vast expanse of blue sea receding into sky. Breathe in the freshness of the air and let your shoulders drop as you do. Feel yourself small and insignificant, yet part of something magnificent.

Come down to the water's edge, let the waves lap at your toes and the wind play with your hair. Then let us walk together, until something catches your eye, a white shell with blushes of pink.

You lift the shell to your ear and marvel: the rush of the sea is right here in your hands.

You had forgotten, or maybe never knew, that everything that has been shaped by the sea holds within it a saline memory: the song of the sea. Each shell, each piece of glass tumbled by the waves, each pebble worn smooth by the tides. Every time you hold it and listen with your whole self, a portal opens to the inner sea. With a pebble you feel it in the solidity of your own bones. In some shells you see it reflected in their iridescence. And in the rarest still you hear it, captured for all time, no matter how far from the shore it is taken.

You hand it to me. I hold it to my own ear and listen.

What is it trying to tell me? I wonder.

I offer you this book, as a naming of the magics of the sea. I invite you to experience the reading of it as a walk along a seashore scattered with treasures. Consider each part a pebble for your pocket, each poem a shell for your ear. You might feel the desire to walk its full length in one go. Or pick out the shells that most catch your eye on each walk. As we stroll together, you might catch sight of a tail above the waves, drop this book to the sand and run out into the depths to swim with it.

There is bountiful flotsam washed up on the shore waiting

4

for you to discover the treasures you need today, and much which will repay your courage if you choose to dive deep. May *She of the Sea* be of service, in whatever way you need it, so that wherever you are you may hold the gifts of the sea in your hands.

Me and the Sea

I cannot remember a time when I have not known in my bones that the sea is a great power.

Carol P. Christ

One cold December day, as I was writing this book, I watched the new film of Daphne du Maurier's classic novel *Rebecca* with my husband. It is a book I have returned to time and again since my teens. He is not familiar with her work, so I explain to him that the sea is a character in her books, always there in different moods. It carries the story along, delivers new events: it is a presence as real as any of the human protagonists. The same is true for the works of many other women writers I love: Iris Murdoch, Virginia Woolf, Jeanette Winterson...

I realise that the sea is a central character in my story, too. She has always been there. Her proximity is felt. Her absence noted. Seeing her is like breathing. Being close is like feeling my own pulse. When the sea is near, I am my most alive. I know that all is well in the world. The further from the sea I get, the further from myself I feel. I find myself parched and on edge, as though wondering where my next breath will come from.

An American friend mentioned that she lived six hours from the sea. I know that this is a geographical possibility. But it is a psychological impossibility for me. Even the thought of it makes me feel trapped. I just couldn't. It seems such a cliché to be so taken with the sea. All I know is that it is my truth.

"I have seafoam in my veins, and I understand the language of waves."[1] The sea is my psychic life blood. She is in my soul and I in her. She is my primal ground of being, a passion beyond reason and logic, a necessity, not a luxury. Admitting the centrality of the sea to my psyche was somehow vital for my journey. Sharing it is too.

I wish I could explain exactly how and why – and this book is certainly an attempt at an answer – but perhaps, even more, it is an excuse to immerse myself more deeply in this passion, in blue and water and words, in soul and flow and magic.

As I begin to try to articulate what the sea means I find a tumble of words, waves of memories rushing towards me all at once: of storms and swells; of sailing and sex; the daily magic of the moon tugging the tides; my fascination with stories of birds that could be goddesses; the way that when I make a spiral of stones on the strand time stands still and a portal opens inside, and each pebble in my hand is a planet, a moon, an egg, each with its own colour and texture and feelings; how I have wanted to walk into the water and not come back; how the chill of winter scares me off swimming even though I really want to try it; how I love to skim stones even though I am not very good at it; how the birds lift off together as one from the shallows and how I talk to them even though they cannot understand; how the inlet has changed course over the years and I wonder how you can know where the salt water becomes fresh, and the time I rowed my boat down that inlet and got stuck in the reeds, and how I bought a little inflatable boat so that my children could have the same adventure but in reverse, so they could know what it means to be afloat with an oar, but how I didn't take the boat down to the beach for years because some sort of shame and fear and practical confusion overcame me…I want to tell you about all this and more. This is what the sea means to me.

"One of the many possible ways to describe a life," reflects Wallace J. Nichols, in his book *Blue Mind*, "would be as a series of encounters with various bodies of water. Time spent in, on, under or near water interspersed with the periods spent thinking about where, when and how to reach it next." This is certainly true for me. And I have a feeling it may be for you, too. We each have our stories of the sea: the way the salt and sand have infused our cells on summer picnics and blustery winter walks, on boat trips and swimming adventures. These are some of those that formed me.

My summers were spent on the shore. There I am with the shaggy dirty blond hair and no clothes, a thin coating of sand on my skin. All the other children wore swimsuits, but me, only sand. Back then I didn't know why. No one did.

I had a little yellow rowing boat that I would row around the bog pond my father had dug many years ago, taking picnics to eat on the island. The pond is now overgrown, the boat was stolen.

There I am, in another boat, this one with sails, side by side with my first love, sailing into the wind each summer. Something about the sea bonded our quite different souls and initiated me to love.

And then, with my life-love, sitting on the damp sand on the strand in the village that we still live. Two teenagers, huddled away from the fire and the party, in the deep blue night, weaving our own world of dreams together to the gentle wash of the waves.

On our travels together we watched whales and dolphins in New Zealand. In Vietnam I kayaked on the ocean for the first time, into sea caves in a limestone landscape of a thousand islands. We swam with sea turtles in Indonesia and snorkelled on coral reefs in Australia. I will never forget that feeling of seeing a totally alien, magical world appear, in vibrant colour, right there beneath me.

It changed something in me. Made me realise the life, the magic, that lies beneath, that we go through our days totally oblivious to.

Here I am again, sat on a picnic blanket on the beach I have spent so much of my life on, watching the waves break on the rocky lighthouse island. My own small children are digging in the sand around me. The other women chat brightly, but I feel strange and cut off from them, trying to find a safe harbour inside, outside, a place to anchor myself in the whirl of their words.

It was on the same strand that I made my commitment to Her, age thirty-three, on my birthday, something clicked in my soul. "Bring it on!" I said to the waves, opening my arms to them. She did. That was the year that Womancraft Publishing was born. It was the beginning of my Burning Woman initiatory process. My journey to self-understanding.

Little did I know where it would lead.

Learning the Sea

I was born in Kazakhstan, without any connection to the sea. I have a very multicultural and multireligious family and every part of my family has its own history of leaving home and to start a new life somewhere else – some of them were forced, some of them decided to move and some were nomads.

When I was six, my parents moved to Northern Germany, where I saw the sea for the very first time in my life. Not just one: I was surrounded by the Baltic Sea and the North Sea. Maybe it is because of my family history that I always feel like I don't belong anywhere. I feel like a nomad.

I feel the trauma of my family (war, violence, religious conflicts, being uprooted and homeless) so deeply. Sometimes I long for roots. I walk in the woods and feel their old wisdom and life. But the sea, especially the North Sea, is the only place where I feel free. The wind and the water make me feel safe. At the sea I feel that it is okay to be a nomad and I realise that no matter how hard I long for being rooted, I won't be happy until I'm on my way again, sailing somewhere unknown...

Lina Garvardt

The Lighthouse

When I was a child, on foggy nights,
The booming wail of the foghorn
Could be heard from the top of the
tower in which I slept.

I am here, I am here!
Rocks ahead,
I am here!

Technology moved on.
The lighthouse keeper left.
The foghorn was silenced.
The light automated.
But still it sweeps each night across the waves
In every weather.
Red towards us here on the rocky land,
White out to sea:

I am here!
Beware the rocks!

My name means light.
Sometimes I feel
That somewhere, at some time, I
agreed to be a lighthouse.

I am here!
Beware the rocks!

Here on my island, with only the flash
of light to share what I know.

I am here!

Belonging

*Our inner landscapes mirror the outer
landscapes in which we live.*
Eila Kundrie Carrico, *The Other Side of the River*

This particular swathe of sand and stormy seas feels as much part of me as my own blood – a contour of coast that I have walked and talked and danced and drawn on, swum and fished and made my own over my four decades thus far. Always, always the sea calls me when the furies race in my head. I walk the strand and allow the wind that caresses my hair to blow the anger from my mind. The ocean unfurls to distant shores, crossed by vast container ships, pocket-sized on the horizon, gently reminding me of my own insignificance. The lighthouse on the island reminds me of solidity and strength when all is foggy and wild. It teaches me, time and again, that storms pass.

I love the liminal times of early morning and late evening, where day slips into night. And whilst it looks most beautiful on blue-sky days, drawing crowds of tourists from far and near, I love the wild, grey stormy days when the seaweeds are piled knee deep, draping the monochrome shore with black, green, gold, brown, hot pink and purple, like mermaids' hair, braided by divine fingers.

All is alive here. It is not just the water but the sand, the sky and time itself that ripples. Each reflects the other. The reedbeds and flowered dunes, the lagoons and pools are connected and then cut off. The landscape is always being remade, redrawn by waves and winds and tides – expanding and contracting – welcoming us in, pushing us away, reminding us that the only thing that is constant is change.

This is a wild place of seaweed and washed-up fishing nets, silver sand and ragged black rocks that cut your feet if you slip. Water so cold it makes you gasp on all but the hottest of summer days. It is a strand where razor clams and lugworms lie hidden deep in sinking sands. No corals or multicoloured fish here, instead our underwater magic comes as shoals of iridescent striped mackerel that run each summer, and lobsters that hide in the rocks. The butter-coloured limpets and spiral shells of periwinkles, shrimps never bigger than your thumb, and the tiny scuttling mottled green crabs beloved by both gulls and children. The rocks are guarded by the lone cormorant and occasional majestic heron that sit sentinel watching the silvery sprats. There are seals and dolphins too, though I have never seen them alive.

Running behind the strand is the bog, a precious limbo land of tufted marram grass, hidden pools and sinking mud, rolling mists and migrating birds rising as a cloud. This is a sanctuary, protected by law. Acres upon acres dedicated to our feathered friends: magical, mysterious, silent and untouched. Wild heaven…with horseflies to keep us real.

And rising up beyond it are the pines and ash of my father's land that he planted as a boy, the only break of tall trees in the whole landscape, which shelter us from storms.

I am a native of coastal places, where land meets water, places of invasions and exiles, of wild beauty and loss, shorelines peopled with stories of giants and pirates, smugglers and fishermen, hidden gold and sunken ships. Fields with mysterious mounds and fairy trees not to be touched. Of strange lights on the cliffs and eerie wails in the night. This is what my ancestors have known: the Celtic shorelines – from England, Ireland, Scotland and Wales.

This little seaside village on the south coast of Ireland is where I feel most at home. It is the through-line of my life, my father's life. And yet…

oOo

The Irish side of my family are 'blow-ins.' We came in via the sea, fleeing a war we didn't believe in, seeking sanctuary in a land our

people had subjugated for centuries. My grandparents arrived looking, longing for a community of freethinkers and ended up here. And
whilst we have lived in many places, this coast, this little sea-edged
village, has kept calling four generations of us back, even though we
don't fully belong.

The Celtic Sea – I only recently discovered – is the official name for
the sea that borders our home. I had always known that the wildness
of the Atlantic didn't quite fit our beneficent stretch of water. The Atlantic Ocean is a different being altogether, whipping up hurricanes,
carrying the gentleness of the Gulf stream to warm our climate. Its
vast expanse crossed by hunger ships to the dream-turned-nightmare
of America where another beloved branch of my family lives, married
to earlier Irish immigrants done well.

Nor is it the Irish Sea, the stretch of water that connects us to our
shared heartland of Wales, my paternal grandmother's homeland –
the place that I have travelled through again and again on my journeys linking my Irish soul to my English body. The journey that my
father and I took on big ferries with little boxes of cornflakes for
foggy breakfasts, to return me to my mother. The journey my husband and I took, sometimes apart and sometimes together, to come
home, to our land, to each other. The voyage that my grandmother
took heavily-pregnant, avoiding German U-boats, to deliver her second child in the London blitz so that it might survive: a fate her first-
born did not get at the hands of the Irish nuns.

Whilst the Irish Sea has bisected my life, the Celtic Sea has drawn
me together: the jagged rocks and slate grey wa-
ters, reaching forth from Ireland, skirting the
northern shore of France, to the lands of
Catalunya. These Celtic coastlines that
cross modern borders draw me back to the
lost parts of myself that don't fit this strange
modern land-life. The water carries on down to
the 'wine-dark' warmth of the Mediterranean.
The sparkling azure sea that felt like homecoming as a teenager, having seen it for many years in

the holiday photographs of my maternal grandmother whose 'itchy feet' always brought her back to the home of shapeshifting goddesses and sea odysseys, ancient ruins and islands covered in sugarlump houses.

Though we humans have a fascination for drawing lines on maps, dividing up the land and her peoples, the sea is one great body of water, one fluidity, going where it will. And so, though we are taught to understand and interpret the world by our land maps, we know it instinctively by the sea and our souls. We are taught to believe that we do, or rather we should, come from one place. We are raised to be proud of the land we call home, to be happy to spill our blood – or the blood of our children – to protect it. But what about those of us that don't come from just one place, just one land? Who find our souls stretched and bisected by bodies of water? Those of us whose identities are more fluid than small tick-boxes on forms allow for. This is the reality of so many of us, whose nationalities, genders or neurology are neither one thing or another, but inherently fluid, both/and. How do we honour this fluidity? We, I think, are perhaps more likely to honour the sea in ourselves, in our identities. We are we of the sea.

The Song of The Irish Sea

Both my parents had to cross the water to find each other, to create me. One from Nigeria, the other from Ireland. But there has been only one sea whose waters have intertwined themselves in my soul: the Irish Sea who trickled her way inland to the stream that runs through my grandmother's farm, that offered play to my mother as a child and fertility to the land and the cattle her brothers raised on it.

The sea was my doorway to adventure. Freedom from the suffocating constraints of London council estate living. This small expanse that called to me, offering all the love, laughter and sanctuary that lay on the opposite shore.

On board the ferry, the grey waves would toss and threaten, and while my mother's face turned green, I watched the waves, feeling their power, knowing it was their choice to let me pass, wondering if this time they would offer me a glimpse of the magic beneath.

Each crossing I knew that not only were we leaving the city behind but all the darkness that often came with it. As we crossed, and she parted to welcome us through, the armour would fall away, an unnecessary weight lifted from our shoulders. I would look back, knowing somehow that she would not allow harm to follow us, you had to be invited, you had to hear her call.

For the first time in forty years, I cannot answer her: my soul sings my half of our duet, but my body is being held here on England's shores. I watch the waves lapping at the coast, I dip my toes and eyes closed pull in her magic. These waters are a part of my blood and if I'm quiet I can hear the whispered stories they hold, of strength, power and resilience. She keeps safe the story of me.

Adeola Sheehy-Adekale

Litera-sea

I must down to the seas again, to the lonely sea and the sky.
John Masefield, "Sea Fever"

I have always been drawn not only to the sea, but to art and writing about it. I have an incessant need to immerse myself in the ocean – literal and interpreted – in order to find myself once more.

I am not alone in this. Galleries are full of seascapes. Libraries are packed with words trying to give voice to what this call of the sea is, why it enchants us so. "The sea," in the words of oceanographer Jacques Cousteau, "once it casts its spell, holds one in its net of wonder forever."

But I found, as I explored this genre of sea-words and images whilst researching this book, that so many circumnavigate shorelines...and feelings. They skirt around the edges in safe descriptions and faithful literal representations of the ocean, afraid of getting wet, getting out of their depths, being washed out by the tide. They allude to, but never fully immerse themselves in, the soul of the sea.

This book dives deep, exploring the sea's role in human culture from many different perspectives: myth, folklore, modern medicine, literature, neurobiology, geology, evolutionary theory, depth psychology, magical and wise woman traditions and most of all, from the least valued of all ways of knowing: lived experience.

We start with the physical sea and shore, the literal ocean of this blue planet, which we are all familiar, but often not intimate, with. We then gradually develop more metaphysical (meaning beyond the physical world) understandings of the sea, worlds more commonly explored in art, spirituality, philosophy and magic, realms of soul, which may be less familiar to some readers. We begin to understand the sea as a portal to other worlds – both within...and beyond.

For the sea is not *just* a literal place to heal and nourish the body and mind. Not *just* a complex ecosystem or natural beauty spot that can engender a sense of calm and belonging. As Mary Oliver so wisely observes in her poem, "The Waves": "The sea isn't a place/ But a fact and a mystery." Every aspect of the sea holds profound metaphorical power. The outer seascape provides so many corollaries for human psychology in general, and women's psychology in particular. This is the reason it has haunted the myths and legends – the psychology before psychology – of so many cultures. And it is why water is present in most spiritual rituals. The sea speaks to the soul. Our ancestors knew that beneath the depths lay much wisdom. They knew that the way to our own depths was through the depths of the ocean.

See that dark line of seaweed, thrown up by the tide, which gathers on the pebbles there, between sea and land? That dark band represents the threshold between one world and another, for at the water's edges, so the old Celtic stories say, you can cross over into the Otherworld. Myth is born here, cast up out of the waves, there for the taking by any beachcomber.

Sharon Blackie, *If Women Rose Rooted*

We have moved from being creatures that have evolved from, with, beside and in the sea, to being alienated from it. The sea, which has woven through our myths, stories, music, food and psyches since the beginning, has become just another resource. In the last century, our culture's respect for the sea has diminished as our ability to traverse her safely and exploit her resources has grown. Patriarchal capitalism has stretched its greedy tentacles out to sea: insatiable, irresponsible, anonymous, rapacious.

This book calls us back to a personal relationship with the wild sea, reminding us of just how intertwined our stories have been from the beginning. It is an urgent call to reweave a new way of being once more that centres the sea in our survival. I want to encourage you to reflect on how we might move from perceiving the ocean as day-trippers or tourists do, seeing it merely as a place of leisure and aesthetic beauty, to understanding the depth of power it holds for us as a species.

The idea of having a living relationship with something non-human or even 'inanimate' may sound strange to modern ears. But this has been the way of most humans who have lived by or worked on the sea since the beginning of our story. Fishermen, foragers, sailors and shore-dwellers had to develop a dynamic relationship, one that respected the vagaries of wind and waves, that followed the stars and honoured unseen forces. They had to trust themselves to the sea in body and soul each time they ventured out, knowing that each trip could be their last. They had to learn to read her signs and respect her power. They lived in reciprocity with her, knowing that as the sea would give, the sea could also take away. They remembered that we humans are only ever visitors to this realm of mystery and awesome power. The sea was part of their prayers and stories, songs and very selves.

So how do we reclaim this for ourselves? I believe we need to find words and images to be able to share our experiences and knowings: we need litera-sea. We will explore many different modes of language to give voice to our growing awareness of what the sea is and represents. In this book you will find poetry, prose, facts and reflections to help you to see and know from different angles, to encourage a multi-perspectival way of engaging, rather than the monolithic logical/intellectual approach that is the norm in our culture. I hope to help you cultivate the witness self that looks outwards to the literal sea and inwards to the inner sea, so that you become more proficient in the reading of signs and their meanings in both. The movement of water over rocks. A shift in the sky's colour, the clouds and the wind. The behaviour of the creatures that live there. All speak of unseen tides, currents, swells, storms... In time, this reading of signs will become second nature, a knowing that creates its own vocabulary: working words for lived experience.

As I was writing this book, an incredible project was underway from Irish cultural and language historian, Manchán Magan, who travelled around the island of Ireland collecting lost and forgotten Irish words specifically connected to the sea.[2] Some that he collected were practical terms for types of waves and rocks, vital for fishermen but few others. But alongside this environment-specific vocabulary, were words and stories that reflected people's implicit understanding of the sea's haunting mystery and metaphysical properties that most of us experience. From the Mullet Peninsula in County Mayo, he discovered the term *caibleadh,* meaning "spirit voices heard on the sea on calm nights." And my favourite, *uaigneas an chladaigh,* which describes "the sense of loneliness on the shore, a haunting presence of people who lived and died long ago." As the man who shared it, Pap Murphy, reflects, "if you would ever walk on the shore alone, whether the tide is in or out, whether it's late or early, there's always a sense there's something spiritual telling you that you are not there alone."[3]

This felt sense of a great presence beyond the physical, which we perceive on, in or beside the sea, is an experience shared by many, and yet one that we do not have the language to express. It is strange, both unsettling and comforting at the same time. It is to this experience, of the places where the outer sea meets the inner sea, that *She of the Sea* attempts to give words.

My own native tongue is English, another island language. One that has woven in and out with Irish to create the linguistic culture of the land on which I live. It is through English that I have learned to see the world. In English, the sea provides us with a rich shared and familiar vocabulary of metaphors that put the ocean, and our relationship with it, at the heart of how we speak about change – both inner and outer. We find ourselves using these words naturally as we describe ourselves as 'drowning' or 'deluged' when we feel overwhelmed and stressed. We are 'out of our depths,' 'in over our heads,' 'all at sea' or worst of all 'dead in the water' when we cannot cope with something. We look 'washed out' when we are ill. We are 'like a fish out of water' when we don't fit in. We 'make waves' when we 'swim against the tide' with the 'big fish.' Opportunities and people 'slip through the net,' but we are reassured that there are 'plenty more fish in the sea.' If we are lucky and 'the coast is clear,' life is 'plain sailing.' But right now, is a time of 'sea change', we are in 'uncharted waters' as a species on this planet. The 'tides are turning' and we are going to have to 'cast our nets wider' in order to find solutions.

As a neurodivergent woman, each of these metaphors creates vivid images in my mind when I hear them. This is why I love to understand myself and the world through the richness of metaphor. Metaphor allows the illogical and mysterious parts of myself to find form and voice, helping me to find pattern and meaning in the confusion and overwhelm of lived experience. I share this approach here with you, in the hope that it might be of value to you too.

Having a shared lexicon can help us communicate what we discover as we dive into the murky depths of our souls. As Clementine Morrigan says, "There aren't words in English for so many of the things that I know."[4] In my experience, the vocabulary of the sea can help us to language our souls, our inner seas, that lie beneath conscious awareness and beyond daily conversation.

As we begin to understand the metaphorical and metaphysical aspects of the ocean, the shell, the pebble, we begin to shift our perception, seeing them not *just* as objects in their own right, but as potential portals to expanded states of being, to the transcendent, the universal soul that so many artists, poets, mystics and storytellers throughout our cultural history have alluded to. Barry Lopez describes it thus, in his award-winning book, *Arctic Dreams:* "Occasionally one sees something fleeting in the land, a moment when land, colour, and movement intensify and something sacred is revealed, leading one to believe that there is another realm of reality corresponding to the physical one but different." This is the realm of the sacred, the divine, the magical, which our modern systems of government, education and medicine seem determined to deny and live without. But this approach is not working for us as individuals, communities or our world.

The promise of the sea is the promise of a journey into the depths and to other lands. To the unknown. To see what lies below and beyond. Far beyond the language of land, the tides pull us into birth and sex and death, into creativity, into new ways of understanding ourselves and our world, into the deep Feminine, the sacred. It is a state of being to which we are called back, again and again.

For those familiar with my body of work, *She of the Sea* combines many threads I have picked up before in previous books and image making: the moon and her cycles; navigating the unknown; healing; the Feminine; harnessing our creativity and spirituality; flow consciousness; learning to live from the soul... In my first book, *Moon Time,* and later in *Full Circle Health,* I explored how to navigate a constantly changing inner terrain – biological and psychological – and how to better understand our cycles. In *Burning Woman,* I unpacked the silencing of the Feminine and what Feminine power can look like through the element of fire. In *Medicine Woman,* I explored women, healing and soul. In *Creatrix,* I reflected on creativity as a flow state, like a river or stream.

oOo

And now, here we are.
The river has brought us here to the sea.
The ocean is where all rivers flow to.
This is the most ancient of waters.
This is where our understanding
Of our bodies, our creativity, our spirituality
Gets deeper still.

The sheer breadth of topics that this book covers has daunted and overwhelmed me often during my writing and editing. I have tried to cut it back, cut it down, make it safer, simplify it many times. *Surely not everything belongs here?* I questioned. And yet it insists it does. Everything I cut out demanded to come back…and more! The book spans from coastal plants to the colour blue, pebbles to prayer, via shapeshifting and suicidal ideation, erosion and immersion, cold water swimming and water birth, seaweed and cyanotypes, from Japanese freedivers and Celtic sea goddesses, to selkies and surfing, and mermaids to Mary. It is intended to be a strange and wonderful deep dive into the inner sea, exploring where the real and the magical, the salty and the sacred meet, within and without, and what implications this has for us as both individuals and a species in these tumultuous times.

She of the Sea

She has called us
Since the dawn of time.
Our elemental longings
Answering the call of the wild self.
She baptises us back into the waters of life.
We come to her, fractured, fragmented, forgotten,
Dusty, dry, half-dead inside
And she washes us clean.
Filling the gaps
Until we begin to remember ourselves.
Remember her.

When the man-made world breaks us down,
Our cells recall
Her eternal promise
I am here.
Our waters
Are of her.
However far we may be from the shore,
Mother Ocean calls us
And we are pulled to her,
As if by magic.

The Call of the Sea

When I decided to leave my Midlands market town life, beckoned by sea-air and the allure of anonymity, a dear work friend who had been raised in a grimy coastal town confirmed to me the necessity of the move. She implored me to walk alongside the waves often, citing their rejuvenating power. We spoke of seagulls, their scavenging ways and the freedom of their flight, laughing as we lolloped around. A few weeks after I hit the coast she died, and I never viewed a seagull the same again. With each one I acknowledged the power of her spirit spurring me on.

Desire drove me to Sussex, it held a magic, promising freedom and release, invoked by memory of escapist jaunts and an estranged love who spent his days swimming for the shore. Being neurodivergent I am accustomed to living on the periphery, feeling safe in the margins, so I found security and sanctuary at the edge of things, meeting many others similarly migrated.

I don't inhabit the seafront often enough to satisfy my friend, and the force of the shoreline easily overloads my senses. Yet just glimpsing it is enough to endow relief, orientate myself and quell any urges not to stay. In the Midlands, visiting water meant walking around reservoirs: all so very still and contained. Here, watched by my daughters' sea blue eyes, I connect to the mercurial water. Once all life gestated and lived there "rocked by the lunar-tidal rhythms" explains Monica Sjöö in The Great Cosmic Mother. The "womb is a condensed experience of the cosmos" with the menstrual cycle "organically echoing the moon-pulse of the sea." There is an omnipresent and unforgiving finality: the possibility of wading gratefully into release.

Claire Robinson

The Sea Sings Through Us

The gift of the sea
Is that of spaciousness
Expansiveness
As far as the eye can see.
When all is busy and chaotic inside,
The sea lulls.
She gives us back our freedom
To soar
To dive
To rest our eyes on nothingness.
She reminds us what it is to be
Belovedly insignificant,
To float and
Know we are held.

There is something almost religious about the call of the sea, the connection we feel that transcends the mundanity of daily existence. It simultaneously reminds us of our smallness and our interconnectedness. It awakens within us the eye of the artist, the voice of the poet, the soul of the mystic. It reignites an awareness that beyond *this* lies something vaster. The water, pulled by the moon, ever-moving but ever-remaining, seems to speak to something elemental within us in ways we can barely find expression for, yet find ourselves driven to try, nonetheless. It has inspired storytellers, artists and musicians of many cultures and genders throughout history. The sea sings through us…if we let her…as we in turn channel ourselves through her.

oOo

In between the binary, the sea, she still can nurture me. The sun, he too sustains this seed, but the sea is always home for me, for she knows my secrets deep. This dysphoric flesh floats out to her subtle surface, silent aching for acceptance. Her waters, minerals and plants, all the life spirit force within, cleanses the trauma this body has endured, from the violence of patriarchy, the degradation of labor, and the entropy of illness, she has been the vessel for my pain. To her I release my tears, the pain that the normals can't understand. She loves me with her secrecy, and allows me to be who I need to be as I float along comfortably. The sea, she holds every part, regardless of a need for gendered affinities.

Through all my confusion and curiosity for me I see, she is a she, she is the She, sacred Feminine, expression of the goddess on this planet and yet non-exclusionary. The sea is the same for me, and he, and they and Xe, and Hym, and them, and Ze, Fae, and Zie and We.

Valerie Moran-Clark

oOo

The song of the sea is a call that cannot be heard with our outer ears, but one to which our inner sea, our waters, our psyche, our soul are drawn, just as they are also pulled by the moon. "Self is a sea," writes Kahlil Gibran in *The Prophet*, "boundless and measureless." *She of the Sea* amplifies the insistent call to a different way of being – of fluidity, flow and freedom, back to our wildness, back to the Feminine, into our bodies, into the depths of consciousness.

So many are drawn to the sea as part of their creative process: swimming daily; taking a week a year beside the sea to restore their spirits; moving to the sea to finish off a creative project; taking a walk on the beach in emotional turmoil; photographing sunsets; singing to the waves in despair or reflection. Its materials – sea glass and sand and pebbles and driftwood – provide the raw materials for their art works. It appears as inspiration in songs and costumes and dances.

oOo

The sea is my second skin.

From my bedroom window I can see the beach and as I awake early each morning, I pull back the curtains and study the sea, the sky, the light to see what today will bring. I feel a flicker of joy, the surge of the pull of the ocean and go down to the beach with my phone and pockets full of selkies. I sit on the pier and watch. Photography, filming the sunrises, welcoming the new day, is a passion of mine.

Alice Grey

oOo

This book shares the reflections of just some of those for whom, like me, the sea is a major part of their life's story. Those who in different ways have chosen to swim against the current of our culture and follow the slipstream of their souls to the sea. Each finds themselves a devotee of a nameless mystery that they find in the waters. These contributors include a beautiful variety of humans of different ages, sexual orientations, gender identities, both with children and without, neurodivergent and neurotypical, from many countries and ethnicities. Some identify as writers, artists, musicians, environmental educators, mermaids, priestesses, and some do not. Each has their own story of swimming or walking the shores, through journeys with cancer and mental health crises, grief and loss, joy and belonging. Each generously and courageously shares an aspect of their identity, their knowing, their sense of belonging and the stretch of sea that sings to their soul, from the Irish Sea to the Caribbean, the Mediterranean and the North Sea, to the Pacific and the Atlantic. Yet more women are included – freedivers and weavers, sailors and fossil collectors – from around the world and throughout history, all united by their connection to the sea as a vital expression of self. At times, our experiences reflect each other, at other times they diverge. Each of us speaks personally to our lived experience. But we seem to share something universal. Something best summed up in the words of French director, Jean Epstein, "I fear and worship the sea. She encourages me to do what I am most afraid of."

She of the Sea is for us all. It is not intended as an insistence that the sea is always or only female (though that has been the dominant assertion throughout much of Western European and in many other cultures). Nor that the sea only speaks to women, for we know that is far from true. But because fluidity and the Feminine seem drawn to each other I bring these connections out to the light here.

Women as a group have often had to push harder for their access to the sea. Women, trans and non-binary people have had to fight for their creative expression, their bodily autonomy, their natural spiritual expression, their right to contribute to human achievement, and have their contributions recognised. And so, this book is filled with voices – some contemporary, some historical – predominantly female, for whom the sea was central to their expression of being, for whom the sea is both medium and message. I hope you will find your own experience reflected and discover many new soul companions for your journey.

Aspects of She of the Sea

I take pleasure in my transformations.
I look quiet and consistent, but few know
how many women there are in me.

Anaïs Nin

The sky is indigo. Or is it the sea? There is no delineation between them. The sand shifts beneath my feet. A gentle rhythmic hush emerges as the waves break on the shore, as liquid meets solid, water meets earth, embracing, dissipating, retreating through the shingle.

Just darkness and sound remain.

The lights of the fishing village over the bay twinkle welcomingly. The lighthouse on the island scans over the rocky shore. One by one the brightest stars emerge overhead. But everything else is darkness. Until a golden line appears, spreading across the horizon.

The full moon is rising. Almost imperceptibly, and yet she is rising. Where once there was just a faint glow, now there is an arc, now a semi-circle. Within moments, or lifetimes, or somewhere in between, she is there full-bodied, gold turning to silver.

Still, she rises. Casting quicksilver and shadows over the waters. Shading each wavelet. A meandering path of light reaching from her to me over the sea. With her emerges the Otherworld.

I am alone on the beach. The children who made the castles and dug the holes that treacherously decorate the dark dunes are all in bed. The fishermen are home. The dog walkers and joggers and horse riders and bait diggers and foragers and kite surfers too.

The dark of night, the fullness of the rising moon, is left for the Sea Priestess, the Water Witch, the Wise Woman, the Wyrd One, the Crazy Woman…

I reach my arms out from my sides, and each one takes my hands. We stand together.

Crazy Woman stands proud and bare breasted in the silver light, clapping her hands to tell the moon that she is here. Trailing moonbeams she spins in circles.

I *am here.*

The Sea Priestess says a prayer of blessing and anoints herself from the waves, before singing her song to the moon.

I *am here.*

The Wise Woman draws a labyrinth in the sand.

I *am here.*

The Weeping Woman begins to wail, her tears blessing her cheeks.

I *am here.*

Burning Woman lights a ceremonial fire.

I *am here.*

Creatrix makes a spiral of stones.

I *am here.*

They sit awhile. The Wyrd One gathers some seaweed for healing baths and shells for her altar. The Water Witch searches the shore for a hag stone to tuck into her pocket.

We *are here.*

They are in me…I shift into them…but I am not them…then they are gone.
I retreat too.
Into a black seven-seater car. Back to the little pink house on the housing estate. Back to electric light and games on the phone and deadlines and meltdowns. Back to my roles as Mother and Author, Wife and Publisher, Neighbour and Friend. Back to what passes for normality.
Yet somehow, what happens on the beach feels
More real.

Connection

I have lived by or near the sea all my life, despite forced moves every few years. Even at the furthest inland, I have had connection to Her through the salty tidal artery of the Thames. It seems that my clan have always been this way, living close to her, carried by her to new lands every few hundred years. She took us from Ireland into Scotland, to Norway and along the coast of Europe, and into Britain across the Channel from France. She is in our blood, alluring, enchanting and deeply powerful mistress, joyful maiden and wise crone. Her ever-changing, shifting nature has always struck something deep within me: a recognition, a longing, a depth of sadness as great as my own. Over the years I have gone to her shores time and again, seeking answers, seeking guidance, seeking comfort, sometimes screaming and weeping into the gales that swept in from her vast expanses, sometimes finding fragments of song torn from my still trembling lips in a language not my own. I can feel my soul in those moments. I can feel the tantalising connection to the great beyond, the realm of the Nokk* and the Fae and all the spirits of the world.

I have never found the answers I seek. That is not for me to know – if I were simply handed them, what should I learn? But I have come to understand my deep-rooted need to be near Her. Water has memory – not in folklore alone, but scientifically, measurably so. For me, She holds the memories of everything I was and am yet to be, the precious moments of childhood, learning how She carved out the shoreline, exposing the history of the land in slices that count aeons like years in a trees' rings. Burying my hands in the careworn pebbles of her shore, closing my eyes and feeling for the tell-tale prick of a fossilised sharks' tooth, smooth and pointed among the rounded stones. The sound of the waves lulling me to sleep in the place I felt safest but that

* Danish term for shapeshifting water spirits.

I rarely was permitted to visit, the home of my Father and my Soul Mother. Now, I have settled where She – the life blood of the world – meets the ancient bones of the land, the mountains. Here I have found my balance.

Make time for Her, and She will gift you with wisdom beyond words. Go to Her with an open heart and She will rush in and overwhelm you. She will touch the deepest places of your soul – if you begin to weep, do not be afraid but let her bear your sorrows away to her farthest depths and understand that you are seen, that you are known. But never forget the awesome force that lies within those waters – be respectful and always give thanks.

Will

An Introduction to Practices and Reflections

I must warn you now if you are new to my work, that reading my books is not a passive process! They require that you open yourself to the energy that is transmitted through them and find ways to let it into your own life. As I said in my previous book, *Creatrix*, "only half of this book currently exists. The half I have written. The other half comes from what you bring to it, what emerges from your bodymind and soul as you read it."

Each chapter will end for you, where it began for me: with reflections and practices. These are ways to embody the material into your own life, rather than simply stay safe in your head, nod in agreement or roll your eyes in bemusement, and move on. I invite you to dive deep with me, to take an active part in the unfolding of this experience, rather than staying safe on the shore. Dare to move into your body, into the fullness of your being.

In our time together we are going to be harnessing many aspects of the sea: its waves…of colour and sound; the sense of groundedness we experience standing on the shore; the fluidity of consciousness; the magic of shapeshifting and perspective. We will be activating your capacity for transformation and creativity – experiencing them through words, exercises, images and sound. I have prepared a multi-sensory experience that should enable you to access the magic of the sea wherever in the world you are.

There are many practices. This doesn't mean you have to do them all. Or do them all now. Some may feel appropriate to where you are emotionally or geographically right now. Others you may bookmark for another time or occasion. There are no 'shoulds', just offerings, waiting for you to bring them to life.

In fact, I would encourage you not to even try to do them all. Choose one. And then just do the first step of it today. Pick an action so small you can't possibly fail. Keep doing it, coming back to that one simple action, until you feel the inspiration or calling to move further. This may take moments…or months.

That one small step might be picking up a pebble each time you go for a walk. It might be lighting a candle each day. Or adding one item to your altar space. It might be putting on the playlist. Don't insist that you must dance or meditate for half an hour a day to the music. Just put on one song, and start out lying down, and simply allow your breath to settle into rhythm with it. You may find movement in your fingers or toes, flowing into the rest of your body, or you may find that today is a day where it needs to ebb into stillness. Take this one action with no force, no expectation of what you might feel, how it might go, how long this action might take. Don't allow yourself to be belittled by perfectionist expectations. Relish the small. Don't force, just observe and go with the flow, learn to follow where it leads you.

I encourage you to reflect on the questions in a similar manner. Questions hold power. Asking questions – even to ourselves, to the wind on the beach, in our journals – stimulates responses. "The answer to your question," says Asja Boros, "lies in the question, the seeker is the portal, every initiation is a self-initiation, the way out is through."

So please don't force a quick, off-pat, clever or rational answer. And don't even worry about trying to get the 'right' answer. There is no right answer. No truth but your own, in this moment. Allow your attention to ebb and flow over the questions like the tides. However you choose to ask them, you will notice that these questions will keep unravelling themselves in your life. Over time, your life will become the answer you seek. You will find yourself brushing up against memories, articles, books, photographs and paintings with whispers of response. Let these questions gestate within. Sleep with them. Take a walk with them. Bring them to your friends, book group or women's circle and discuss them with others.

Do not limit yourself to words in answering your questions. Images can be powerful ways of discovering what lies beneath and making original connections. You may want to draw, paint, sculpt or stitch in direct response to the questions, or simply reflect on a question as you create. If you would like to make images but your critical mind gets in the way, collage is a powerful tool that creates layers of meaning. Pictures can be taken from magazines, newspapers, printed from the internet, scanned from treasured photographs, and then combined simply by cutting and sticking, or integrating your own creative additions.

I invite you to do whatever works for you. I invite you to try new approaches too. Please do give yourself the opportunity to live into these inquiries.

Reflections

The Call of the Sea

What does the call of the sea mean to you?

What milestones of your life are connected to the sea?

What childhood memories do you have of the sea?

What artwork makes you feel connected to the sea?

How often do you get to the sea now? Why do you go? Why don't you go?

What do you fear about the sea?

How do you like to move along the shore...and the sea?

Is another body of water more meaningful to you than the sea? Are you someone who has a deep connection with lakes or streams or swimming pools instead...or as well?

Lega-sea

Where do you come from in relation to the sea? Try to answer this on as many levels as you can: geographically, genetically, culturally, intellectually...

Has the sea found its way through the generations of your family? What did it mean to them?

Who was drawn to the sea? Who was lost at sea?

What was shared and what went unspoken about the legacy of the sea?

What skills, wisdoms, songs or stories were passed down to you about the sea?

What do you love about your legacy?

What traumatic memories do you or family members have connected to the sea?

What do you try to hide or ignore about your inheritance?

What have you not been told about it? What family secrets might it hold?

The Inner Sea

Which water metaphors do you use frequently?

Which sea words, images or symbols have an inner resonance for you?

What does 'inner sea' mean to you? What might it look like?

When did you first discover it?

How does it correspond to the literal sea?

What does it feel like to be on the surface…underwater?

Can you see any traces of where you have been? Or do you have any idea where it might be taking you?

Are you alone here? Do you have any sort of guide or companion?

Can you draw, paint, write or collage your inner sea? Can you make a map of the areas you have already visited?

Altar Practice

I highly recommend you make a special physical space in your home on which to collect objects that reflect your journey through this book. I call this an 'altar space.'

If you are hesitant about creating an altar or are new to this concept outside of mainstream religion, please know that this is not about worshipping anything that is on the altar, but appreciating the beauty and sacredness of each item, as well as what they represent symbolically to you. The altar acts as a portal for you, its creatrix, between the daily world and the realm of soul: a way of connecting with and entering your inner sea with ease. For some the focus is magical, for some it is purely about celebrating nature, for others it may be spiritual in a different way.

For me, creating and tending an altar space is a focal point of my creative and spiritual life. It is a way of making visible the ideas, colours and symbols that I am working with, creating a snapshot of my inner world that my outer eyes can land on throughout my day. It is a theatre for the psyche.

Altars can be made on a windowsill, shelf, small table, mantelpiece, the floor... They can be temporary or semi-permanent, private or shared with others.

The act of purposefully placing objects with intention and focus is healing in itself, helping to regulate the bodymind, allowing us to connect to deeper layers of consciousness as we keep our hands and brains busy with the act of cleaning then ordering and organising meaningful objects. Using items that have connections to special places or people helps to bring the energy and consciousness of those times and people to be with us here and now. Adding blessings, inquiries or prayers, we allow these objects to become a focal point for this moment in our lives and what we need to remember, discover, embody, celebrate and release.

Building your Altar

The first step to altar building is completely mundane and practical: finding a suitable place where things won't get knocked over by curtains, windows, doors or breezes, and that will remain untampered with by animals or other members of your household.

Next you need to clear time and clear space.

Make sure you will be undisturbed as you focus on making your altar.

Get a cloth and some water with a couple of drops of essential oil that is fresh scented – lemon, grapefruit, rosemary or lavender would be my go-tos. You may also want to add some sea salt to it.

You might want to play the *She of the Sea* playlist on Spotify as you create your altar.

Clear the surface and allow your mind to clear as you do so.

As you begin, you may want to say a few words of blessing or inten-tion. You may want to wash your hands with the water or put a dab on your forehead or heart space. Then wipe down the surface, slowly and methodically, imagining that you are also wiping yourself clean inside. Then dry the surface with a clean, dry cloth.

You may choose to cover the surface with a blue or white piece of fabric or paper or simply leave it bare. You may want to burn incense, dried rosemary, or a scented candle to change the energy of the space.

You may want to start by leaving this book on your altar, or the journal that you will be writing in as you read.

We will be adding to the altar as our journey here continues.

2

SEA SHORE

*Shorelines are where the known world
drops away into unseen depths.*

Charlotte Runcie, *Salt on Your Tongue*

Walking the Shore

The shoreline is where we begin our journey. This liminal space between land and sea is where we start to become aware of the moods of the sea, what she's like in different weathers, tides and seasons. We can walk beside her and begin to look for patterns, search for her gifts from the safety of the shore. Here we start to become familiar with the birds and the plants, the shells and the rocks, without getting wet. The shoreline holds the most incredible ever-changing offerings from She of the Sea, if we will only pay attention.

I love Molly Remer's words in *Walking with Persephone* when she says, "I stand in the waves and realize that when you are facing the ocean, filled with her sound, it doesn't really matter how many other people are around, there is still a sensation of solitude."

Solitude is a recurring theme in women's writings about the sea. "Women need solitude in order to find again the true essence of themselves,"[5] reflects Anne Morrow Lindbergh. In *To The Lighthouse,* Virginia Woolf shares what this solitude means to a woman's soul: "For now she need not think of anybody. She could be herself, by herself. And that was what now she often felt the need of – to think; well not even to think. To be silent; to be alone. All the being and the doing, expansive, glittering, vocal, evaporated; and one shrunk, with a sense of solemnity, to being oneself, a wedge-shaped core of darkness, something invisible to others…and this self having shed its attachments was free for the strangest adventures."

Solitude is what so many of us are hungry for in this busy world. It is right there waiting for us on the shoreline.

Sea Dance

I feel the rush of the wind and waves race
through me and I long to run,
To raise my arms along with the oystercatchers
and curlews, the dunlins and lapwings
And fly.
I long to spin and never stop.
I can't understand why everyone is not
intoxicated this way by the sea.
How can they plod along, collars up, heads down?
I do not want to walk sedately along
the shore like these dog walkers
In their sensible jackets.

I want to dance to the percussion of the wind and the waves.
Can they not hear the invitation to dance?
Are they, like me, using every last bit of willpower to resist?

I can bear this walking no more.
Subtly I take her lead, I change the rhythm of my feet:
One-two, one-one-two.
Then look around me.
Is anyone watching? Am I safe?
The coast is clear.
Arms come up from my sides.
One-one-two, sweep around, scarf trailing, hair streaming.
Around and around and around.

West shore, island, sea, east shore, sand, shingle, bog.
Again and again,
Faster and faster, sea blurring into bog, east shore
into west. I feel the tension rise from my chest. I
spin and spin. Mind lightening, breathing easing,
smile emerging from behind the grey clouds of my
mind. The birds wheel. The wind blows. I spin.
Another walker emerges.
Their dog jumping and spinning and barking in wild delight.
I drop my arms and still myself.

Why do humans only have to walk,
When the wild wind calls and the waves crash?
I long for the freedom to move as myself
Through this world
Without apology for my strangeness.

A Pebble in My Pocket

Some beaches are fine sand, some mud, others are pure shingle. Ours is an ever-shifting mix of the three. Silver sand, sometimes scattered, sometimes deep ridged, with pebbles of varying shapes, sizes and colours, with underlying patches of boot-catching mud.

Each time I walk the beach, I pick up pebbles. Some days, it is one of the small yellow ones that look like kernels of sweetcorn. Other times, grey with white quartz veins that fits perfectly in my palm. Sometimes, jet black and smooth as a baby's cheek, which seems to suck the energy into it. I have pebbles in coat pockets, windowsills and the car cupholders.

My fingers are often drawn to these pebbles as I go through my daily life, especially when I am feeling anxious. I silently turn one over in my hand and it brings me back to a place of clarity and connection. It gives me a sense of solidity. I only learned when I was writing this book that this type of stone has a name: a palm stone or worry stone. They are used for grounding you emotionally.

Previously, grounding had always been a slightly woo-woo word for me. Something you did in your head by imagining you were a tree with your roots going down into the ground. It was self-hypnosis, imaginative self-soothing…wishful thinking as far as my cynical analytical brain was concerned. But then I realised something that blew my mind: when you hold a pebble, you are holding an ancient piece of the ground in your hand, millions of years old. This physical example of solidity grounds you, literally. It also provides an energetic connection to the place that you gathered it and that time when it first calmed you. "There are times when you need the extremity of rock, the hardness of an old, cold place against which you can measure yourself," reflects Sharon Blackie in *If Women Rose Rooted*.

As I was reflecting on this, I happened upon a book extract about Dr Malidoma Somé, a Dagda shaman and his approach to mental health from his tradition. It made so much sense to me, as someone who finds it hard to stay grounded, and feel a sense of solidity and belonging:

A common thread that Dr. Somé has noticed in 'mental' disorders in the West is "a very ancient ancestral energy that has been placed in stasis, that finally is coming out in the person." His job then is to trace it back, to go back in time to discover what that spirit is. "In most cases, the spirit is connected to nature, especially with mountains or big rivers," he says.

As part of the ritual to merge the mountain and human energy, those who are receiving the 'mountain energy' are sent to a mountain area of their choice, where they pick up a stone that calls to them. They bring that stone back for the rest of the ritual and then keep it as a companion; some even carry it around with them. "The presence of the stone does a lot in tuning the perceptive ability of the person," notes Dr. Somé. "They receive all kinds of information that they can make use of, so it's like they get some tangible guidance from the other world as to how to live their life."

"People think something extraordinary must be done in an extraordinary situation like this," he says. "That's not usually the case. Sometimes it is as simple as carrying a stone."[6]

Is this not what some part of us is doing when we instinctively collect these pebbles? Dr Somé is from Burkino Faso, a land-locked African country, where the sea would not feature so much in the lives of ancestors or their beliefs. Whereas in nations with large coastlines, that call of nature and our ancestors speaks to us from the geographical feature that surrounds us most: the sea. We feel a deep need to connect to the place that has shaped us, woven through our ancestors' lives, that has brought us together and divided us, over and over. We are called to carry her with us in the wave-tossed pebbles and the seashells we collect on her shores – they provide a portable four-way connection: to self, place, natural world and past. They are amulets of belonging.

Pebbles have been a passion of mine for as long as I can remember. I am not alone in this. Many of my friends and family members have windowsills in bathrooms or altar spaces with rocks of various shapes and colours: hag stones, heart-shaped stones, flint arrow heads and pebbles striped with quartz. Much less glamorous than the crystals and gems that we also treasure, duller in colour and sheen, still they draw us to them. In our family we gift each other pebbles and crystals. Little solid gifts of love and belonging, passed from hand to hand, soul to soul, to mark special moments.

When I went backpacking around the world in my early twenties, I picked up black lava rock and greenstone, pyrite and coral from beaches in New Zealand and Australia: colours and textures and formations that we simply do not have here on the south coast of Ireland. They were so exotic compared to the purple-grey, blue-grey and white-grey stones from my own beach at home, and yet there they were just ordinary beach stones, scattered everywhere in profusion!

Soon I doubted myself: *who carts rocks around the world with a baggage weight limit?* I ditched them somewhere – these little parts of places where I had found…and left – bits of my soul. I dearly wish now that I hadn't.

Pebbles have been connected to my creative work throughout my adult life. My blog has had a photograph of a stone spiral as its logo for most of its decade and a half. The spiral was made with a special group of women on International Women's Day, out of the pebbles on our local beach. It was the beginning of my spiral making, which continues to this day. My creative work returns again and again to spirals, in particular making spirals of beach stones, gathered on my local strand.

This spiral of pebbles takes me back to my graduate degree at Cambridge University, when I was pregnant with my first child. There was an art gallery in a former curator's home called Kettle's Yard, that we often visited. In the sitting room was a dark oak table in a sunny window with a beautiful spiral of round white pebbles carefully arranged on top. In the midst of uncertainty, the disorientation of a first pregnancy far from home, it was deeply grounding and soothing.

Not long after my son was born, I read Judith Duerk's book *Circle of Stones*. She uses the metaphor of a circle of stones for a circle of wise women who hold space for you. Women who ground you and help you find your centre again.

In her book Judith Duerk asks: "how would your life be different, if you had a circle of women to go to?" I was feeling lost and at sea. Newly settled in the land of my birth, the village beside the sea that had always called me back. I needed to find a circle of belonging as the woman I now was, not the child who had visited in her holidays. Her words gave me the impetus I needed in calling in a community. I typed this question up on little pieces of paper and handed them out as invitations to the women I felt closest to at our local breastfeeding group.

This women's group has been my rock for well over a decade. We have shifted and evolved, as women have moved here or moved away. But still we join together most months, to discuss our lives and struggles, to share a meal and book recommendations, and celebrate the seasons. In pandemic times, we have gathered on the beach. They are my circle of stones that have held me through the greatest storms of my life. I am so eternally grateful to them.

Hag Stones

The connection between women and stones runs deep. A few years ago, I found out about hag stones – pebbles that have a hole naturally eroded all the way through them. I had seen them without seeing them all my life. Like much of women's culture and magic, I was missing them in plain sight, because I didn't have the words for them.

Also known as Witch Stones, Fairy Stones, Druid Stones, Holy or Holey Stones, they appear in stories and folklore from Scotland, Wales, Ireland, England, the Netherlands and Germany. They were strung up and used as amulets of protection for boats, keys, homes, livestock and loved ones.

The word *hag* is often used to mean a witch, old or wise woman. The sort of woman usually associated with magic: a woman connected to her wisdom, a woman who knows. They were so-called, apparently, because the hole was considered a tool in seeing the Otherworld, the world of spirit and soul: it was said that looking at the ocean through the hole of a hag stone may help you see a mermaid.

But before you race off to the internet to purchase one, it is said that a hag stone must "cross your path" in order to do its magical work. They should not be bought or given…so be sure to look out for one the next time you are walking the shore.

Gifts from the Sea

Each winter, we pack up our business into a trailer and travel with our family to a small island in the Gulf Coast and spend a month living on the beach. There is something about being on an island that quite literally transports you into another world. The sensation of stepping out, stepping off, and stepping into is palpable as we cross the bridge to the island and settle into the slow, quiet rhythm of island life, guided by the tides, the moon, and the rising and setting of the sun. Our sleep and waking schedules change. Our priorities shift. Our to-do lists become very short.

As I shed layers of myself at the beach, watching dolphins, running with my children, picking up shells, walking hand in hand with my husband into the setting sun, life feels simple, and what I need and want feels very clean and very clear. My intense self-motivation and drive softens, my itch to get more done fades away, and I am left with the core of myself and discover, anew, how very much I like her.

This year, the morning after we arrived at the island, my husband and I headed to our favorite part of the beach where the shells are the biggest. My favorite shell in the world is from a moon snail. Round, smooth, and beautiful, curling in a wave to a perfect tiny spiral in the center, with colors ranging from brown to pale blue. Many of the moon shells we find are small, the size of a quarter or smaller, my holy grail (holy snail) is a palm-sized moon shell that will fill my hand.

But on our way to the beach we are stopped at a little guard tower and told we cannot continue. When we inquire why, the sour-faced man tells us that the beach was "gone": it had been destroyed in a hurricane last fall.

We returned to our beach house in a state of confusion and shock. Our long walks on the beach, our hopes for the new treasures we would discover, the part of the island we so love and have so many happy memories of, all swept away. We walked on a different part of the island feeling a genuine sense of distress and grief. How could the beach just be gone? Does the island now just abruptly drop away into the sea? We feel a sensation that something had died.

We walk in silence for a time and then realization dawns. There is no way the beach we long for can actually be "gone." Back in the beach house we Google to discover that yes, the beach sustained significant hurricane damage in the fall...We make some enquiries and a day later receive a pass to enter it. The parking lot is damaged, but the beach itself is still very much there and very much alive.

As we walk, I stop to take a photo of one of my goddesses on a piece of faded green driftwood. I am in that state of total presence that I experience often in our island walks, the complete immersion in the moment, stripped of all other purpose or task, but simply myself, walking on the beach. It is a type of what I call "stepping through," like I have stepped out of myself, out of reality, and into a different plane of relationship with the natural world. We find several fighting conch shells fairly close together and as I turn away from the driftwood to continue walking, just as my husband's foot begins to come down on the sand, I see it.

I grab his arm and pull him back, and there it is, a sun-bleached moon snail shell that exactly fills the palm of my hand. I laugh with joy and exhilaration and nearly cry in my delight. I tell my husband I feel as excited and happy and full of wild euphoria as if I've just given birth to another child. This is one of the best moments of my life! I crow, laughing semi-hysterically.

Then, realizing what I have said, I laugh some more. Is it sad that some of the best moments of my life has been finding perfect shells? No, I decide, I adore being the kind of person who sees with island eyes and who discovers the best moments of her life simply by paying attention to what is happening on the shore.

Molly Remer

Plants of the Shore

On the peach-coloured wall of my girlhood bedroom in England hung a beautifully illustrated poster of coastal plants. Each night before I went to sleep, many miles from the shore, I would breathe in the shapes and colours and names of these hardy plants that survived by rooting into seemingly inhospitable sand and shingle: thrift, yellow horned poppy, rock samphire, ribwort plantain, sea holly, marsh mallow…an incantation of the sea.

Whilst most of us love the cultivated beauty of garden plants, and many the wild wonder of abundant hedgerow plants, the plants of the shoreline are stranger creatures: low-growing and tough, they show us just how adaptable nature is. These are not plants that we make bouquets out of, or even notice, unless they are in flower. They are overlooked, trampled on in our rush down to the sand and the waves. Most of us have been taught to disregard them as weeds.

When we think of the wild foods of the sea, our minds tend to go to the creatures: periwinkles and shrimps, mussels and crabs, fish of all sorts. But these seaside plants would have been an important part of our ancestors' diets. The Northern European shoreline has so much to offer: oraches, samphire, watercress, alexanders, sea buckthorn, sea beet and sea kale, most of which until recently were never sold in a shop, they were the gifts of the sea, available only to those who knew where to look and when to pick.

We are remembering these wild plants, their salty flavours and nutrient rich gifts, their appearance on tables in restaurants and homes in recent years testifies to this.

We are remembering what the shore has to offer.

We are remembering the wonders of the wild places in nourishing us.

Rosemary

Rosemary, the highly scented hardy herb, is a native of the Mediterranean shores, recently recognised as part of the plant family that includes sage and mint. Its name literally means 'dew from the sea', from the Latin ros (dew) and marinus (sea), because it is so hardy that is all the water it needs to survive. It is sometimes known as the Rose of Mary, who is said to have laid her cloak over its flowers and turned them from white to blue.

Rosemary has been recognised for several thousand years in many different cultures for its ability to cleanse, purify and heal and was considered sacred in Ancient Egypt, Greece and Rome. According to Greek myth, rosemary was draped around the neck of Aphrodite as she rose from the sea. In the language of flowers, rosemary signifies remembrance, so I always add a sprig of it to funerary flowers.

As well as adding it to food, or cleaning the body and hair, it can be burned, fresh or dried as a bundle, as a way to cleanse space.

Seaweed

God created seaweed. The seaweed made the world.

John B. Keane

The tough, low-lying weather-beaten cousins of clover, bindweed, rose and poppy are recognisable enough where sand meets land, but when we walk down to the water, the plants get stranger. Tentacle-like fronds in browns and greens, red and hot pink, that come to life underwater, flowing and dancing in the currents. They are both so familiar…and so utterly strange. Beautiful and alien, these primitive plants of the algae family, which pre-date humans by 1,200 million years, speak of lost worlds and different ways of being.[7]

The waving fronds of rockweed remind me of the tiny cilia that we learned about in school biology, that waft our eggs down our Fallopian tubes. The bewitching translucence of sea lettuce speaks of magical underwater picnics. Deadman's bootlaces, spongeweed, sugar kelp, dulse, carrageen moss, bladderwrack, feathered wing weed, sea oak, Devil's tongue, sea horsetail, landlady's wig, dabberlocks, oyster thief…just the names of many of our common seaweeds are enough to set your imagination going!

And that they did. In Ireland, the language and folklore are rich with seaweeds. There are hundreds of native words for different species and sub-species of seaweeds, as well as the tools and traditions associated with them.

In coastal areas of Ireland, the UK, and Northern Europe, seaweed was put to a vast array of different uses from food, fertiliser, fuel, to predict the weather, as medicine… Seaweed gathering and cooking was generally associated with women. In Irish there is a word specifically to describe the work of women gathering seaweed on the shore: *cannabhaireacht*.[8] Even its use in roofing was women's work, as a modern thatcher from the Danish island of Læsø shares: "Since the male islanders were often out at sea, the women were left to look after the farms and houses. 'They were alone on this island and taking care of themselves. They found a way to make these roofs, which is not seen elsewhere in the world.' Around 40 to 50 women would work on the roofs together [...] treating the eelgrass almost as if it were wool by twisting it into large *vasks* (ropes) then tying them to the rafters to serve as the base."[9]

Seaweed in all these folk uses fell out of fashion for much of the twentieth century, replaced by other materials and technologies. But as interest has grown in local native plants, foraging and sustainability, it has enjoyed a revival.

Seaweed is eaten in different ways around the world. In Japanese food it is probably best known as nori, dried into sheets and served wrapped around sushi or sprinkled on top of rice. It is also enjoyed as a pickled salad, served in soup, and to flavour stocks in both China and Japan. In Wales, it is fried with onions and oats to make laverbread. In Ireland, carrageen is used to make a set milk pudding, as well as being served as a syrup for coughs and colds, both of which my father fed me growing up.

No wonder it has been a dietary mainstay in places where it is plentiful. Seaweed is an extremely nutrient dense food, more so than any land-grown vegetable. Rich in fibre and naturally organic, seaweed is packed full of many vitamins especially B12, C and E, and is between 20-50% pure minerals when dry.[10]

Most of us are lacking in these essential minerals that are found in the oceans – namely iodine and magnesium, as well as Vitamin D (that we get through our skin on a sunny day on the beach). Omega 3 fatty acids – vital for brain development and functioning – considered to be a core component of how our species developed far larger brains than our primate cousins, mainly come from our consumption of fish and algae. Research consistently shows that the healthiest diets for longevity – Mediterranean, Japanese and Scandinavian – are all high in seafood.

Seaweed can be bought as a ready-made condiment or added to all sorts of stews, soups and salads, just as any green vegetable would be. According to Professor of Botany and practicing herbalist, Ryan Drum, it can take up to four months for the body's gut flora, when it has not previously been exposed to seaweed in the diet, to be able to recognise and fully digest it.

Iodine

Iodine is vital for the healthy functioning of the thyroid – the butterfly shaped gland in our necks that manages our metabolism and energy levels.

Iodine is rare in land plants, but plentiful in seaweeds, as it is concentrated in sea water. Just 5 grams of most seaweeds (dry weight) will provide the recommended daily allowance. We tend to get the majority of our iodine from eating fish and sea vegetables as well as from food grown in coastal iodine-rich soils.

We not only take in iodine through our diets...but in the sea air. Iodine released from seaweed boosts thyroid levels through inhalation, according to research published in the Irish Medical Journal. Researchers discovered that the levels of iodine in the blood diminished in direct proportion to the distance people lived from the sea.[11]

Women's need for iodine rises hugely during pregnancy and breastfeeding, and varying studies from around the world show that anywhere from 16% to a staggering 84% of pregnant women are deficient in it.[12] Thyroid issues are already at epidemic levels in women, due to our adrenaline-fuelled modern lifestyles and our heavily processed diets, leading to slumping energy levels, continual exhaustion and depletion. Perhaps one of the reasons for our being drawn to the sea is an intuitive response to our bodies' cries for iodine.

It is not just the nutritional and health benefits that attract us to seaweed. Something seems to draw artists – women specifically – to doodle, embroider, press, paint, sculpt and draw this form. Something about seaweeds seems to captivate us. Which is a little odd as they are so different to the flowers we have been taught to love and identify emotionally with since childhood. There is something primal in our attraction.

This love affair between women and seaweed is not a modern phenomenon. Seaweeding – collecting and pressing seaweed samples – was a popular 'women's pastime' practised by many, including novelist George Eliot and even Queen Victoria – during a flourishing of amateur female botanists in the Victorian era.[13]

Amateur or not, Victorian women's collections are now being used to help us understand the changing nature of our seas. "Seaweeds, which we think of as fragile and gooey, actually hold that history, not in their DNA, but in their tissues,"[14] says Kathy Ann Miller, curator of algae at UC Berkeley's University Herbarium. The collections of these women have helped scientists look back an extra seven decades in time, to the early days of mass-industrialisation to understand more about this vital ecosystem and our impact on it.

To me this is just one example of how women, so often kept out of the 'serious work' of scientific and artistic endeavour throughout our history, have bridged the gaps between science and art, refusing manmade delineations of how we are taught we should see the world, and instead choosing both/and.

Let us seek to know more…and let it be beautiful. Both/and.

Seaweed Baths

Seaweed baths are a great way of bringing the sea to you (especially if you live far from the ocean, hate swimming in the sea or don't like eating seaweed)…as well as letting you turn up the temperature so you can wallow more comfortably! Seaweed baths and treatments are also now offered at many spas, so you can treat yourself and luxuriate without any effort in gathering… or clearing up afterwards!

A rich source of minerals, seaweed baths naturally destress and detoxify the bodymind and can be especially helpful for those with aching joints, back pain and exhaustion, moisturising the skin and helping clear rashes, including eczema, acne and psoriasis. Seaweed contains extremely high levels of melatonin which helps our bodies fall and stay asleep, so try a seaweed bath just before bedtime if insomnia is an issue for you.[15]

If you live near the coast, seaweed can be gathered from the shore without any damage to the environment. Go down to an unpolluted seashore, especially after a storm, and the beach should be thick with washed up fronds of seaweed. This way you know what you are getting is fresh, but you are not cutting roots or damaging living weeds. Collect what you need in a bag or box fresh off the beach…leave it be if it's super stinky and has been decomposing on the strand for weeks! When gathering from the seashore ensure it is legal to do so. Gather respectfully and sparingly, aware of your impact on animals and plants that may live on or under the rocks.

Seaweeds are categorised primarily by colour: green, red and brown. The most nutrient rich of all the seaweeds are the brown seaweeds, especially bladderwrack and dulse, which are abundant on Northern European shores.

Bladderwrack (see below) is the easiest to identify: dark browny-green, almost black when dry, it has fat fingered fronds, and little air chambers, like bubble wrap. You can take a book or app with you to help you learn to identify the different species. If you live in tropical climes, you'll need to find out which native seaweeds are best for bathing. Unlike foraging for mushrooms, there is no need to worry, any seaweed is better than none, and no fresh seaweed will harm you.

Once you have gathered your seaweed, rinse off any sand. If you are not going to have a bath right away, you can keep it wet in some sea-salted water for a couple of days, or leave it to dry in the sun. Once dry it can be stored in a dark place for years.

If you do not live close to the shore, seaweeds can be purchased from health food shops or online from sustainably harvested sources, but can be pretty pricey for what is essentially a fast-growing, wild plant. Seaweed extract is also used in many bath products, for all the goodness, without the mess!

Making your seaweed bath

I had my very first seaweed bath as I was writing this book. I was both apprehensive and curious when my friend spoke about its trance-inducing, almost hallucinogenic, qualities.

Trying is believing. Our naturally limestone rich 'hard' water became super soft. My skin felt as though it had been immersed in the most luxurious moisturiser. My hair, when I washed it, was thick and luscious, like a mermaid or a lady on a shampoo commercial. Trance? No. Relaxed and extremely pampered? Most definitely.

To make your seaweed bath, put the plug in and then put the seaweed in the bath. Don't tear up the seaweed, as you don't want it blocking your drain! Run the hot water over the seaweed – this will help to release the saponins from the weed, which feels almost slimy to the touch. The hot steamy air will help to release the iodine for you to breathe in deeply, just as you do when you walk on the beach. You will also be taking it in through your skin. You can remove the seaweed from the bath before getting in, or go for the full sensual experience and have the fronds in with you as you bathe.

You will notice that your skin and hair become slippery with all the seaweed goodness, and your hair will be glossy and shiny after. For a final boost to skin, hair and nervous system, you can rinse yourself with icy cold water before drying your skin vigorously with a towel to get your circulation going.

Remove the seaweed into a bucket or bowl before draining the bath. It can then be placed in your garden if you have one, directly onto flower beds or into the compost bin, where it will decompose into the most beautiful nutrient rich fertiliser for your plants.

Reflections

What are you most drawn to on the seashore and why do you think this is?

What gifts from the sea have you found?

How do you display or honour them?

How do you feel about seaweed? Does it fascinate you or repel you?

How might you incorporate seaweed as something nourishing into your life?

Practice

A Pebble for your Pocket

Find a stone or pebble to put in your coat pocket or purse, that you can take out and hold when you need something to ground you. Hang a hag stone around your neck, in your window or on your bunch of keys to protect them.

Altar Practice

The next step in creating your altar is gathering what Anne Morrow Lindbergh so beautifully calls "gifts from the sea." This might mean a walk on the beach or searching out items from around your home that you purchased or found at an earlier time. These should preferably be natural items and might include – sea glass, shells, pebbles, driftwood, dried seaweed, a dried starfish or seahorse, feathers…

Place them on the altar in a mindful way – you may choose to create a mandala or spiral, or arrange them in another way that has meaning to you.

3

HEALING WATERS

I went down in the afternoon
To the sea,
Which held me, until I grew easy.

Mary Oliver, "Swimming, One Day in August"

An Invisible Essential

Water. We are so surrounded by this fluid medium – in our baths, showers, toilets, water bottles, urban fountains, mountain streams, swimming pools and oceans – it is so ubiquitous as to have become all together unremarkable to our daily minds. When actually it is nothing short of miraculous.

Without water, there is no life.

We are drawn to water, because water means life for us. Scientists search for one thing on new planets to see if it can support life: water.

Our beautiful blue planet is almost three-quarters water, 95% of which is salt water. Our brains are hardwired to recognise, notice and move towards it, and not just for food, leisure or travel. According to biologist E. O. Wilson, we have spent most of our evolutionary history – 300,000 generations – living in close proximity to the sea. And still today, four in five of the world's population lives within 60 miles of a large body of water.[16] So, of course we are naturally attuned to it. Our bodies and minds work optimally when in proximity to water. Recent studies show that simply "being near it can calm and connect us, increase innovation and insight, and even heal what is broken."[17]

Humans have been drawn to the sea to reflect, recuperate and heal ailments, both of the body and psyche, throughout history. When we are sick, we instinctively know that water heals: we run a burn under a tap, cool a fever with damp cloths, wash a graze, gargle with salt water, soak our aching bodies in a hot salt bath, ice a sprain, hydrate with drinks or intravenous saline drips. "The cure for anything," the wise saying goes, "is salt water – sweat, tears, or the sea."

The sea positively affects us on so many levels: psychologically calming us through the wavelengths of sound (that our nervous systems perceive as soothing), and light (which we perceive as colour) – we are naturally calmed by blue.

Time and again, research has shown that a lack of time in nature has measurable negative effects on our physical and mental health.

We need a bare minimum of two hours a week outside to see the effects.[18] But the distinctive benefits of the sea are not the same as being outside anywhere else, nor is it simply the physical exercise that we might get walking the shoreline or surfing or swimming in the sea – though these do contribute to raising feelgood endorphins, lowering cortisol levels, and strengthening our muscles, heart and lungs. The sea impacts our physical and emotional well-being in a vast variety of unique ways that no other natural setting can.[19]

Matrix

Water is in every cell of our bodies. Our very essence is an internal ocean.

Giving Birth in the Ocean, *Aquadural*

We are bodies of water...birthed from bodies of water...drawn to bodies of water.

In the words of Albert Szent-Gyorgi, discoverer of Vitamin C: "Water is life's matter and matrix, mother and medium."

Matrix...from the Latin meaning *mother*.

Matrix...meaning *underlying structure*.

As Azra and Seren Bertrand reflect in *Womb Awakening*, "Everything is birthed through a womb, and the fabric of creation is a pregnant ocean of dark matter: the dark mother, the dark birther, a dynamic but creative shimmering Void of luminous darkness. This great sea births us into life, and eventually we fall back into her living waters."

The gametes that made us found each other in flow. Fast-swimming sperm and slow-drifting egg met and melded. Our bodies were water-bound for their first nine months, floating in their own private ocean in our mother's womb. Our immanence was heralded by the breaking of these waters: a gushing flow precipitating our arrival on dry land. We are 78% water when we're born, decreasing year on year, until it makes up just 60% of our bodies in old age.

We can know the importance of water with our pre-frontal cortices in certain ways. Through scientific research we can understand the structure of water molecules, the impact of minerals. We can know water through our senses – what it looks, feels, sounds, smells and tastes like. But what we know about water extends far beyond this. Understanding water as mother takes us somewhere deeper. Somewhere primal. Somewhere both ancient…and new.

The Sea, The Sea, The Deep, Deep Sea, It Holds All the Treasures of Humanity

I can remember in my twenties I went in earnest search of who I am. Asking G.O.D. for an answer I was not sure I would ever find. But yearning from the inside to know why and what I was all about.

After weeks spent in asking, praying and contemplating, I had a vision.

I saw the entire world as a body of dark, ink-colored water with all of life connected and inter-connected to each other. In this large body of water, we were all the same. There was no colour or differences in distinction.

The water was calm, soothing, relaxing and pleasing to be in, as it continuously moved and flowed through me. I was one with everything as it was one with me. It was as dark as ink, but I could see every human being as if we were all encased in bubbles that separated us and then blended us together continuously moving, continuously flowing.

There was this blissful feeling of being inwardly relaxed and at peace. Joined and attached to everyone and everything. No separation.

I came away from the experience with more questions than answers, but what remained in my body from the experience was this sense of belonging.

It was that same feeling of belonging which I had experienced as a little girl when comprehending what death was like when I was five years old.

My mom, true to form as a Christian, gave me her biblical version of death, which seemed to soothe me for a short while. But there were still questions that no one could or would tell me, even though I asked.

I was finally told to stop asking.

So, left to my own devices, I began imagining what death was like and what becoming nothing felt and looked like. I only ever saw blackness.

Which brings me back to the beginning, where I wound up in my twenties still asking the questions that were answered in the vision. Blackness was the beginning and ending, it was everything. No separation.

Sharyn Ginyard

Medium of Transformation

When we think of water as matrix, as a vital part of the underlying structure of life, it teaches us that fluid change is at the heart of existence. It models transformation so beautifully, as it changes from blue-hued icebergs to deep grey brooding expanses of ocean, to fat raindrops kissing the parched earth, to snowflakes, to pebbles of hail, mighty flowing rivers, rainbow-laced waterfalls and mist over the forest. It transforms from solid to liquid to gas, from crystal to fluid, over and over and over again, yet always, in its essential nature, simply water.

Water has been acknowledged as a symbolic and elemental conduit between states of existence by cultures around the world for as far back as we are aware. For many spiritual traditions it is considered the matrix of transformation, its fluidity allowing us to move from one state of being to another. Many cultures acknowledge the sea as a portal to sacred or magical realms beyond, and water itself as an earthly sacrament. In Celtic culture the sea was what separated this world from the Otherworld. The Norse floated their dead out to sea in burning boats, as did some Polynesian cultures. In India, Hindus still sail the ashes – and sometimes bodies – of loved ones down the sacred Ganges to the sea. In Christianity, Jesus was baptised in the Sea of Galilee, consecrated to God in an act repeated over two millennia by hundreds of millions of Christians as a mark of belonging to the divine.

In my book *Burning Woman* I wrote extensively about the baptism of fire. But what of the baptism of water? I want to reclaim this act of transformation for each of us beyond the limitations of religious dogma. It is a powerful magic. By using conscious immersion in ritual practice, in our daily lives, we can begin to remember, to reclaim what it means to be directly connected to the matrix. To The Mother: Mother Nature.

Water allows us to touch magic.
Be touched by magic.
To embody magic.
To be held.
To be transformed by the elements.
The sparkle of sunlight on water
reminds us of this promise.

Sea and I

She and I have a complicated relationship.

I was brought up listening to Her whisper. I could see Her from my bedroom window as a child and She soothed me on many teenage nights fraught with anxiety and self consciousness.

But at 23, when I landed my dream job, and was basking in my ego's triumph, I returned home from London one weekend and didn't recognise Her voice anymore. I'd become immune to Her call. I couldn't translate Her into this new language that was taking over my tongue.

In London, I felt a part of me was missing. The only time I felt even close to whole was on the riverbank of the Thames, but He was never home. He wasn't Her. He was a dirty, compromised, tidal waterway that lapped suggestively against concrete.

I fled London for France, seduced by Her Sister Sea, the Mediterranean. She was a flashy, turquoise blue. She was ancient, She'd seen it all. Nothing surprised Her and She accepted all who swam in Her shallows. She was a private sea, a narrow vagina at Gibraltar opening to a womb of nations. She didn't mind Her international stardom and the story that She was the playground of the rich and famous. It kept the world's attention away from Her Eastern and Southern shores, from those ones She carried away from terror, war and famine.

I certainly knew nothing of the thousands who journeyed across Her on flimsy rafts and tattered dinghies. She did Her best, but it's not Her fault that men are greedy, and governments are merciless.

Returning to Ireland in the first decade of the new millennium, I shrugged off my deep need to be beside Her. I lived in the city and waved to Her occasionally from the train. It wasn't until my own waters filled with life that I listened and moved back by Her shore, back to the childhood window but deaf to Her voice and illiterate to Her words.

Then I began to understand how She stretched, how She laboured, how She never, ever rested but ebbed and flowed ceaselessly, pulled by the insatiable Moon. Then I began to hear Her grey anguish. It started quietly, innocently enough. It was a soothing rock-a-bye, a constant I could depend upon as I toiled away, striving, giving, living to the edge of my extremities.

Until one day in November 2016, quite out of the blue, She invited me under Her cool blanket. It wasn't even an invitation really. A suggestion? No. An order? Not quite. A resigned, callous insistence that I shrug off my trappings and disappear under Her deep.

For many years, I spent Sunday mornings at church services either preaching from a pulpit or watching clingy children in a crèche. There wasn't space or time for me to worship or bask in the Divine Presence. I would come away empty. I would envy my non-religious friends their Sunday morning swims.

Didn't the Spirit of God hover over the waters?

Now I go to church every Sunday – the church of sea salt, a lot of women, clear water, laughter and sunshine. And my cup runneth over!

Melanie Clark Pullen

Bathing

Stroke by
stroke my
body remembers that life and cries for
the lost parts of itself—
fins, gills
opening like flowers into
the flesh.

Mary Oliver, "The Sea"

The journey of She of the Sea requires that we acclimatise ourselves to the sense of immersion, the feeling of having a second skin: the water. We start to remember who we are beyond our current physical confines and limitations. We allow the flow of soul in and out of our skins. We top our bodies up on the minerals they have been lacking. We begin to reclaim the feeling of fluidity in the comfort of a bath or swimming pool or hot tub or the sea. We activate the relaxation response, allowing our nervous systems the chance to switch from high alert, to resting and repairing.

For many of us this requires a degree of courage.

oOo

When I was nine, I came close to drowning, in a swimming pool when an older boy sat on my shoulders depriving me of the abil-
ity to surface. I'm sure that somewhere in my mammal brain that memory of not being able to take in air still lingers with every immersion I make into the sea on my doorstep in Plym-

outh...and yet that isn't the whole story. When about to enter I stand and feel the sea and know that I am in the presence of Otherness in a way that should engender a respectful fear. I am often figuratively and literally out of my depth when sea swimming and my awareness of that generates a frisson, an emotional high, a sort of endorphin kick that expands my sense of safety ever-so slightly with each time.

For me there is no feeling of at-oneness with its vastness and power and energy so readily available to my senses through the pull of currents, tides and daily nuances of behaviour. I would say the sea and me have a relationship based on a...morbid fascination with each other...because I keep returning again and again to see how far it can push me. Likewise, no at-one-ness with nature for me when swimming – in fact, for the sake of authenticity, the experience exacerbates my sense of separateness from it...and yet...swim I must.

I am unable to articulate why I sea swim so often given my feelings. It speaks to another part of me that is a-verbal, non-cognitive, a part beyond, beneath, above, simultaneously transcending me whilst also moving through me. For that I have no words, only a compulsive sensing that the sea is beyond my understanding – and that is what I am attracted to, to be silenced by her.

Gia Daprano

oOo

Bodily immersion is one of the most literal ways of connecting us to the water and feeling its physical and psychological benefits.

Bathing for health and wellbeing goes back at least as far as the Romans in Europe, where people would flock to natural hot springs to soak in the mineral rich waters. In the eighteenth century sea bathing became extremely fashionable in England. Doctors prescribed 'taking the waters' to those suffering from mental health issues, recuperating from illness or suffering from rheumatism or gout.

Bathing in all its forms is experiencing a resurgence, thanks to the boom in the wellbeing industry. From natural hot springs in New Zealand, Japan and Iceland to modern spas in hotels, as well the massive rise of cold water and wild swimming, people are flocking to take the waters once more, knowing instinctively and experientially how much good it does them.

Sea Swimming

I awake in my warm comfortable bed most mornings after a restless night. I inherited my mother's insomnia. I am, however, looking forward to the time I can get up. Why? Because I have my 8am daily beach date, for an invigorating dip in the Atlantic. The very best way to start the day!

If I am honest with myself, it doesn't always pan out like that. The thought of dragging my head off my pillow and body from beneath my cosy duvet to an icy beach in my swimsuit and entering the chilly water is as appealing as it sounds! However, we (my equally crazy winter swimming buddies) have a saying that rings in my head if I dare to hesitate or consider sending a wimping out text to the 'Ladies Who Swim' WhatsApp group:

"You never regret going, but you will regret not going."

It is true, and the lure of the après swim buzz and euphoria is always too much to resist.

This daily dose of cold water, sunrise, beautiful scenery and a brief coffee catch-up with likeminded friends, definitely sets me up positively for the day ahead. I must admit to a smidgen of smugness too – no harm to feel personal pride, however small the personal achievement.

So, I pop on my swimsuit and snuggly Dryrobe and pack the basket of essentials: a flask of warm water for sandy feet and freezing fingers, wetsuit booties and gloves, coffee and super warm loose clothes, socks and sheepskin boots to jump into after swimming.

I started these swims a few years ago when a friend was going through a particularly difficult time. The swims were her escape from the stress in her life and looking forward to the next swim kept her focussed on the positive. Spring, summer, autumn, winter...a different experience every time and we often find ourselves saying, "This is the best swim ever!" regardless of the season. It makes us giggle every time!

A year after we started swimming, I found a lump in my left breast. My sister and a couple of first cousins had already been through breast cancer treatment, so I had done the genetic test a couple of months earlier. When I got the result, I had convinced myself that I would be a passive carrier. But fate had other ideas.

I was diagnosed with breast cancer and kept swimming through three months of chemotherapy: the support from my friends and nature was invaluable. Swimming did not prevent me from getting, or cure me, of cancer (nor did I expect it would), but it undoubtedly supported me physically and mentally throughout my treatment, and subsequent health, mind and body challenges. The health and wellbeing benefits of sea swimming are widely celebrated. Speaking personally, being in the sea throughout the year makes me feel really alive and wonderfully connected with nature. Maybe it is because over 60% of our bodies is water, maybe it is just because I am being active. Maybe it is simply having a focus, aim and a daily achievable goal that benefits me personally.

That the benefits of submerging myself daily in the freezing but beautiful Atlantic Ocean are still a mystery is part of its magic. However, whatever it is, it is having a positive effect, and I am not prepared to find out by stopping.

Life is thankfully good and healthy now and my cancer-compromised immune system seems to be hardy, as are my supportive pod of 'Ladies Who Swim'... The sea is a good friend to us all, and I intend on nurturing my friendship with it for as long as physically possible.

Helen Cuddigan

A Portable Prayer

After a scary Burning Woman initiation, that sucked my soul from my body, a beloved wise woman suggested I plunge myself in cold water.

I know for many it works. My sister and brother are avid proponents of it, and I know of women healing from cancer, managing grief or trauma who swear by cold water swimming in the wild to boost their endorphins and energy levels. It is recommended by many doctors and therapists for depression and anxiety, shocking the system into functioning in a different way and toning the vagus nerve to calm the nervous system.

But for me, the tenuousness of the connection between bodymind and soul feels so small, my stress levels so high, that I fear it will do the opposite: shocking me away from my body for good.

When traumatised I need the safety of the swimming pool, the hot tub, the bath…the gentle warm waters of a surrogate womb space in which to float, with as little human contact as possible, to come back to myself. To unfreeze. To fill my body with myself once more.

But getting into the water is still hard. There are many times when I cannot put on a swimsuit and face the judgement of strangers. When water in any form is too much. I cannot bathe or shower or swim or even wash my face or walk the shore. Though I live a mile from the sea, there can be months between my visits. Though she heals me, often she is too fierce for me, even in her gentle days. Her light too bright, the shoreline too exposed. When my inner sea is churning so violently I fear it may wash me away for good. I dare not approach it. I put up my sandbags, build my barricades, hunker down to survive this internal storm.

This is when the numb frozenness can only be borne, not bathed. When the sensuality of water is a sensory step too far. When nothing but bed is safe or quiet enough.

The wind roars outside my window, bringing the scent of seaweed and salt. Reminding me of the sea that I cannot venture to.

During lockdown the local pool that had become my sensory lifeline was shut for months on end.

In a moment of clarity, I realise that I need to bring the water to me. And so I head online and order an above-ground pool. It feels brave, risky, daring and irresponsible.

This pool is a portable prayer. A harking back to the turquoise bliss of three summers ago when the seeds of this book were planted. Before the rumbles became a storm. Before our lives were flooded, washed away. Before this house became both jail cell and lifeboat. A time when we could venture out into the world, visit the beach, as a family.

It arrives…during a hosepipe ban, after the driest May on record. We build it together as a family, raking stones, slotting pipes, stretching tarpaulin, in anticipation of the forecast summer storms.

The rains fall. Day after day. The pool fills with storm water. We add salt not chlorine.

In front of our house, we now have a shrine to water magic and healing. A site for immersion in the front garden parking place of a busy modern housing estate. A turquoise cauldron of salt water behind a hedge, to dissolve our anxiety on safe home ground.

I listen as three children, who cannot normally spend time together without anger or tears, are laughing and splashing. The water is working its magic. Their laughter breaks my spell of numb isolation. I emerge from the house in my swimsuit and join them in the blue.

Sacred Bathing

I am going down to the dark, dark places I know best
I am going down to swim
in the warm-misted sea.

Patricia Monaghan, *Seasons of the Witch*

We each may have different abilities to access bathing water, dependent on our location, circumstances and health. Some may be able to get to the sea itself, for others it is too far, too polluted, too cold or dangerous to access. For some, a swimming pool is a fabulous alternative. The bright blue or turquoise of the lining also gives a hit of colour therapy, along with the fluidity of movement, the sensation of floating and the ability to totally submerge ourselves in safer waters. Obviously, the quieter the pool, the more relaxing the experience: Saturday afternoon at the local public pool is not a time for a reflective soulful swim!

Swimming pools, whilst wonderful in many ways, do not provide the minerals that you get from a dip in the sea or natural spa. For those with access to a bathtub, I offer some additional ways of accessing full body immersion from the comfort of your own home. If you don't have a bath, why not use a large bowl as a footbath.

In my house we use showers for quick day to day washes, and baths for relaxing, decompressing and coming back into contact with our many layers of self. A sacred bath tends to have candles, each lit with a prayer or intention, and salts and scent added to the water. You might also choose to put on the *She of the Sea* playlist. Close the door and allow yourself to slip into another world. Soak your body and let the wisdom of water flood you, fill your cells, immersing you in the sacred.

Salt

Salt has been deeply valued by cultures throughout history for culinary seasoning, food preservation, healing and spiritual reasons. It has long been associated with wisdom and trustworthiness – a good person is described as 'the salt of the earth' in a phrase taken from the Bible into common usage and someone who is to be trusted in their work is 'worth their salt,' a phrase dating back to Roman times when soldiers were paid part of their wages in salt.[20]

Salt, like water, is an elemental substance which is used for physical, spiritual and energetic purification. Salt is considered sacred by many. Pagans and witches use salt for protection. A protective circle of salt may be cast around a practitioner at the beginning of a ritual, to delineate sacred space. It is often used to cleanse crystals. Interestingly, many Christians use 'blessed salt' in similar ways to holy water – to protect a home and for exorcisms.[21] Growing up I was taught to always throw the remaining salt from a pinch in cooking over my shoulder – to keep the devil away – a folk practice still common in England amongst people of no religious belief.

Salt water is extremely healing for many skin issues and is used to cleanse wounds to prevent infection. Saline drips, energy drinks and diarrhoea treatments include salt to rebalance the body's electrolytes. Breathing in salty air, often referred to as halotherapy,[22] is recommended for depression and some respiratory conditions, hence the practice of using salts in bathing.

When I was growing up, bath salts were definitely the preserve of my grandmother's generation, but they have enjoyed a recent revival.

Today there are many salts to choose from: Epsom Salts, Himalayan pink salt, sea salt magnesium flakes…but which to choose?

Epsom Salts were originally from Epsom in England, where magnesium rich waters were first discovered in the early seventeenth century, making it a much-visited spa town. The spring has not been used since the early twentieth century, but magnesium and sulphate, which are found in many natural sources, have since been combined and used, retaining the name Epsom Salts.

They help in replenishing the body's magnesium supplies, through the permeable barrier of the skin – much as bathing in natural mineral-rich water at a thermal spa or in the sea does. Used by those with arthritis and rheumatism as well as athletes, salt baths are known to detoxify the body, easing aches and pains. I take a handful and scrub my wet feet and legs with them before allowing them to dissolve in the water, ensuring an invigorating direct dose of magnesium that makes my skin tingle.

Magnesium has been shown to be a powerful anti-inflammatory, lessening the severity and number of hot flushes during menopause and decreasing migraine. It has been suggested that one reason for women's chocolate cravings during the pre-menstrual phase is a lack of magnesium in modern diets.[23] According to recent research by the US National Institutes of Health, "Magnesium is involved in 80% of known metabolic functions. It is currently estimated that 60% of adults do not achieve the average dietary intake and 45% are magnesium deficient, a condition associated with disease states like hypertension, diabetes and neurological disorders, to name a few."[24]

Magnesium is best absorbed through the skin, rather than through the stomach lining, which is why bathing in Epsom Salts, **pure magnesium flakes,** or spraying yourself with a magnesium spray after bathing or showering is much more effective than taking it as an oral supplement.

Himalayan pink salt is mined in the foothills of the Himalayas. The salts were deposited by ancient oceans over 250 million years ago, as these mighty mountains were emerging from the sea. Covered by snow and ice for tens of millions of years, these salts are considered particularly powerful in terms of their healing properties, and free of many pollutants found in other salt sources. Coming in beautiful crystals of orange, pink and white, it contains a large assortment of trace minerals.

Sea salt is made by evaporating water from sea water to leave the salts, containing many trace minerals that are known to support optimal immune function and hormone production. Some of the most well-known sea salts are from Maldon in the UK, prized for cooking, and the Dead Sea, located between Jordan, Israel and Palestine.

Whilst the Dead Sea and the Himalayan salt mines are large, they are also non-renewable sources of salt, unlike other sea salts, and so I tend to avoid them.

Whichever salts you choose, I recommend purchasing them unscented (as most of the scents are artificial) – and getting them in bulk, from chemists, veterinary suppliers or major online retailers for the best prices and to minimise packaging waste. For most benefit, you need to be generous with them, a good cup or even two are needed. Then add your scent, in the form of a few drops of essential oil, chosen to relax the body. Lavender is a classic, but rosemary, grapefruit, bergamot or rose geranium are other favourites of mine.

Today's the Day to Go Swimming

It's been going on seven years nearly. Six and a half and a bit long years. Six and a half and a bit short years. Six and half and a bit years since I swam.

Today is the day I went swimming...

I didn't listen to music afterwards for a long time, and then one day I was ready and it was right. I didn't go back to yoga for a long, long time afterwards and then one day I just knew that I could. I didn't dance for a very long, long time afterwards and then I just did. Each time I never pushed myself, just went with the flow and when the joyful urge bubbled forth to partake I just did it. Swimming was the last thing...the last afterwards undone thing. It was the first thing I planned to do with her after she was born, me, her big brother and her. And afterwards I never swam again. I wasn't even aware that it was a thing I didn't do any more until about three years into grieving. Even after I wrote a poem just before her second birthday I didn't twig I had a swimming block. But by three years in I knew it was a biggie. It was huge.

> Today's not a day to go swimming
> I might just want to breathe it all in
> And dissolve into my grieving
> In the Universal Womb
> I want to wade right in
> Little darling

Maybe it was all that water, the element of our emotions. A whole great big ocean of my emotions. Maybe it was because the planned water birth never happened, because of the burst water-main which happened as I went into labour and the water was shut off in the whole area and the pool stayed empty. Maybe it was too womb-like. Swimming in the amniotic fluid of the Great Cosmic Mother. Maybe it was other, darker things...

> Oh I want to go swimming
> With you little darling
> I don't want to do living
> No more

Two years ago I bought a swimsuit, but I knew I wouldn't wear it that summer.

Last year I thought I might swim. I was almost ready, but not quite. This year I knew I would swim, but didn't know when. This summer passed. Every opportunity and invite to swim seemed the wrong one...a hesitancy in my gut, and I listened to it.

Today I won't go swimming
I'll stay on land where it is dry
And let my heart fall from each eye
In drops that I see you living
Form a sea that I could swim in
little darling

But...today, as summer moved into autumn and the last rays were deep golden in a sky so blue, I just announced that we were going to go to the beach. I found myself putting on my swimsuit, calmly as if it were the most everyday thing in the world, then donning my clothes. The decision made unconsciously, so sweetly it didn't jar or feel odd. I know me. I know me so well and if somewhere, on some level inside me, I have decided that this is okay, and suddenly announce this to the world and to my surprised self, then I trust that this is okay and will not hurt.

I grabbed the only two white roses in amongst the freesias from the vase, wrapped them in damp tissue and we headed to the nearest sand and sea. As I drove I was aware that I was headed to the beach nearest to where my daughter is buried.

We found a quiet patch in amongst the other sunseekers. Then I discovered within myself an urgency and a joy...I had to get in the water. No fear, no overwhelming sad emotion just a desire. And in I went.

I cannot even relay to you how blissful it felt. So wonderful, so warm, so cold, so playful, free and delightful. I had my quiet moment of absorbing the relief to have somehow got to this place inside myself. To find myself at this point in the journey of Izzy and me. I shed a tear, but it was okay. I danced on the sand beneath my feet, spinning in the water up to my waist, my hands trailing the surface in rainbow sparkles of water and sunlight.

As I turned to face the horizon, I noticed a solitary seagull bobbing up and down too on the waves. And me and the seagull had a moment. A real moment. About a year ago, Seagull came to me as a new power animal, for me to work with Freedom specifically. And in that moment I knew what Freedom was. To be free I have to live from pure desire emanating from the Self connected to Source. That creates a blissful life free from fear and self-imposed limits.

I had this long moment bobbing together with the seagull and felt truly free, present and happy. And then it flew off.

Afterwards we visited Izzy's little garden. A proper woodland now, so many of the trees have really shot up this year, hers included. We laid out white roses. I hugged that little hawthorn tree and I sobbed so many tears. "I swam without you."

I'm so glad I trust myself to heal and to know.

I'm so glad I don't force or push myself, just doing what I need to do and when.

I'm so glad I listened to my heart every time it told me "today's not a day to go swimming"

And I'm so very glad I listened and took the plunge without hesitation when my heart whispered to me "today's the day to go swimming."

Heidi Wyldewood

Reflections

What does "water as matrix" mean to you?

How might this inform your interaction with it?

How might we have a two-way relationship with water? How can we become more aware of its impact on every level of our existence? How might this communication look?

What scary experiences have you had with water? Have you managed to process or integrate them? If not, how might you begin to?

Are there times when you find water healing?

Are there times that you cannot cope with water? How do you respond at these times? Do you force immersion or allow retreat? How does this work for you?

What new ways of experiencing water would you like to try? How can you make this happen?

4

DEEP BLUE MAGIC

*Suppose I were to begin by saying that I
had fallen in love with a colour.*

Maggie Nelson, *Bluets*

Out of the Blue

If magic was a colour,
That colour would be sparkling blue:
Aquamarine, cobalt, lapis, turquoise, sapphire,
Blue...

It was the blue
In a dozen shimmering shades
Azure, cyan, deep sky,
Prussian, Egyptian, navy, cerulean,
That began the healing process.

Cornflower, teal, peacock, electric, baby, powder...
I seek it out in paints and inks.
Phthalo, indigo, true, royal,
Mermaid, pond, stream, denim
Ultramarine...

I call up these names like mantras,
Watching them spread in the silent
pools of water on the page,
Fingers stained with their vibrance.
I drink them in through my eyes
Like a dying woman gulps water.

But however hard I try, I can never capture
the layers of intensity of those days
And what it felt like to be immersed
In the blue.

To be skin deep,
Soul deep,
Bathed in blue.

At the time
I thought it was the warmth,
The lack of deadlines,
The juicy ripe fruit.
But when I close my eyes,
It is the blue that returns.

I drank it in, from sunrise to sunset.
The pale blue of the sky,
The glittering aqua of the pool,
The blue of pens on paper in the morning sun.

But my longing was only fully sated
By the vast expanses of Homer's wine-dark seas
Growing turquoise in hidden coves,
Which called the white sailing boats to them
Like doves.
The desire for full immersion in this
blue heaven was hypnotic.
She called us all,
Even high on the barren hilltop
And we were powerless to her silent voice.

Alchemy

*For many years, I have been moved by the blue
at the far edge of what can be seen, that colour of
horizons, of remote mountain ranges, of anything
far away. The colour of that distance is the colour of
an emotion, the colour of solitude and of desire, the
colour of there seen from here, the colour of where you
are not. And the colour of where you can never go.*
Rebecca Solnit, *A Field Guide to Getting Lost*

Humans get hungry for blue, it seems: to hold the sea in their hands, to wear the sky in their hair, to drape them-selves in the hazy blue of distant mountains. Blue is more than a colour: it is a feeling. We don't say that we feel orange or purple, but we say we feel blue when our souls are sad and heavy. We play or sing or listen to the blues to express this sensation. Like any colour, it cannot be adequately described with words, only experi-enced, known through the eyes and the soul.

Making blue has always been magic: the domain of alchemists since the beginning of human history. To find red only required blood or berries or the smearing of red clay. To make brown was as simple as reaching down to the earth beneath one's feet. White chalk is plen-tiful in many places, or can be replaced by fire ash. But blue appears rarely in forms from which paints or dyes can be made…blue re-quires earthly magic.

The creation of blue pigments for art and writing required craftsman-ship and carefully followed recipes of alchemical reactions, heating and aging and additions of other compounds…or the grinding and binding of rocks from a landlocked, mountainous and often war-torn country.

Blue was a secret lost and found at many times and in many places during human history. It has played hide and seek with us, leading us forward in longing. Amongst ancient cultures it was the Egyptians who first mastered and treasured the manufacture of blue paint.[25] Their secret was lost in the European Dark Ages. In Celtic lands woad was used as a dull blue dye for clothes and manuscripts until the arrival of the more vivid indigo from The New World and the rare ground pigment of lapis lazuli arrived via the Silk Road.

Its arrival was celebrated by the adornment of Mary, Mother of God, who shed her dark mourning clothes and emerged in Medieval art draped in resplendent robes of ultramarine. Bejewelled rose windows appeared in cathedrals featuring this magical new blue. The upwelling of devotion to the sacred Feminine was echoed in the poetry of courtly love to the dark maiden, the beloved but unattainable woman. Blue spoke to the longing of our souls for the Feminine. Blue became sacred once more.

There are so many of us who understand Robert Macfarlane on a cellular level when he says, "I love that blue with all my heart, dreamdive deep into it, drown in its hue."[26] In fact, in survey after survey around the world, blue emerges as our favourite colour.

There is something in blue against white that enchants us. Perhaps because it speaks to us of the sea. First developed by ancient Mesopotamians, to mimic lapis lazuli, cobalt blue glazes on white backgrounds have decorated the most expensive and desirable ceramics: from priceless Chinese Ming vases, through Islamic mosques bedecked in the most exquisite mosaics, to Dutch delftware and English willow pattern Wedgewood, to contemporary designs.

As I child, I lived next to a Victorian rubbish dump, in an abandoned chalk mine. It was my favourite place to play; littered with fragments of broken blue and white china, glass marbles and blue bottles, which I unearthed and displayed in my own little museum. As an adult, I love to collect sea glass, looking out for the glint of frosted blue and green amongst the grey pebbles.

Most of our rubbish today, however, is far less beautiful. Plastic bottles and nets and old shoes and straws dumped out at sea, this floating plastic reaching places otherwise untouched by human culture, creating blue, green, pink and yellow granules that will outlast seven generations.

This is our collective legacy. And it breaks my heart.

I want to leave beauty.

Blue Prints

When I was studying A Level Art at school, I spent many happy times in the dark room, gazing by dim red light into trays of dark shimmering liquid, watching as the images appeared as if by magic in front of my eyes. I loved that dark room.

Discovering and making cyanotypes during the writing of this book helped me remember the magic of photography: it is the echo of light captured forever.

Cyanotypes, from the Greek "kyanos" dark blue and "typos" image, "blue prints," were the earliest form of photography. They were later used by architects and engineers as a cheap way to reproduce their plans to share (hence why these are still called "blueprints").

Cyanotypes remind us of a technology more primitive than our high-tech digital photography, but more visceral. We see the magic happening before our eyes. We observe transformation in real time.

The technique was made popular by Anna Atkins, a British naturalist and illustrator in the Victorian era who started out working alongside her father (her engravings of shells are found in his translation of Lamarck's *Genera of Shells,* published in 1823, Lamark being the author of an alternative understanding of evolution.) She then followed her passion for natural forms, especially those of the sea, to capture seaweeds using cyanotype. She self-published these in the first ever book to contain photographs: *Photographs of British Algae: Cyanotype Impressions* in 1843.

Interest in her timeless, haunting images has reawakened after a recent exhibition of her work. Described by Ansel Oommen in *Exposure* magazine as "visual magic [...] fixed in a blue dream,"[27] the seaweeds she photographed look as fresh as if they had been gathered yesterday, each frond carefully arranged. They are the echo of time, water and sun made real and visible.

I was so excited to have discovered her work. Another creative woman, enraptured by natural forms and the sea, who decided to publish her own work, rather than trying to appease traditional publishers. She felt like a kindred spirit.

Seeing Anna's prints made me want to enter this timeless blue world myself. I went down to our local beach, gathered some seaweed and brought it home to our garden. The sun was shining and the sky above as blue as the strange blue paper I was about to cast a sun spell on.

The process itself is magic in action. You start with a chemically treated blue paper.[28] You place your leaves on the surface and watch as the colour bleaches out of the uncovered parts of the paper over the course of a couple of minutes – hence they are also often known as sun prints. The area under the leaves remains blue. Then you wash the paper under the tap and the print disappears completely. If you're anything like me, you start to freak out that you've washed the beauty away. But then gradually, gradually it appears – reversed – in front of your eyes and darkens over the next few hours.

Blue Rocks

Since I was a child, blue and turquoise have always been my favourite colours. I had several books of rocks and crystals when I was young, and used to pore over them. My mum always had lots of crystals around, and I am so delighted that my own daughters seem to share this passion. Since writing this book, this interest has bloomed into an obsession, as I have found myself filling my space with different varieties of blue stones.

There is something reminiscent of the different moods of the sea and ourselves, in crystals, from the surface shine to the depths changing colour according to angle and light. They give the appearance of liquidity, and yet are portable in the way the sea is not. The crystals most commonly associated with the sea, would of course be salt crystals – magnificent cubic forms. Like a pebble or a shell you might collect from the shoreline, crystals can be held in the hand, strung around the neck, worn on a finger, or put in pride of place on a window sill or altar space. Their entrancing colour heals, soothes, calms or uplifts, depending on the stone.

Crystals are representative of ancient earth magic at work unseen deep inside the planet we inhabit. They remind us of the potential beauty that results from transformation, the shapeshifting of earth's elements from one state to another. They remind us that under great pressure and stress and heat, magic can happen.

I have always chosen crystals as jewellery, rather than the precious gemstones our culture values. The vast majority is lapis lazuli, turquoise, amethyst, quartz, moon stone and opal bought from jewellery artists and market stalls. I have a few larger raw pieces in each of my creative spaces and also use them in creating altars and personal healing.

I am intuitive in the way that I select and use crystals, so it was interesting to discover, as I delved further into them for this book, that blue is used for dealing with fear, anxiety, self-expression and creativity – my biggest struggles. Sea-coloured crystals are said to cover the upper chakras that regulate our physical and spiritual energy flow – from green (heart), blue (throat), indigo (third eye) and white (the spiritual chakra, situated above the crown of the head). They are generally considered cooling (because of their association with water), and are used for calming and balancing the bodymind, as well as helping to reduce inflammation, such as migraine, swollen joints or glands. They are connected to the voice, helping with creative expression. They are associated with the Feminine and intuition…you can see why I am sharing them with you in the context of this book!

Initially I was going to suggest a couple of crystals, but quickly found myself falling fast down a rabbit hole of sparkly delight in every shade of the sea (at one stage this section ran to seventeen crystals!). I found myself reclaiming a lost love.

These are just a few of my favourites…

Larimar

Often known as "Stone of the Ocean" or "Atlantis Rock," larimar looks like sunlight on the turquoise Caribbean Sea, which is where it originates. This has become my favourite crystal, and was one I only discovered when writing this book. It is only found in the Dominican Republic and, as a reasonably rare stone, is quite pricey…otherwise all the larimar would be mine! Larimar connects us to the cooling peace of the ocean, it is said to alleviate guilt, fear, and dissolve energy blockages. Its properties include freeing creative self-expression and calming anxiety: it was made for me!

Aquamarine

From the Latin for "sea water," this pale green crystal is a cousin of emeralds. It is said to give protection for those travelling on the water. Like many of the blue-green stones it is used to support vocal expression, and ease swollen glands.

Blue Calcite

With white and turquoise or baby blue waves and base layers of golden rock below, blue calcite is particularly stunning carved into pointed columns, where it looks like the sea in solid form. (I may have been coveting some beautiful specimens on Instagram when I wrote this!)

Unpolished or carved, it looks like a baby blue version of rose quartz, but is actually calcium carbonate. Its soothing qualities mean that it is used for anxiety and depression. I have a polished worry stone that fits beautifully in the palm of my hand, which I hold to help me feel calm and balanced. It is said to aid the development of your inner vision, dreaming abilities and clairvoyance. It is often used in combination with aquamarine for unlocking the throat chakra, and aiding the communication of deep emotion.

Labradorite

So-called because it was first found in Labrador, Canada, labradorite is not blue or green, in fact, at first glance, it looks a little like a deep grey granite. However, when polished, it reveals an incredible internal opal-like iridescence, known as "labradorescence" that appears to move and dance inside, like the Northern Lights: sometimes gold, sometimes green, sometimes blue. It looks truly magical and has to be seen to be believed. Labradorite represents the dark moon goddess, and it is no surprise that it is known as the "Shaman's Stone," and is used in healing in order to bring to light things buried deep within.

Fluorite

The word *fluorite* comes from the Latin verb *fluere*, meaning "to flow." It comes in a wide range of colours, blue and green being some of the most common, often with layers of purple and clear crystal. So-called because it fluoresces under ultraviolet light, it looks spectacular lit up from within as a lamp. It is said to illuminate the mind and magnify the positive and so is often used to support meditation.

I bought myself some beautiful sea green fluorite fairy lights that go bright turquoise when illuminated that I have strung up beside my bed.

> **Note:** There are many ethical and ecological considerations when it comes to the mining of crystals, so please, please buy from reputable suppliers that know the source of their stones. Cheap stones usually either mean fakes…or stones of dubious environmental and human cost.

Reflections

What is your relationship to the colour blue?
What role has it played in your life so far?

Altar Practice

The colour blue is deeply healing on every level: allow yourself to be immersed in it.

Add more blue to your altar or living space, perhaps some crystals, or blue glass, as well as a cyanotype or other blue artwork. You may want to add blue or white fairy light or candles.

If you have a blue crystal necklace or bracelet, take it out and wear it…if not, could you gift one to yourself…or ask for one for an upcoming birthday?

If you like to create with colour, blue comes in many hypnotic and vivid forms – alcohol inks, acrylic inks, marbling inks. Make your own blue art magic with whatever you have to hand. Write or draw with blue ink in your pen, dip your brush or your fingers into blue paint. Smash old blue plates to make a mosaic. Rip up blue magazine pages to make a paper mosaic or collage.

If you're not up for an art project right now, give yourself some time to go around your home and collect blue objects: blue buttons, crystals, Lego, books, images, clothes, crockery…collate them on an altar space, perhaps take a photograph, which captures this blue essence for you to gaze at whenever you want.

If you want the feeling of full physical immersion, wear a blue silky scarf or skirt and lots of blue jewellery to get a feeling of flow as well as the colour hit!

5

SACRED SEA

*Standing looking out to sea can be like
standing at an altar. You wait in silence for
some kind of benediction. If prayer could have
a physical destination, this would be it.*
  Jean Sprackland, *Strands: A Year of Discoveries on the Beach*

The Oceanic

Almost a century ago, as the modern world was being born, Sigmund Freud, the founding father of psychoanalysis, wrote a book called *The Future of an Illusion,* in order to scientifically dismiss the roots and practices of religion as the infantile superstitions and wish-fulfillment of primitive man. In response, a respected friend and mentor let him know that in his wholesale intellectual dismissal of religion he had entirely missed the point of spirituality. The root of religious experience, the friend explained, was a sense of the 'oceanic':

> *It is a feeling which he would like to call a sensation of 'eternity', a feeling as of something limitless, unbounded — as it were, 'oceanic.' This feeling, he adds, is a purely subjective fact, not an article of faith; it brings with it no assurance of personal immortality, but it is the source of the religious energy which is seized upon by the various Churches and religious systems, directed by them into particular channels, and doubtless also exhausted by them. One may, he thinks, rightly call oneself religious on the ground of this oceanic feeling alone, even if one rejects every belief and every illusion.*
>
> **Sigmund Freud, *Civilization and Its Discontents***

Echoes of Freud's sentiment lie at the heart of today's science, which has no place for the sacred, no space for mystery, no time for the sentimental or emotional. The soul is unverifiable to science. Unprovable. And so, whilst this intellectual scepticism has loosened the totalitarian control of religious dogma, allowing for the flourishing of science, technology and liberal culture, it has ensured that much of meaning and deep importance to the well-being of the human soul has been pushed to the very margins of our culture.

Freud was able to intellectually dismiss the roots of religious experience – the oceanic – because, by his own admission, he had never experienced it personally. I feel sorry for him. But I also resent his approach. It is a common occurrence within patriarchal culture – that those who have had no experience of something but hold cultural cachet, seek to dismiss or negate it, fast becoming the respected experts and authors of our cultural narratives. Whilst the contradictory personal experiences of the non-male, non-neurotypical and non-white 'others' are invalidated, silenced or ignored.

Those of us who know the 'oceanic' experientially find ourselves totally out of step with our culture and the modern world. We may be perceived as odd, quaint, immature and, thanks to Freud, perhaps a little neurotic. And none of us wants that. So, we tend to stay quiet about our personal experiences of the magical and mysterious. We tend not to speak of what really matters to us, to our souls. We rationalise our experiences of the inexplicable and wonderous, sharing them perhaps with a close friend or partner, but not allowing them to challenge the cultural narrative, because we don't want to be perceived as crazy.

Believe me when I tell you how much I know this. In the writing of this book, I had to confront, time and again, my internalised cultural dogmas about not speaking about the sacred or magical with my female voice. I had to confront the shame that this silence brings if you are not writing from the role of an expert – a priest or academic – but rather from lived experience. It is very real.

It is because of this silencing that such experiences seem out of the ordinary. Because we tend not to speak of the sacred or the magical in daily life, we don't realise how much of a shared experience it is. How common and everyday. How downright mundane the mystery is. We do not admit to ourselves or others how vital it is for our souls. How we suffer and struggle without it. How rich and alive we are when we live immersed in it.

This is how patriarchy thrives, on our silence.

Muddy Mysticism

The earth sloped gently when we reached the shore and there were thousands of square feet of water-logged sand, firm to run upon, glistening in the lowering sun, decorated with sea-crab bubbles. There were vast stretches of the liminal space between land and sea, where I am accustomed to only a small swath of tidal zone. There were occasional sea anemones grasping the rocks.

It could have just been simply, the ocean. It could have simply been a blessed moment in the wild. And it was both of those things, but when I tipped my perspective ever so slightly, that liminal space became our sacred ground. And our steps became our prayers, even while they remained our steps. In some ways, all that changed was that I stopped and took a deep breath before I ran toward the water.

Our son, Jude, ran with all of his strength, pumping his short arms, his mop of brown hair splayed out like wings in the wind. The roar was tremendous and we had to yell to be heard. When we finally reached the water and were soaking our cramped toes in the breakers, Jude looked out at the vastness. He opened wide his arms and shouted, "This is the ocean. This is the ocean."

Yes, my dear boy. This is the ocean—in all its fierceness and power and gloom. In all its strength to give and take life. In the way it rushes through us. These are the ocean's prayers: this teeming swarm of movement, this freedom and vastness and depth. These are the ocean's prayers and these are ours.

"And those are the eagles..." he continued, embracing the sky and following the birds' motions with his arms. They were actually seagulls. We did not correct him. Sometimes the role of mother feels impossible to merge with the identity of mystic. And other times, oceanside, it is completely natural.

Sometimes all it takes is the simple power of looking and naming to recognise the sacred. I think that's what happened for Jude. It sure is what happened for me as I listened to him and looked out at that which he named in such a childlike fervor. The water was dark, the sky still light. We stood in the middle of the ocean bed. We stood and we knew God in just that water's edge way. The water's edge graced with my son's huge presence became my sanctuary. For a few blessed hours, I lived the life of a mystic who cannot steal away and who doesn't even want to. In other words, I surrendered.

Natalie Bryant Rizzieri

Remembering Magic

Magic lies waiting in our blood and bones,
waiting for us to open to its presence.

Aidan Wachter, *Six Ways*

Magical. This is a word that comes up a lot when people share their experiences of the sea. People who in their daily lives have no time for magic seem to reawaken to it on the shore. When they recall the way that the sun broke through the overcast sky, transforming the water

97

from battleship grey to teal. When they tell of the emergence of a pod of dolphins that leapt and wove beside their boat. Or the discovery of a treasure on the shore. Or the eerie sounds made by the wind in a cave, which sounded like ancient song. Or the way that swimming in cold water shifted something profoundly in them.

As Alice Tarbuck wonders in *A Spell in the Wild:* "What is magic? Is it a subjective feeling? Is it a scientific fact? Why does landscape make us feel things?" Magic is a word that we use to express a sense of awe and wonder at the inexplicable or unexpected. It is how we reference the way that the rational, logical world seems to vanish from our eyes and another stranger, wilder and more beautiful one takes its place. One where our relationship with our environment is alive, vital and visible. One in which we are active participants. Where the creative imagination is a force as powerful and undeniable as gravity. Where birds and waves seem to heed our voice, where the sun harks our call, where time stands still and the mythic re-emerges. Where the impossible becomes not only possible but real. "Magic is, for me," concludes Alice Tarbuck, "the practice of removing any barriers that exist between myself and the absolute, total apprehension of the world through my body." Clementine Morrigan describes it as "a way of being in the world, of being open to relationship. Magic is the practice of recognition: seeing the liveliness of the living universe, seeing the liminal. It is a practice of wonder, curiosity, remembering."[29]

I write for each one of us who is remembering what magic is… what it means…what it can be… We, who are remembering that it matters. We, who are exploring how to better work with the power and cycles of the natural world. We, who are learning how to unite our will, voice, intention, imagination and action to make the impossible possible.

The sea helps us to remember that magic is all around us, if we have the will to see it.

It is the flicker, the glimmer, the moment that causes a sharp intake of breath, the unexpected, the rediscovered, the cherished, the improbable, the miraculous in the midst of the mundane.

It is sunbeams dancing on waves and moonbeams silvering the land. The eerie glow of bioluminescence illuminating a dark sea and fog's disappearing spell.

It is the stars appearing each night, rainbows hidden in water droplets and the silent power of riptides.

It is a flock of birds flying patterns in the sky, traversing oceans to the same nest. The majesty of a school of whales breaching together. The haunting sound of their song traveling for miles through the water.

It is a heart-shaped pebble waiting to be seen by a broken-hearted lover. A feather found in answer to a prayer.

It is the iridescence of an abalone shell, the pull of the moon on the ocean, the creation of a pearl from a grain of sand.

It is energy in flux, the fluid and ever-becoming, the perfectly formed, the microcosm reflecting the macrocosm, the hidden revealed. It is the impossible just out of reach, the delightful, the colourful, transformation as it happens…

It is the unseen soul in action. Everywhere.

Magic happens in the edge spaces, where consciousness meets unconsciousness, energy meets matter, soul meets world. It takes place in the liminal space of birthdeath, here-not-here, on the edge of possibility. It requires a state of consciousness where we are able to perceive – and potentially influence – the connections between the material and the spiritual, the literal and the metaphorical. It is the imaginal realm, where all that is first comes into form. It is what arises naturally in us, if we allow ourselves to remember the miracle of our very existence and that of this habitable planet.

Reclaiming

*If you look for evidence that the world is
made of magic, for evidence that your life is
magical, you will find it everywhere.*

Molly Remer, *Walking with Persephone*

I am reclaiming my belonging to something deeper than dry land. Reclaiming the magic of turquoise and black, shimmer and sparkle, the dark unknown. Reclaiming this vital aspect of myself that has nearly blossomed many times…but has shut down through busyness and fear of others and living in a small community and professional visibility.

I am discovering the currents of my own soul. Reclaiming what living in flow could feel like, be like, here and now, day to day. I am reclaiming my connection to myself through the natural world, reclaiming magic as my natural religion, re-imagining the divine in the fluid Feminine and knowing this as tangible in the world.

This knowing of what the sea means to me rises to the surface.

It feels as though I am being immersed, submerged, flooded with an oceanic longing or knowing or remembering. The sea is leaking into me and I into her, as I remember in my surface self what I have never forgotten in my depths. Knowing on every level of my being that it is real. That it is not wrong or to be feared. Nor am I making it up.

I am one who is dedicating her life
to this…whatever this is.
I am reclaiming the parts washed away on the tide.
Reclaiming my soulskin.
Reclaiming myself.
Reclaiming my magic.
I am here.
This work makes me strange in the eyes of the world.
Swimming naked against the current of our culture.
I am a freediver of the soul.
I dive into the depths of being and
bring them to the light.
This is how I remember who I am.
This is how we remember.
This is how.
This is.
THIS.

God and Magic

The face of the divine changes. I use different names
as I need God differently. Often these changes are
initially disorienting—it can feel like I have lost God.
But I wonder if the divine is too alive to remain static.
God changes, perhaps not in essence, but in shape and
color and form, like the late autumn light hearkens
us toward winter—preparing us for what is to come.
Natalie Bryant Rizzieri, *Muddy Mysticism*

There are two things I know to be true…and yet often doubt the reality of when I am exhausted and broken and overwhelmed by land life: God and magic. Both feature heavily in human stories throughout time and place. They are at the root of all cultures, but are not considered contemporary realities by our intellectual or scientific communities.

Since the emergence of Judeo-Christian faith, it has been insisted that God and magic inhabit two different realms: God was good and light, and magic was dark, evil and dangerous. God came through priests and kings. Magic came through witches and magicians in concert with the devil. And yet few seem to remark on the fact that they deal with the same 'thing' – a mysterious, unseen, greater-than-human force, one that is imminently connected to the elements and speaks through nature. This timeless and untouchable entity seems to want to come through human bodies into the world. It can be petitioned by its adherents, and when harnessed gives them superhuman powers and can make the seeming impossible, possible. This force is understood as being both in-dwelling and external. It holds sway over both life and death, over fate, success or failure. It is capable of blessing and cursing, materialising and dematerialising.

Growing up in England, the two were most definitely separate. But here in Ireland, below the shine of modernity and the patina of Catholicism, there is a common understanding of the sacred – magic and God – as coexisting in a primal way that is connected to the land and that is always in communication with us. "The *Día* [god] of Irish is an expansive, supernatural entity rooted in nature," explains Irish writer, Manchán Magan, "the god of all things, of every raindrop and honeysuckle petal – an illuminating lifeforce that infused everything with sanctity."[30]

Over the years I have come to understand that God(dess) and magic are not dark and light, good and evil. This is a myth of patriarchy, to keep us (especially women) from direct engagement with the power of nature and the magic inherent in our own souls.

They are one and the same.

They are yearning for us as much as we are for them.

O r i g i n s

There is an aliveness to this earth, which was here far before us. It is
here still. And will be here long after us. There is something greater
than meets the eye at work here.

This is what I know when I walk the shoreline, looking out to sea.

There is, and has been, a deep human knowing of our primal connection to the waters since the beginning of recorded history. Many
creation myths from around the world focus on the separation of sky
from sea, light from dark at the very beginning of time, and connect
this to our own origins.

In Ancient Egypt, Nut, the goddess of primeval darkness "represented the undifferentiated dark sea of potential energy that existed
before all manifest creation." The indigenous Kogi ("Jaguar") people
from the Sierra Nevada mountains in northern Columbia believe
that, "In the beginning there was blackness, only the sea. No sun,
no moon, no people...no animals, no plants, only the sea. The sea
was the Mother...She was memory and possibility...the mind inside
nature."[31] These understandings of our genesis deem so resonant with
Sharyn Ginyard's intuitive insight that was featured in Chapter 3.

In ancient Greek myth, in the beginning was Chaos. From her
emerged Gaia, the earth, Tartarus, and Eros, god of love. Chaos also
gave birth to two darknesses – Erebus, of the netherworld, and Night,
the darkness over the earth. Their coupling gave birth to Ether, the
heavenly light, and to Day, the earthly light.

Meanwhile Gaia, without help, gave birth to Uranus, the starry sky,
and Pontus, the sterile sea.[32]

The creation myth of Japan states that, "Long ago all the elements
were mixed together with one germ of life. [...] A muddy sea that
covered the entire earth was created. From this ocean grew a green
shoot. It grew and grew until it reached the clouds and there it was
transformed into a god."[33]

At the very beginning of the Christian story that I grew up with,

the first words of Genesis speak of a creative intelligence giving order
to the elements of nature:

*1 In the beginning God created the heavens and the earth. 2 Now
the earth was formless and empty, darkness was over the surface
of the deep, and the Spirit of God was hovering over the waters.
[...]
6 And God said, "Let there be a vault between the waters to
separate water from water." 7 So God made the vault and
separated the water under the vault from the water above it. And
it was so. 8 God called the vault "sky." And there was evening, and
there was morning—the second day.
9 And God said, "Let the water under the sky be gathered to one
place, and let dry ground appear." And it was so. 10 God called the
dry ground "land," and the gathered waters he called "seas." And
God saw that it was good.*

The Book of Genesis

I have always loved these words. There is an inherent beauty in
them. And power. The God in these verses is the God(dess) I know.
A force beyond gender or dogma, nothing to do with the vengeance
and retribution of tribal cultures, or moral control, rather it is a description of the generative, creative impulse of the intelligent and
mysterious lifedeath force, creating, witnessing, being with creation
and knowing it as sacred.

The primacy of the sea and the (Feminine) darkness in our story
of existence, in the world's story of existence, has been there since
the beginning of human cultures. Even in science we speak of life
emerging from the primordial oceans and of the universe itself being potentially formed within mysterious black holes. But only now,
in the hubris of our own technological advancement, that we have
forgotten the wisdom of the darkness and the waters, and that our
origins and fates are entangled.

"In the beginning, in the time that was no time, nothing existed but the Womb," writes Barbara G. Walker in *Restoring the Goddess*. "And the Womb was a limitless dark cauldron of all things in potential: fluid as water yet mud-solid with the salt of the earth; red-hot as fire yet relentlessly churning and bubbling with all the winds. And the Womb was the Mother, before She took form and gave form to Existence. She was the Deep."

She *is* the Deep.

Holy Water

The song of the sea
Is the call of freedom.
The summons to surrender to a wild power
Vaster than ourselves.
The sea, our first god:
Expansive, ineffable, eternal,
To which we are called
Instinctively
To immerse ourselves,
To venture into the misty unknown.

She calls us when our binds to being human chafe,
And living in a human-sized world
is no longer bearable.
We feel ourselves breathed by the wind,
Pulled by the waves,
Freed from our own interiority.
We get a sense of something so much vaster and wiser:

Holy water
Calling us home.

Praying isn't what I learned in school.
It is something so much more primal,
Embodied.
Hands on earth, stone in hand,
Lips on love,
Flow moving through this body.

The sea is the closest I can come to God
On earth.
The closest I can come to Her.

The ocean is a body prayer
Of feet on sand, salt on skin,
Of becoming onewith,
Escape and arrival,
Ever becoming, ever unbecoming.

The song of the sea is the hymn of the liminal,
Psalm of freedom.
It is the mystery
Calling, calling, calling…
Looking for our response,
Waiting to hear our echo in the shell of Her ear.

What Lies Beneath

*The hidden well-spring of your soul must needs rise
and run murmuring to the sea; and the treasures of
your infinite depths would be revealed to your eyes.*

Kahlil Gibran, *The Prophet*

I want to write of the oceanic…mystery…the soul…of God(dess)…
magic…the sacred…that which lies beyond words. Because the repeated, deliberate seeking of connection to this is at the heart of what
I do and who I am. It is my creative and spiritual practice.

I want to speak of this so that you can close your eyes, turn inwards
and smile, knowing, just knowing. Until our conversation can continue without words. Even though true knowledge lies far beyond
language, my dearest wish is that my words can act as a bridge or
vessel, they can bring us part of the way there together.

I want to share what I have known, and for it not to sound strange.

And yet, strangeness is its nature. The soul is not of this world.
It is not rational. The sacred is not logical. But nor is this chaotic,
magnificent, contradictory and complex world of ours. And yet we
insist on pretending that it is…and being disappointed, afraid or
bemused when it shows us its reality again and again. As Jeanette
Winterson says in her book, *Lighthousekeeping*, "I do not accept that
life has an ordinary shape, or that there is anything ordinary about
life at all. We make it ordinary, but it is not."

Be assured that I am interested in reality, not fantasy.

Understanding what lies beneath matters deeply to me. I long to
comprehend it more fully. To engage with it as it is, not how I have
been taught to interpret – or dismiss – it. I want to be able to interpret
my lived experience, to share it and hear your experience, so that we can
dive beneath the shallow stories of what our culture tells us reality is.

This is what I live for. But speaking openly of it scares me. My bodymind resists, with migraines and panic attacks, trying desperately to keep me safe on the shore.

The sacred, for me, is not something I take on faith nor access through the ministrations of others. I know it to be as real as I am, more so. It is full aliveness, that I have felt again and again in this body, in this time, here on earth. Not through prostrations or belittling and repenting, but through true connection – to the body and soul of another, to myself, to the natural world, through words or music or images, the sound of waves, a candle flame. Suddenly it is just there, has always been there. The world takes on extra dimensions, only I have not been able to perceive them.

What lies beneath is a real, tangible presence, an intelligence and interface that I feel the lack of when I am not connected to it. To be connected is to be fully alive and at peace. It is to know, on some deep level, that all is well, and that all is part of a much, much larger mystery. The constant thread for me is to draw ever closer to it, to channel more of it through, to dedicate my life and work to it more fully. And this is what I see reflected in the lives and works of others of disparate beliefs and practices: those who are following the trails of spirit and soul. Though we may differ here or there, in the shape and form of our language or ritual, the path to the sacred is ultimately one.

The oceanic is always here. It is the basis of psychic life. Of life on every level. Ours is a journey of remembering. Again and again. Of reaching through pain and distractions and busyness and numbness and denial and forgetting and bad news and remembering once more: this is what is real.

This is what we are for.
To know ourselves as sacred.
To know the world as sacred.
To know the sacred.

The sea teaches me the 'oceanic' in an embodied way. It reminds how to embrace liminal states of being, the paradoxical mystery of lifedeath...where the gap is taken out from between them and they merge into one fluid continuum of becomingunbecoming, where love is right there, where beauty is right there, where a voice both booms and sparkles from beyondwithin in a silence that is more solid than anything I have ever seen. It is a place I know, where I am held.

Alice Tarbuck writes of it so beautifully: "The world does this: demonstrates, occasionally, that it isn't just connected to us, isn't a network in which we are one distant, autonomous node. Rather, it is us. We are, then, overpowered by it, entered by it and transformed. And in the same way, we enter the world, daily, and transform it, for better or for worse. Every time we act, every time we think, even, we are shaping the world and it is shaping us, and there is no escape from either. [...] Learning how to enter them, how to court them, how to cause them: that is magic. Magic happens in all those moments when the world and you aren't separated any longer by any sort of barrier."[34]

I have found this place through meditation, though it takes me a lot of fighting with my mind to allow myself to practice. I find it easier through writing and art and music and sex and dance and birdsong and floating in water...this sense of being doubly alive.

My dreams allow me to be fully immersed in this state, body and mind.

And so does the sea.

But, like the sea, I cannot hold it in my hands. The tide comes in, the tide goes out. This seems to be a vital part of being human – we are connected, then we're not. In the moments of disconnection, we can despair. This, it seems, is what it is to be human: part conscious being, part unbridled soul, part instinctive animal, always immersed in mystery, often convinced by our fear that we are alone.

The tide has gone out and stayed out for so many people. They do not have their personal connection to the sacred, to magic, to mystery, to the oceanic. Instead, there is busyness and stress and the life of the automaton. Some, but fewer nowadays, access the sacred through faith in the connection that others have or claim to have. But many live without it, dry and disconnected, reliant purely on the vagaries of their distractible minds, which fixate on the sparkly things of the world like money and lust – rather than the spark of the sacred.

And so, we are here. In a culture transfixed by manmade sparkles, and the blue light of screens. Not the azure sparkle of the sea and immersion in the sacred.

Disconnected. From ourselves. Each other. Nature. And source.

As she starts to understand what healing means to her, our Heroine sees the way home to her Self open up before her. She follows the trail of stars from the desert all the way back to the shore of the Sea of Sorrows.

Vanessa Oliver-Lloyd

The call of the sea is the call of the matrix, the first Mother, life behind life, back to soul, to the sacred, to the oceanic, back to our essence, our primal nature. It is a reminder that what lies in the depths needs to come to the surface, to be witnessed, to be known, to be loved.

And whilst on one level I know this and seek out this immersion in something greater than myself, whilst I love it with every cell of my being, as with the sea, still I resist it, fearing the repercussions.

This is the dance…
That I do with the humans I love.
This is the dance I do as I create.
This is the dance I do with the divine.
This is the dance I do with the sea.
This is the sacred dance
Of becomingunbecoming
Of remembering flow.

Mary Star of the Sea

The church rising high on the hill across the bay is dedicated to Mary, Star of the Sea.

Her designation as *Stella Maris,* "Star of the Sea," is originally thought to have been a mistranslation by St Jerome in the 5th century BC: Mary's name in Hebrew is *Miryam,* which also means "drop of the sea." The connection of the Mother of God with the sea has endured for over 1600 years. The association of her name with the North Star, used for navigation by seafarers, and her distinctive blue robes, seem to have cemented her role as both guide and protector of all those who travel the seas – literal and metaphorical.

For most from Christian backgrounds, Mary has been the only intimation that God could have a Feminine face. Her veneration in so many cultures around the world is a clue to our hunger for a Mother God.

Here in Ireland most towns and villages have their own grotto to Mary, surrounded by rocks and flowers, with benches for quiet reflection and prayer. In coastal places she is always looking out to sea. Mary was my first exposure to the concept of the divine feminine, and it is she who I, schooled in my teens by Catholic nuns, still call upon, in times of fear – "Hail Mary, full of grace, Blessed art thou among women."

Personally, Mary as archetypal Mother Goddess, comforter and protectress, is what I connect with, rather than her role in the Christian story. And her roots go back to the ancient mother goddesses of land and sea, the ancient animating principles, the soul force, the life behind life, which for me will always emerge from a female form, as this is what life on earth does (except for in the miracles of seahorse papas and trans men.) For me the Mother Ocean, and her representations that I can hold in my hand, are a more tangible way into God(dess) here on earth, than the Sky God of my childhood. My God(dess) is deeply rooted in the elements here and in my own body, immanent and transcendent, both.

The worst thing we ever did
was put God in the sky
out of reach
pulling the divinity
from the leaf,
sifting out the holy from our bones,
insisting God isn't bursting dazzlement
through everything we've made
a hard commitment to see as ordinary,
stripping the sacred from everywhere
to put in a cloud man elsewhere,
prying closeness from your heart.
The worst thing we ever did
was take the dance and the song
out of prayer
made it sit up straight
and cross its legs
removed it of rejoicing
wiped clean its hip sway,
its questions,
its ecstatic yowl,
its tears.
The worst thing we ever did is pretend
God isn't the easiest thing
in this Universe
available to every soul
in every breath.

Chelan Harkin, from Susceptible to Light

Returning to Source

*What happens to a female when all her life she hears
sacred language indirectly, filtered through male
terms? What goes on deep inside her when decade
after decade she must translate from male experience
into female experience and then apply the message to
herself? What does the experience imprint inside her?
Does it keep exclusive maleness functioning inside
her, at least at the level of experience and symbol?*

Sue Monk Kidd

For me God(dess) is another way of saying the source of the sacred,
an energy matrix, capable of communication, that is
woven through all things. God(dess) is
both the pattern-maker and the pattern
itself, the flow beneath the flow, life behind the life.

Our bodyminds are wired to connect
with this, because they are made of this.
We are made to be more alive, happier, healthier when we
are connected to source. Every single one of us is capable of a relationship with the sacred if we desire it. Because we are all capable of
contact. The water, and her magic, can seep into our bodies, whether we have language or not. Whatever age we are. Whether we can
move independently or not. Our awareness of it goes beyond all these
factors. Magic is innate to the waters. It is there. We are born of the
water. It touches us. And we touch it.

It can pour through our own hands, hearts, bodies, words…no
translator required.

We don't make magic up.
We are participants in it, channels of it.
Our job is to keep ourselves open.

The sea is an outer portal to this state of being. As are all the things that have been touched by it. The sea reactivates our flow state, if we will let it. This flow passes into and through us…if we are open to it. It is not whether this is real, but whether we perceive this or not. And how we respond.

As we learn to heed the voice of She of the Sea, we remember what it is like to inhabit a world where magic is real. Where the sacred is alive and sings in the Feminine.

Attuned, entrained, enchanting, enchanted.
We remember who we are.

"Everything we know and have and are was created by magick," writes Cassandra Snow in *Queering Your Craft*, "Everything we know and have and are is maintained by magick. Magick is a skill. Magick is a love song to yourself and the world around you. Magick is internal, external, and beyond even that. Most of all though, magick is your right, and responsibility—as a human living on this Earth […]The living of your life is a magickal act."

The world needs a soul infusion of source
magic on a scale unprecedented
Right now.
She is calling
Each of us
To dive in.
To get wet
To cry
To feel

To channel the oceanic through us
To dive into the flow
And become one with it.

Reflections

What do you understand by magic? And God?

How do our understandings of God and magic coincide or differ?

Do God(dess) and magic go together in your belief system?

The term God(dess) is one that I am exploring using…how does it work for you?

Do you have a personal practice or relationship with God or magic? Have you developed this yourself or were you taught it by someone? Does it still accurately reflect your lived experience?

What excites…and scares you…about magic?

How does your understanding of the sacred find form in the world?

Altar Practice

What representations of the sacred or magical can you add to your altar space?

6

FLOW

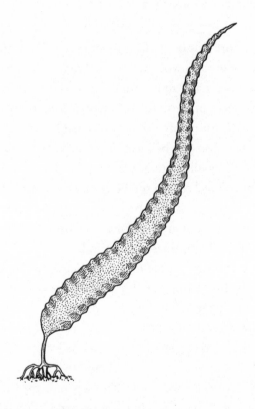

The creative act is a letting down of the net of human imagination into the ocean of chaos on which we are suspended, and the attempt to bring out of it ideas.

Terence McKenna

Reclaiming Fluidity

All my life I have kept one foot on the shore and one in the sea...
In order to swim, we cannot forever hug the shoreline.
One foot, then the other must be raised from the seabed.
We must trust ourselves to the water.

As I write this book, I find that every area of my life has become infused with water-based practices to help me reconnect body and soul, torn apart by trauma.

At the beginning of the process, I wake each morning and anxiety is already there, churning my stomach and making my thoughts race in circles. This fear stops me being able to touch and work with my own inner flow. My default setting is to block it out, with a book or my phone. I want to feel safe in my body, in the world. To do so I have learned that I must physically practice returning to it each morning. I try to set up a consistent rhythm of practises so that my body can reclaim me from the riptides of my mind.

I take up swimming on the recommendation of my therapist. But not for me the fifty laps before breakfast and a cold shower. Instead, I glide, luxuriating in the feeling of support and experiencing myself suspended in spacetime. I trust the weight of my body to the water and feel myself held by invisible threads. As I do, I allow my cells to remember another way of being. A sense of safety. Of being held. I am one with the water, and yet my skin separates me from its fluidity. I streamline myself, become a line like a stream, flush with the water. As my ears submerge, the surface world becomes muffled, like on a snowy day, and the strange sounds of underwater emerge. I am the closest I can get to flying.

After almost a year of swimming, I get up the courage to try aqua-jogging in the small, deep, dark dedicated pool. I put on the float vest and immerse myself. Round and round I run through the water, the solid bottom far from my feet. I am weightless in this small circular pool, the large float around my middle removing gravity, my arms and legs flowing by themselves. On land I am a slow and awkward runner, my joints ache, my breasts bounce. Here I am suspended. I move as though in slow motion in the dark water, creating my own whirlpool, the ripples catch the lights: I am entranced. Round and round, my brain switches gears to flow consciousness, time drifts away. Occasionally my eye lands on the clock, only to see another five minutes has evaporated like steam. Round and round. Water flowing through my partially open fists as they thrust smoothly through the water, reminding me that I am a channel: life flows through me. This is elemental being. Me. The water. The darkness. The light. And the wisdom flowing through unimpeded.

My mind drifts from surface certainty.

What if the world, that I have been treating as solid and fixed, is not?
What if understanding it as fluid would be more real?
What if flow is our natural state?
[It is].

Creative Flow

Water does not resist. Water flows. When you plunge
your hand into it, all you feel is a caress. Water is not
a solid wall, it will not stop you. But water always
goes where it wants to go, and nothing in the end
can stand against it. Water is patient. Dripping
water wears away a stone. Remember that, my
child. Remember you are half water. If you can't go
through an obstacle, go around it. Water does.

Margaret Atwood

The water has transformed my images too. I have moved from painting in bold acrylics to the more fluid medium of watercolour. I love the way that the colours bloom and swirl and merge, their magic released by the water on the page.

"What I do," says Mexican artist, Ana Maria Calderon, on the watercolour painting video I am watching, "is to take the water and put a few drops on each colour that I'm going to use. It frees up the colour so that it flows better." I have come to love this flow, as I have learned to work with this technique over the last year of writing this book. Previously, watercolours had both scared and bored me. They seemed like an old-fashioned medium, one of traditional staid seascapes and clichéd views of misty hills.

A couple of years back, I wrote a blog post about how I had inherited my grandfather's paintbox – and my relationship with God had felt the same. The old-fashioned colours didn't fit me…yet my soul was hungry for what they offered. I knew I needed new ways of connecting with the oceanic, with flow, which fitted me, that belonged to me, a woman in this modern world. Over the last few years I have learned them afresh – both painting and praying – from women.

I have gone from finding it hard to make time to paint, to it becoming a new passion, doing it first thing in the morning and last thing at night, with a sneaky quickie in the middle of the day. First it requires my learning how to utilise water as a flow medium, through which the colours could bloom and transform and shapeshift, rather than painting in the way that you do with most other mediums. I learn not to need to be in control, but rather to become a participating witness. I seek out my colours, artist grade pigments in liquid watercolours, far more vivid than my grandfather would have used: raspberry pink, turquoise, peacock blue, hot orange…these are vital colours for my soul.

I have spent weeks struggling to do the final edits on this book and instead spent my days painting watercolour pebbles obsessively: tiny pebblescapes on bookmarks sprinkled with seaweed, sea glass and shells. These help me bring the seashore to my home. Into my body. Bringing myself into the flow. Into direct creative connection with the sacred here at my kitchen table.

One of my favourite newly-learned techniques, is to sprinkle table salt into the still-wet paint, and watch the colour retreat from each crystal, making tiny stars, echoes of magic, right there in front of me.

I discover painting as prayer. I relish the joy of being in flow with my soul once more. For me, creativity is the authentic expression of soul, liberating it from the prison-guard of the mind and straitjacket of the body. It is a conscious reclaiming of our original and natural state of being.

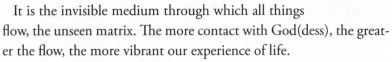

Water is like God(dess).

This thought hits me as if from nowhere. Floating up to consciousness as I watch the cerulean blue come to life on my paper as it blossoms in the water.

It is the invisible medium through which all things flow, the unseen matrix. The more contact with God(dess), the greater the flow, the more vibrant our experience of life.

Then, the thought simplifies.

Water is God(dess).

Oh. My.

This stops me in my tracks.

Can this be true? And if it is…how does that change my relationship with water?

*What does it mean for water to **be** God(dess)? For us to understand water to be the sacred source?*

Sea and Creativity

My daily walks on the beach are my medicine and the tide table my bible. I love simultaneously the sameness of everyday on the beach and the subtle differences. I make new discoveries: the amber glow of the sunshine illuminating flowing fronds of kelp. Seagull feathers like arrows insisting upon a change of direction. Patterns of black sea coal, etched onto yellow sand, depicting the ancient forests it once was, millennia ago. I find treasure in rock pools, as pebbles glow like precious stones, in billowing luminous green seagrass, in the delicately flowing fronds of sea anemone. And all against a backdrop of that vast huge spacious sky. I am in relationship with the North Sea, I talk to it, share my thoughts, my ramblings.

My ceramic work is increasingly inspired by myths and fairy tales of the seal. I feel a kindred spirit with the Celtic stories of the selkie. The creature part woman, part seal who lives a rich existence partly in deepest depths of the ocean and partly with humankind, this duality mirrors my own life. It allows me to live as a mother and teacher and also to dive deep into my creativity. I make sacred objects inspired by the ocean: selkies, goddesses and yonis. All of which are about our relationship with the sacred Feminine. It is the ocean which allows this alchemy. When working with clay I make internal space and invite the creative piece to arrive in my hands. The sea is never very far from my thoughts. I am constantly surprised by what I make and know that my conscious mind has very little to do with this process.

Sometimes I struggle with the slow, repetitive rhythms of hand modelling the clay, of drying, of bisque firing, of colouring then the glaze firing. I want a quicker more immediate result and yet I know that this slower pace is good for me. It mirrors the rhythms of the tides and the seasons. Later I take the finished pieces down to the beach and work with them in nature. Here I use photography to add depth to their meaning. Sometimes as sacred mandalas, sometimes being simply washed over by waves. I get excited by the magical interplay of light and water, which is a natural backdrop for my ceramic work. This is how I weave my work with nature and create a sense of the Wild. My photographs and ceramics work in tandem together, each one informing the other, both of equal importance.

Alice Grey

Flow Consciousness

The flow state of consciousness is something I return to again and again in my books: it is, for me, the holy grail of human experience. It is what I would consider the state of magic-making: relaxed but active, attuned to the inner witness, almost superhuman in our abilities to focus, sense and respond, in a co-creative state with the mystery.

When I am in flow I reach through time, to a place beyond. In writing, art, dreams and sex I am able to forget the challenges of being on the spectrum and fully embrace the positives: immersion in pattern, flow mind, shapeshifting and the powerful ability to make fluid, novel connections. I get to be myself in multi-dimensional technicolour: to move at my own pace, to heal, to meet former and future selves in a moment of transcendence, to allow the flow of time to wash us together on the shores of my self.

Flow is not just a metaphor or poetic concept – it is an accurate description of how information travels through our brains and bodies. Flow is a positive psychological state, an expanded state of consciousness, where our senses are heightened and our perception of reality is shifted.[35] It is, I would argue, the healthiest, most satisfying, spiritually attuned and creative psychological state that humans can experience. It is my favourite way of being alive.

Water seems to be a medium that facilitates flow consciousness – perhaps rather obviously. In water our bodyminds *remembers* what flow *feels* like. They get a direct transmission: water teaches us fluidity experientially. It slows down our breathing and brain functioning, heightening our other senses whilst calming the nervous system. And whilst immersion tends to be the most powerful, research shows that even simply being in the presence of a body of water brings us back into entrainment with flow consciousness.[36]

In his book, *Blue Mind,* Wallace J. Nichols dives deep into how water, especially the ocean, impacts our minds, an effect he calls "Blue Mind." He describes this as "a mildly meditative state characterized by calm, peacefulness, unity, and a sense of general happiness and satisfaction with life in the moment. It is inspired by water, and elements associated with water, from the colour blue to the words we use to describe the sensations associated with immersion. It takes advantage of neurological connections formed over millennia."

I believe we have a lot to learn about who we are and how our bodyminds work from the sea. It seems to me that water – flow – is a more accurate metaphor for consciousness than the more mechanistic frameworks popularised during the Industrial Age of machines. Our brain is more like the sea than a computer, with information and energy flowing through branching nerves like tendrils of seaweed.

It makes me wonder how this might inform how we live, as individuals and communities? How could accessing flow consciousness, and living and working from it as a normal, rather than a rare peak state, impact us as a species?

Reflections

When have you experienced flow consciousness?

Do you have practices that allow you to regularly access it?

What prevents you entering the flow state?

Are there certain places where it is easier to enter? Certain times of the year, the moon's cycle or your menstrual cycle, if you have one?

Practice

Try some sort of fluid art, my favourite media include:

> Marbling inks
> Alcohol inks
> Watercolour paints
> Fluid pouring acrylics

Allow yourself to become a witness to the flowing of the medium, and to play with it, rather than forcing it to your will. And of course, add some of the products of this creative play to your altar space.

7

THE FEMININE

Water [is] an ally, a shortcut into a woman's deep, primal self.

Giving Birth in the Ocean, *Aquadural*

Women and Water

The sea has his-storically been portrayed as feminine – fickle, alluring, enchanting, unpredictable and ultimately destructive. For much of history, women have been explicitly banned from being in – or even on – the water. In many European cultures, a woman's presence on a boat was considered unlucky, thought to tempt fate and disaster. "Women were bad luck on board because they distracted the crew, which would anger the sea, causing treacherous conditions as revenge. However, conveniently for the male crew, naked women calmed the sea, which is why so many [boat] figureheads were women with bare breasts."[37]

Even a woman's proximity to a sailor on land was considered dangerous. In Ireland, "a fisherman would have to return home if he saw a red-headed woman on his way to sea."[38] The behaviour of a woman *on land* could influence the safety of her man at sea: "A woman should never wash or comb her hair when her men are at sea."[39] Note that a woman's body (especially her hair), her sexual allure and the sea are understood to be intimately connected. A woman's metaphysical power is both acknowledged, and prohibited, simultaneously. Hers is the power to influence the sea. She must therefore be controlled.

And so, men have dominated the surface of the seas, sailing to fish, to fight, to travel to new lands, to escape, proving their strength and manhood through dangerous conquests. The collective story of the sea thus far in our culture, has been a heroic one of masculine overcoming – the stories of Odysseus and The Ancient Mariner, Columbus and Magellan, Moby Dick and the D-Day landings. The role of woman was to be on the shore awaiting her lover, caring for his children, doing all the work that keeps daily life going on shore. Or she was mythologised into the ultimately capricious, seductive but dangerous mythic icons of femininity: the siren, the mermaid, the selkie.

Where the masculine is solid and reliable, our culture tells us, the feminine...the female...is fluid: she changes dependent on the container you pour her into. In a culture that prizes the strength of individual identity, the fluidity of the feminine and those who embody it, have been read as unstable, unreliable…dangerous. When, in reality, all of us, regardless of sex or gender, have a fluidity that we are not allowed to express within the dictats of patriarchal culture. Trans bodies cause ripples of discomfort with their shapeshifting. And cis-gendered female bodies are required to hide their hormonal tides, the way that they are pulled in and out through menstrual cycles, pregnancies, births, post-partum, and later through menopause. We have been taught to live in denial of our shifting reality.

Women, throughout patriarchal history, have had their freedom limited. Women's clothing and moral expectations in many cultures have prevented them even entering the water. Whilst they have been forbidden from being on, or in, the sea with men…women have found ways to answer the calling of She of the Sea.

There is a quieter, more intimate story of the sea, if you have ears to listen. The Feminine story of the sea. Women have had a more personal and intimate experience throughout history, it seems, one with less fanfare or acknowledgement within our culture. Women's experiences have tended to be with the liminal places: the shoreline…and the depths.

Women were the majority of shoreline food foragers in most cultures since the dawn of human emergence. In Wales and Ireland up to the twentieth century, gathering, preparing, preserving and selling shellfish was the domain of women at times when it would have provided a much larger part of daily nutrition than today.

In Korea, the *haenyeo* freedivers of Jeju are exclusively women who have fished for generations. In Japan, the Ama (literally, "sea women") also dive without equipment to collect abalone and pearls, a tradition that dates back two millennia, and again is predominantly female. In Sardinia, the now almost extinct tradition of diving to gather sea silk, was the preserve of women, passed down from generation to generation. This delicate fabric when dyed and woven was valued as more expensive than gold, and worn by emperors and pharaohs.

The Feminine

Surfing

Surfing, which for much of its white history has been dominated by men, in Hawaiian culture was considered an activity for everyone, from queens and female chiefs, to mothers, grandparents and children. Surfing was far more than just a sport. Like the other sea activities here, it was also considered sacred, a practice passed on to humans by the great goddess Pele, she of fire and volcanoes, creatrix of the Hawaiian islands, and her younger sister, Hiʻiaka.

According to Lauren Hill, author of *She Surf*, "Historians of ancient Polynesia acknowledge that it was women who seemed to stand in the highest regard for their skill, grace and poise as surfers. Woven deep into the chants and lore of our surfing culture's roots are the stories of revered women who rode waves with utmost grace and athleticism. [...] During the ancient times of the gods and goddesses, Punahoa was a revered surfing chiefess. One epic tale recounts when her surfing skill was challenged by a group of men. She was celebrated for never losing her board and asserting her confidence in the water, with her surfing surpassed only by the supreme skill of goddess Hiʻiaka."[40]

I find it fascinating that each of these disparate groups of women sustained not only a rare and valued skill – freediving for valued gifts from the sea – but also a divergent belief: an animist, feminine spirituality, centred around their intimate connection with the ocean. Each of these groups are reported as praying to the goddesses of the sea for bounty and protection. Rather than the mundane and the spiritual being considered separate realms, as they have been on land, work and soul are indistinguishable, and the sea is an intimate partner in their way of life. It is this female telling of what the sea means – on both a physical and a spiritual level – that fascinates me. It speaks to an innate part of our psychology that dry land and patriarchy have no language or value for.

Each of these women's sea skills is an art on the verge of extinction. One which mothers and grandmothers have initiated daughters in for centuries, millennia even. But sadly, the modern world is too fierce a competition, with fewer women willing to forgo the comforts and relative safety of modern life for the sacraments of the sea. Just as fewer men are following in family footsteps becoming fishermen, and this work has been taken over by industrial fleets, manned by people with little connection to or love for the sea. In a world that values the fast, the cheap and the plentiful, arts that take time and care and a lineage of skill have been devalued.

Despite this, it seems that our collective yearning for communion with the sea has not diminished. Instead, it has grown stronger. We are finding other ways to answer the call of the sea: wild swimming, freediving, scuba diving, sailing, marine conservation, surfing, foraging, sea-priestessing, and sea-tinged creativity are all experiencing massive growth, as practitioners cultivate new communities of humans intimate with the sea, dedicated to experiencing the flow state as their norm.

Freediving

Freediving is a pastime that seems to attract a disproportionately large number of women. These modern-day mermaids, with their monofins and neoprene skins, dive into the deep blue on nothing but their own breath. The world's greatest freediver, Natali Vadimovna, could hold her breath for nine minutes, and whilst our dolphin cousins can only dive to 45 metres, her deepest dive was 101 metres.[41]

To describe it as a sport or endurance feat seems to miss the point entirely. Time and again, these women describe it as an embodied spiritual experience.

"You are truly free while you are diving. You go down, you

forget about everything. You only feel the universe, the sea and the soul. To me it's the closest thing to praying or meditating." (Raghda Ezzeldin, Egyptian record-breaking freediver.[42])

Freediving is often described as being like meditation. Diving deep, you leave the world and its noise and demands behind, and dive into a bubble of pure blue. Until it is just you and the sea. You and your own aliveness, your own abilities. You and your breath.

In the words of Sarah Campbell, English World Record-breaking freediver, "You're allowing yourself to fall deeper and deeper into the ocean, away from our most direct source of life force that is the breath. Some people say it is crazy, but those who have experienced it recognise that there is some real magic and profoundness in the free fall, literally and figuratively."[43]

Scylla, Glaucus, and The Sea Re-Imagined in the Black Body

I think of the sea, I think of the way that monsters were crafted out of the female form. These stories range from tales retold about women who call to men leading them to their doom, to the monsters who left the wake from countless ships within the lungs of Black female bodies. These same Black bodies that would go on to be reframed as the main villains.

The story of Scylla turned monster because of a man's scorn* is stitched into the idea of the Black female body and its history in America. The Glaucuses of that story have created tales of horror, disgust, and assumption from one continent to many others within their bottomless hunger. For the Black female body, the Scylla now transformed not of her own will, salt water never leaves the veins. It becomes something passed down to her children.

---

* In Greek myth, Scylla was a beautiful freshwater water nymph who was turned into a man-eating sea monster by the sea-goddess/witch Circe. Approached by the sea-god Glaucus to create a love-potion, Circe, who wanted Glaucus for herself, instead created a potion that she poured into the water where Scylla was bathing, turning her into a sharp-toothed, six-headed monster that guarded a sea channel, devouring sailors who passed.

I always wondered if the automatic love of the sea was just in the blood, passed down through the veins. Most white men I was in relationship with would be quick to say, 'I am a fish, I must be near water.' I wondered if piscine attributes were a birthright while others like myself spent time dodging the water for one reason or another. In high school, taking swimming as an elective was painful because I remember how the chlorine damaged my hair. Along with that damage came a whooping as I was blamed for not properly tending to my hair.

oOo

I did not realise that the ocean was missing from my reality until 2008. I was on a road trip with someone who I did not yet recognise as my Glaucus. Water to him meant ocean, pond, anything that allowed his body to become submerged, while I would usually sit on the rocks or the sand as silent observer.

The first night we arrived at Tybee, he wanted to go to the beach. I stood, guarded, on the shore. In this moment, I told myself that maybe I could like it. Maybe I too could become like this Glaucus letting the water take my body. Yet, I refused to go any further into the water or the darkness.

My body remembered not being allowed to go near the bigness. I vaguely remember being tethered to my mother. I was not allowed to trust letting the bigness of the sea swallow my body. Mama mentioned something about needles washing up on shore. Maybe it was one news story, then again, that is all it took, one story to add one more public place to the list of other public places that was deemed unsafe for my Black body, at least according to mama.

I thought of all of this as I stared into the darkness conflicted about the joy of feeling the salt water on my feet. Maybe it was safe to wade in, but not now. Now, my body was content with being swallowed by the dark.

oOo

'I can't believe the water is that blue, it really is blue', is something I kept repeating after my first visit to St. John, in the US Virgin Islands.

131

Before then, I really thought that television just did camera tricks to make water look that blue. As a kid of the inner city, I had no knowledge about what the sea or any other bodies of water looked like within its natural element. Trunk Bay seduced me from afar. In the daytime, I could not be swallowed. I let the water guide my body, but something still prevented me from giving myself over.

oOo

Several months ago, I finally get a chance to read Dr. Christina Sharpe's *In the Wake: On Blackness and Being.* I do not quite know what to expect until my eyes land on this sentence, "...I argue that rather than seeking resolution to blackness's ongoing and irresolvable abjection, one might approach Black being in the wake as a form of consciousness." Dr. Sharpe's connection of the inevitability between the Black body, the slave trade, and the way that every aspect of the forced salt water experience lives in our lungs is something that I re-examine in my own life.

I see of all the times I tried to step outside of my Black body to have access to the sea or other bodies of water yet ignoring the pause or foreboding that enveloped me while I was in any large body of water, even when there is a buffer of a kayak.

I see the moment in India in 2011 of walking along the sea in a full moon wishing that I could get closer, let the water wash over my feet but was too afraid to do so. I see the moment of me going to stare at the ocean every day in Goa, and how I was more content staring at the vast open of the water, yet, never drawn to go in for a swim.

My mouth salivates over stories of what may be missing at the bottom of the ocean floor because I think about what else lies there, the treasure in the form of ancestral bones that have become whale fall. And instead of whale carcass, within these stories of what is hidden, I start to hear bones that refused to stop signaling.

They told me to hold still my body because I already carried the salt in my veins.

Shanta Lee Gander

The Descent of Woman

*Water has played a much greater part in
human evolution than previously thought.*

David Attenborough

It is interesting that women are leading the field in freediving…
whereas in land activities they do not, because of the inherent differences between cis-male and female physiology. Does this offer us
clues about our ancient history as a species?

Evolutionary theories have been developed by men, about men:
why we are what we are, how we developed, where we came from…
Or rather where *man* came from…why *man* is as he is… Because
whilst the term 'man' was used to talk about both sexes for the majority of written history, it was only (cis, white) man that these men
were interested in. Only his story mattered. Woman has always been
merely a footnote, an irrelevance.

In the Victorian era, Darwin's *Ascent of Man,* the ever-upward arrow of evolution, began to replace a millennia-old story of the fall of
man (due to woman's sin) and the afterthought of woman, created
from man's rib by a male God. In the 1950s, the story of man as pin-
nacle of development was further solidified by "The Savannah Theory" of man the hunter by Raymond Dart and Robert Ardrey, pop-
ularising the science of "a hard, violent vision of human origins."[44]

In the 1970s, Elaine Morgan, author of *The Descent of Woman*
and *The Aquatic Ape,* took some evidence that an eminent Oxford
scholar had been too worried about losing his career over…and ran
with it. She questioned this male-centric vision as prejudiced hypoth-
esis, rather than fact. She asked uncomfortable questions about the
assumptions that male scientists were making. *Questions that she was
most definitely unqualified to ask,* they retorted.

Evolution couldn't continue, she argued, *if it only advanced the male.* In *The Descent of Woman,* her speculative alternative version of human evolution, from a non-patriarchal perspective, Elaine Morgan uses scientific evidence to challenge The Savannah Theory.

She suggests that rising temperatures on the African continent meant that scrub, grassland and trees were reduced and modern humans' predecessors were pushed out from the centre of the continent to the coasts. They would have been tree-dwelling on the whole, and far more vulnerable on the ground to the many large predators. Finding themselves without tree cover on the coasts, she posits that our ancient ancestors would have had to run into the water to get away from predators. Females would have had to do this far more than males, as they would be slowed down by carrying small infants or being pregnant and so were less able to climb to escape. Being "somewhat bipedal" they would have been able to stand on two legs, up to their chins in the ocean, "in a way that a feline who doesn't like getting wet wouldn't be able to." In this posture, they would also be able to hold their baby above the water to keep it safe.

Morgan looked at the anomalies in the story of human evolution and wondered: *why – if humans lost hair to keep cool when hunting (as current theories suggested) – did males (the hunters) retain more hair than the females? And why did other hunting animals in hot countries retain thick fur?*

She suggests that the females' fur began to disappear over millions of years as she spent more time in the water than her male counterparts: gathering food, escaping from carnivores, birthing…similar to the way that the hippopotamus, walrus, manatee and other water-going mammals have minimal hair and smooth skins. Whereas males, who spent far less time in the sea, did not adjust in this way.

She looked at women's bodies and wondered why women have a much thicker layer of subcutaneous fat than men – the fat that modern women are shamed into shedding for 'swim-suit ready' bodies. Fat that we need in order to be able to menstruate. Fat that is laid down further during pregnancy and breastfeeding. *Could this be for buoyancy and insulation?* she pondered. This layer of fat, just under the skin, similar to a whale's blubber, is unique for humans in comparison to any other primates. Whereas all other aquatic mammals have it.

As we have seen, our species is consistently drawn to the sea, whereas our ape cousins live as far from the coasts as they can…and are unable to swim (note the moats around monkey and gorilla enclosures in zoos). Our ability and aptitude for diving remains unique amongst primates.

She looked at the large size of our brains and wondered if they were helped along by a diet rich in fish oils, the omega threes that we are now being sold at high prices in health food shops to make up for modern diets low in seafoods.

She looked at human babies and wondered why they have vernix – the white greasy substance covering the skin at birth – when our nearest cousins, the apes, don't. Only seals and sea lions do, both mammals whose young would enter the cold water soon after birth.

She wondered about our mammalian breath-holding reflex when we put our heads in cold water, that our young have most strongly. And the fact that babies are instinctively able to swim underwater at birth, yet cannot walk for well over a year, whereas most other land-based creatures walk almost instantaneously. She pondered our ability to control metabolic processes when diving deep, which we share with seals, a skill that freedivers and escapologists use today.

She mounts up yet more biological evidence: the residual webbing in our hands and feet and the development of ear locking mechanisms in those who swim a lot, even today. Our bodies, it seems, know the water to be our second home: they remember a different way of being, which the direction of human culture has, on the whole, steered us away from.

She gives much reflection to the different way that we have sex, in comparison to our ape cousins and other land mammals. Practically all land mammals solely use the rear approach to mating, whereas the majority of aquatic mammals use the frontal approach. She suggests that the angling of the vaginal cavity in humans is a normal marine modification, "retracted and covered to reduce salt water and sand intake." The fact that we can have heterosexual intercourse just as easily from both in front and behind is, again, pretty much unique to our evolving both on land *and* in water.

Does it not make sense, therefore, she wondered insistently, *that for a significant part of our evolutionary history, we were a shore-dwelling, water-birthing mammal, where female food gathering would have been a key part of our development?*

She is not the first to posit such an idea. Around 546 BC, the Greek philosopher Anaximander "postulated that mankind had sprung from an aquatic animal species. He thought that humans, who begin life with prolonged infancy, could not have survived otherwise."[45]

As a non-male, non-scientist, despite Elaine Morgan's hypotheses being rooted in the writings of an esteemed Oxford professor and proven biological anomalies, her work was dismissed by most. But it has persisted, influencing many researchers, and in recent years has been championed by the greatest living naturalist, Sir David Attenborough, whose understanding of natural history has been shaped by seventy years of documentary making, and an enduring fascination with our oceans.

"People have a deep emotional connection to the sea," writes Callum Roberts in *The Ocean of Life*. "The oceans inspire, thrill, and soothe us...our relationship to the sea stretches back through time all the way to the origins of life itself. We are creatures of the ocean."

More and more evidence is being discovered showing that the ocean and shoreline have had a significant impact on our physical and cultural evolution at every stage. Our earliest tools were made of pebbles. Cowrie shells were known to have been one of the earliest forms of currency in China, East Africa, India, Brazil and amongst some Native American tribes. The earliest musical instrument ever found was a 17,000-year-old conch shell, adapted to be played...and cave paintings show our ancestors playing them.[46] Just as cave paintings dated to 9,000 years ago far inland in Egypt show our forebears swimming.

The ocean has made us who we are today.

Water Birth

My first baby was supposed to be a water birth. Having heard the stories of my brother's water birth at home in front of the fire, and having a traumatic history with hospitals, I knew that I would birth at home. As part of my preparation, I watched a fascinating documentary of Russian women ice bathing when pregnant, and women around the world water-birthing.[47] It reassured me that although this practice was new to me and unusual here in Ireland, it was a trusted form of birth in many cultures around the world.

We borrowed a pool – but my son arrived a week early, and fast! We didn't have a hose to fill the pool, so he was birthed on dry land on the sitting room floor. But we bathed together within the first half an hour, me and my child who smelled of the musky salt tang of orgasm.

My second was born on the bathmat beside the bath. It was a strange birth. Blue faced and slippery, she looked otherworldly as she emerged, umbilical tentacle tied firm around her neck, in need of oxygen. Lifedeath was especially close to us that day.

By my third, I had read the theories of Janet Balaskas and LeBoyer and interviewed Michel Odent. I was not just open to a water birth but actively wanted one.

This time we had the pool inflated a fortnight before, just in case. When labour started, the night after full moon, I remembered renegade midwife Ina May Gaskin's words: *when your throat opens, your cervix does too, both sphincters need to be open and relaxed for birth to flow well.* I found myself singing *London Bridge is Falling Down* on repeat, rocking through the contractions until the pool was full.

And then the bliss, the ease, of submerging into it, the falling away of intensity. The water created inner space, where the sensations could be integrated. I felt fully in my body – awakened to my primal self – I could surrender myself to the water and be supported by it, as I rested between contractions.

Seeing my second daughter floating out of me from my waters into the pool was a timeless moment. She was suspended. Totally at peace. As were we all. United in the wonder that is gentle natural birth. I took her in my hands, and gently moved her under the water for several minutes, marvelling at her grace underwater, before gathering her to my chest and life on land. Still joined at the cord. Me and her, in our own watery bubble, with the arms of my husband and the midwives behind us. Smiling. Crying. Quiet, deep joy pervading us all.

Mapping the Feminine

Women and coasts are constantly changing and physically redrawing themselves in cycles.
Charlotte Runcie, *Salt on Your Tongue: Women and the Sea*

What if we have spent our lives hearing how faulty we were, only to realise that the theories were not written about us, that the words did not describe our lived truth? What if women's bodies were made for the water with their buoyant fat stores?

And not just our physical bodies. What if theories of consciousness were culturally prejudiced and narrow? What if the picture of us inside and outside didn't fit the man-made maps we were given? What if the stories of God and spirituality were too small and narrow too, excluding, as they do, the Feminine face of the sacred, and our ability to commune with Her physically?

Most of our stories of what it means to be human, until very recently, were written with a male pen: words and theories based on male knowings and experiences. One of the founders of modern psychology and a hero of mine, C.G. Jung, talked of human consciousness as a house, with many floors, and the unconscious as the basement. This used to work for me, but the more I have reflected, the more I do not know this solidity of being. I rarely experience myself in this way for more than a moment at a time.

My natural state of being, though I have spent my whole life resisting it, is fluidity. I am unpredictable, fluent in something other than staying the same. I have repeating patterns and currents, but this skin barely holds me together as I float jellyfish-like through this world of permanence.

I know now that much of this experience is down to my autistic neurology and unstable health. But not all.

For most women who menstruate, I think that our way of being is more fluid, more tidal, because of the constant surging of our hormones. And yet we have been raised to prefer the mirage of a solid structure, rather than the reality of the sea, as a self-image.

Rather than a building on land, perhaps our natural state of being in the Feminine is the sea.

The song of the sea seems to emanate from here. When we hear it, we hear the echoes of this ancient world, calling us, reminding us of this other way of being that was lost to the sea. This world that honours the Feminine, and speaks to our souls, lies in ruins, under the waves.

Freud would say, no doubt, that this is because the archaic, deep Feminine is associated with our pre-egoic, pre-conscious state in the womb and early infanthood, when we did not experience ourselves as separate to our mothers. And this may well be a psychological root of it. But to him, this would be to dismiss it as infantile, a relic of dependency and childishness to be overcome by the mature self. Whereas I would consider it a psychologically important state of wellbeing and safety. This feeling of containment by the primal Feminine should be celebrated and remembered on a cellular level as our genesis, and replicated for ourselves and others as the ultimate way of feeling safe.

What if God, the sacred source, was not only in the heights, but also in the depths? Not only He but She? How can we move beyond God as being outside, above, a Sky God of light, doling out judgement, retribution and punishment, to remembering and embracing the Goddess of the depths, the waters, the dark womb, and complete nurturance?

What if these were sacred too?

(*They are*).

How would we relate to these parts of ourselves, each other and the world if we knew that this was true? What would happen if we gave these elements of world and self the same consideration and reverence?

The magical lunar waters of our feminine time in the womb and the Womb Consciousness that is generated by it become the dark, disturbing shadow waters of the lost feminine soul where our inner monsters and demons lurk and where our inner treasures call us. [...] Our solar-focused world has forgotten and forbidden all memories of the mysterious womb realm of shining darkness that every human was created in, but these memories live on in a place we call the unconscious.

Azra and Seren Bertrand, *Womb Awakening*

Why has this oceanic Feminine been so little charted? My guess would be because most of our culture's celebrated explorers of land, sea, spirit and psyche were cis-gendered men...who saw things through the masculine lens, they interpreted what they found through a masculine narrative...of progress and adventure, solidity and rationality, and the development of an individual, independent ego, unconstrained by anything, especially the feminine: the small and suffocating, and emasculating domestic world of first mother, then wife.

The urging of Western psychology has been individuation. Whereas the longing of the female soul seems to be both freedom (of movement and expression) and merging – with lover, child, the sacred... To stay healthy a woman needs both, and frequent transitions between the two. There is no shame in the desire for merging – it is what our bodies require of us – during sex, pregnancy and nurturing. The tides of our menstrual cycles teach us again this two-pronged necessity for our health and psychological wellbeing – the need for merging and freedom. Both.

Wild Waters

for years
i watered
myself down
let myself
become
something
to quench your
thirst

now i know
the power i hold
i could destroy
you in a
single swell

Laura Lewis

The Voice of the Feminine

Throughout his-story we have all been called back to the ancient sea world of the Feminine – through the songs and tales of mermaids and sirens and selkies, the ancient unknown sea creatures that have been made monsters in our tellings. Each were considered dangerous to men, with their enchantments and haunting songs. And so, we assumed they *were* dangerous. We learned to distrust the voice of the Feminine. We learned to fear the depths. Learned to dissociate from and call monstrous the traces of these that we found in ourselves. Because our stories told us to.

But we forgot to notice who was telling the stories.

This song of the sea, which told of the ways of water, this song of enchantment which led the way back to the Feminine, that calls us to leave the man-made world behind was condemned as evil and be-witching...**because it threatened the dominance of the patriarchal narrative and values. It threatened the masculine.**

But we are beginning to remember another way of being: the deep and primal Feminine. She who emerged for me through one of my earliest adult paintings, the Fish Goddess of the depths. She who in shame and confusion I painted over with sea, not recognising her. She lies hidden beneath the blue void of my all-time favourite paint-ing, invisible to all, except for her texture. But I know she is there.

This strange image emerging, and then disappearing again into the blue was my own intuitive understanding of Goddess. It wasn't until more than a decade later that I learned that "The ancient Mother was associated with fish, seashells, seawater, salt, ships and fishermen. She often appeared in mermaid form with a fish tail. In her honor fish were eaten on Friday, which was her official day, named after Freya, her Scandinavian incarnation. Latins called it the Day of Venus." (Barbara J. Walker, *The Women's Dictionary of Symbols and Sacred Objects*)

I remember. I am remembering.

But still there is shame. Still a habit of silence.

We left this place so long ago. We have been taught to not speak of it. Not think of it. To forget.

But the ocean remembers. She still calls us back to remembering, in a song so deep and ancient it pierces our hearts, making us risk all to freedive to the heart of oblivion, to be kissed by the waters and to remember who we are.

Who we can be.

She reminds us what we were like before patriarchy defined us... and our world. She whispers to us what we could be like after...

We are mapping this domain for ourselves, together. We are learn-ing to trust and follow our inner tides, to read the patterns of na-ture, to surrender ourselves to the flow. We are remembering what it means to co-exist with magic and leave space for mystery. We are making new maps and passing them on to our sisters and daughters, sons and lovers.

But to do so, we can no longer hug the shoreline. We must explore the depths we have learned to fear. We must trust ourselves to it. We must do it in our own skins.

She Calls Me

I want to skip over the sparkling surface,
Like a skimming stone.
But this is not my path.
I am a pebble
That plunges the depths.
When I cannot live any more, it is
the water that calls me.
The first time she called me
The closest I could get to the sea was a bath.
I filled it full.
Stepped in.
Lay back.
And back.
The water closing calmly over my new-formed breasts.
My ears.
The noise of the dangerous unstoppable world shut out.
My eyes.
Deep breath.
Last breath.
Water flooding.
Over my mouth.

My nose.

Just one more breath.

And then forever silence.

But the life within me wouldn't let me.

I rose like a whale breaching.

Life charging me to the surface.

I lay

In my porcelain wombspace.

Salty tears.

Shock.

Sadness.

Alone with my secret almost.

Alive,

But still not knowing how to live.

Dark Waters and Riptides

Oh, the sea she washes me, oh the sea she softens me
oh, the sea she frightens me, oh the sea enlightens me.
[...]
When I dive to the deeps
when I'm floating and free
when she roars and I roar
when we sleep once more
when I dive to the deeps
when I'm floating and free.
[...]

Oh, the sea she heals me, oh the sea reveals me
oh, the sea embraces me, oh the sea replaces me.

"The Sea", Eleanor Brown (from the album Spirals)

I have spent my life clinging to my own shores for safety. Flying like a bird above the storm waters of my own body, too scared to land. I guess that is why the sea floods in to visit me. I have been too frightened to venture out into her depths alone.

The central core of me is dark and churning, I can only sense it vaguely. It scares me with its power. As a late-diagnosed autistic woman, I realise that this experience is partly neurological...my sensory abilities are all hyper-aroused on the surface, and my nervous system melts down when it becomes overwhelmed in everyday places. But my ability to know what is going on within is flawed. Instead of an accurate information readout, there is a big, dark, unknowable mass within. I am sailing blind without map or lighthouse within my own skin. It feels a very scary place to have a life sentence. This is why I write: to attempt to find words for what this big scariness is, to try and find images to give form and name to the wild churning expanse.

Dark Sister Below

This is
The inner sea.
The place of cupped breasts and floating hair, of
hot pink and deep blue so dark it is black,
The starless sea lit only by moon and the deep mind.
A place of fantasy and shipwrecks
That evades the searchlight of the lighthouse mind.
It traces the surface,
Illuminating the waves,
But not the caves beneath
Wherein I lie.

What is the me I cannot see?
Over the years I have discovered so many parts,
Like a marine biologist
Carefully labelling my samples.
But still so much lies unseen,
Unseeable?
It makes up the bulwark of my being,
This self that lies beneath
That reveals itself only in darkness
And in multicoloured dream displays.
My words are hooks,
I send them down
Not knowing what they might bring up.
Again and again, I sail away
Empty-handed.

And then, on a full moon night,
Something twitches in the net.

Gelatinous, fluid, writhing, morphing, tentacled,
Luminescent,
Glowing.
Deeply, darkly, disturbingly strange.
I long to turn on the light, to explore it,
But to do so may kill it.
Kill me.
I let it slip back
Into the underwater caverns of my being,
Far from prying eyes.
Sensuous, undulating, I feel it come to the surface of my skin
In sex, in dance, in writing words like these
The dark Feminine rises,
She of the Sea
Within me.

Reflections

What in this chapter was new to you, and how might you integrate it into your self-knowledge and understanding of us as a species?

Have you had the experience of a Glaucus in your life? How did you respond?

How have you experienced yourself as fitting, or not fitting, with traditional psychological models?

What does the Dark Feminine mean to you? How does it make you feel?

Practice

Ways of bringing the sea to you

I am so lucky to live only two minutes' drive from the sea. But there are many times when I cannot get there for weeks or even months, because of my inner sea. For many, a trip to the sea, and all the benefits it brings, can be a precious and infrequent treat. I want to share with you lots of ways that you can bring the sea to you, wherever you are, however you are:

Sound

Listening to sea sounds
The 'white noise' of the ocean is deeply soothing to our bodyminds. If you can't go for a walk on the beach, then there are hundreds of sea recordings available for free on Spotify and YouTube – some with panpipes and synthesisers…and others completely *au naturel!* There are several ocean recordings included in my *She of the Sea* playlist on Spotify. Pop on your headphones and immerse yourself in an aural bubble of bliss and relaxation, or put them on at night to fall asleep to. If you want something even more immersive, why not invest in an inexpensive LED projector which projects calming images of waves onto the ceiling.

Sight

See the Sea…Every Day
If you are stuck inside or sick, often one of the nicest ways to connect with the beautiful shapes and colours of nature is through the lenses of others. A free way to do this is by curating your own miniature world, either on Pinterest or Instagram. Take a look at my Water Therapy Pinterest board for inspiration: pinterest.ie/dreamingaloudnt/water-therapy

Create your own sea view without even moving house! Make your phone or computer background an image of the sea, as I did during the writing of this book. Purchase, find or create a calming sea image and hang it on your wall or altar space.

If you want multi-sensory immersion, why not watch one of the films recommended in the References section at the back of the book. They range from shorts to feature length films.

And if you are able, why not spend the day at an aquarium.

Touch

Create a sand box to drag your fingers through and draw labyrinths in. It can be a big pit in the garden or a small tray on your lap.

Organise pebbles or shells into beautiful arrangements – spirals, circles, hearts, mandalas, flat lay arrangements – on a table or the floor.

Enjoy water in whatever way feels good to you – a bath, shower, foot bath, paddling pool…

Movement

The following exercises help us to remember our fluidity and the sense of being detached from the surface world and immersed into a slower, more profound state of being. Where our body moves, our mind follows.

Body Flow Meditation
This is the meditation I have been using mornings and evenings and stress times when writing this book.

Get yourself into as dark and peaceful a physical place as you can. If you have comfortable headphones then use them, or a good speaker.

Put on a relaxing track. I use "De Profundis" by Terry Oldfield (you will find it on the *She of the Sea* playlist on Spotify, or on YouTube.)

Close your eyes and let your breathing fall deeper and deeper into your body. Allow the muscles in your forehead and jaw to relax.

Imagine you are sinking into the music. Continue to do this as you move your attention down your body, as though you are falling into the depths of the ocean's embrace. Allow the muscles in your shoulders and arms to relax, your belly, your pelvis and buttocks, your thigh and calf muscles. Allow your mind to stay softly focused on the music. Any time you feel it starting to weave stories or worries or plans, gently bring it back to rest on the music.

When you are finished give yourself a couple of minutes to experience yourself embodied in silence. You may want to draw or write something in your journal, to move your body or simply take a long, deep breath into your belly to carry into your day.

Underwater Dance
This was inspired by watching Julie Gautier's breathtaking underwater dance in a short film entitled *Ama*.

The music is Ezio Bosso's "Rain, in Your Black Eyes," a fluid piano piece which you will find on the Spotify playlist. In this exercise you can experience the sense of weightless fluidity, without having to be a world champion freediver!

Press play on the music, having it as loud as is comfortable and feasible, allow your body to move through the music as though it were water. Let a slow-motion flow of movement travel from the shoulders, down the arm, through the fingers, allowing yourself to feel weightless and suspended as you move slowly as though underwater. Allow your breathing to come into this slowed state. Use a nearby wall, sofa back or chair to lean on to raise a foot or leg slowly off the floor in the same tempo. You may want to do it with your eyes closed, imagining yourself under the water.

8

WEEPING WOMAN

When spirit becomes heavy, it turns to water...
Therefore the way of the soul...leads to the water.

C.G. Jung

The Women of the Shore

H ere are the women. Crouched on the shingle in a group, wrapped in their dark shawls. The caption on the photograph says it was taken on a West Cork beach in 1910, but the women are timeless. It could have been any time in the last three thousand years. Any coast. Women, from young girls to elders, gathering seaweed and shellfish, flanked by gulls, exchanging stories.

They know She of the Sea as both generous and cruel. They understand that all who are touched by her beauty and blessed with her bounty are also touched by her pain.

These are the women who have wandered the shores through the centuries, looking, longing, waiting, grieving, calling out to the sea, hoping for a call in return, not the echo of her own voice against the wall of fog and fear.

Sifting the Wreckage

I find myself
Looking over the wreckage
That years of storms have washed up.
Driftwood, debris,
Seaweed like hair, torn out at the roots.
I walk the strand,
Finding parts of myself:
My ideals, my energy, hope, courage,

The belief that I could do it differently,
That I was different,
That I was in control.
This, more than anything else, is the lesson of the sea.
And one that is learned hardest:
You, dear small creature, are not in control.
The tides roll in, and there is nothing you can do.
No magic words, no act of will, no
barricades of sand will stop it.
The tide rushes out
Taking what it will.
Including you,
And all you love.

I have been storm-tossed by the
waves these past few years,
Rearranged until I barely know myself.
Everything that I thought I was,
Was toyed with in the dark by the
crashing, smashing waves,
My head pushed under again and again.
In the darkness.

Many times it felt like death would be easier.
Many times it felt like death.
Many times I begged the waves to take me.
But it was not time for death.
Not yet.

Weeping Woman

*After such a deep shift within her, our Heroine realises
that she has to let part of her story go. Or rather, she
has to let a story she has been telling herself die.*

Vanessa Oliver-Lloyd

In the darkness, a wailing blows in on the wind, through the windows
to warm beds. Her cry, splitting the night air, is a dreaded sound in
these parts.

They call her the banshee, from the Irish *bean si,* meaning fairy
woman. She who wails to foretell a death. She who brings awareness
of what is to come. She who scares us. She remembers the future to
us. But she does not cause it.

Lifedeath. The wheel has turned again, she reminds us.

And now the women in black shawls are gathering around the body.
Like a flock of black-winged birds, channelling the sound and salt water
of pain through them, echoing into the space made by the lost loved one.

This ritual of grief is an expression of the trapped feelings of all
those gathered here, channelled by these women, learned in the arts
of loss. Their role is to break the barrier of silence and reach between
this world and the Other with their voices, to help the soul of the
dead move freely onwards from this earthly plane.

These are the keeners. Once common from Irish to Mexican to
Muslim to Scottish funeral ceremonies. Not long ago these black-
garbed weeping women were invited, welcomed, paid. Now their
service is no longer required. In our husk of a culture, even the per-
formance of grief has been shut down.

There is nowhere left that it is okay to grieve. No way to grieve.
Nothing large enough to be acceptable to wail publicly for. Not the
loss of a partner or a parent or a beloved…or even the whole world.

Our grief is shrouded in silence, hidden behind smiles.

oOo

Many of us have been taught that grief is only appropriate when the body of someone we love dies. This is such a limited definition. Grief is a natural result of significant change. And change is constant, which means grief is a natural and ongoing tool and ally for our inner selves to keep up with and healthily move through change. It is our main tool for inner growth, I believe. When things change, we are invited to let go of our inner gripping to what was, so that we may live in the energy of the present rather than keeping psychological and emotional ties to the past. When we let go these ties through the grief process, so much energy is released to become reorganized within us to support our current experience. [...]

Grief opens the channel for the soul to express itself. Grief unclogs the passage for the inner gifts to come forward. Grief is the red carpet for inner truth. Grief is a death and a rebirth rolled into one. Grief is the most powerful way to move energy through your system that there is. Grief is inner alchemy.

Chelan Harkin

oOo

They used to brand weeping women hysterical. Connecting an excess of emotion with the wandering womb. Some still do. A hysterical, weeping woman could be locked away, judged to have taken leave of her senses.

But they cannot lock us all away.

Perhaps the way to be rid of the patriarchy – inner and outer – is to wash it away with our tears, with this sacred salt water. To grieve our losses together. To learn to feel again together. To express it together. Rather than hide it away in fear and silence and shame.

As I write this, I think of the weeping women that I've seen in news footage from around the world: the Mexican mothers, the Indian mothers, and most recently English women mourning together, in public, grieving the rape and murder of their daughters, their granddaughter, their sisters, their friends. Women who are then arrested, beaten, intimidated in order to silence them once more.

> *Enough silence.*
> *Enough violence.*
> *This healing flow of our tears*
> *Is rain in the desert,*
> *Washing our prayers through,*
> *Bringing us back to life.*

The Wisdom of Tears

Crying occurs when people have reached the limit of
what can be said in words and what they are capable
of managing on their own. This does not mean that
their words up to that moment are necessarily good or
true or to be trusted, but it does signify that a breaking
point has been reached. It means that it is time to
pay attention to the systems the tears point towards.
Heather Christle, *The Crying Book*

It seems like there should be a right way to cry. A right time. A right amount. For the right things... It's just that crying didn't get the message. Tears well unexpectedly in the wrong places, about the wrong things. And at the times we may be expected to cry, there is often nothing to demonstrate what we are expected to be feeling... and no words either.

We are taught not to cry. Because to cry is to feel deeply. It is to register loss and pain and hardship in a culture that requires the expression of only positive emotions. The uncontrolableness of grief, of tears, threatens chaos: it is a breaking of the social contract that everything is under control.

But it's not, it's not, it's not.

Crying is a healthy response found in humans of all ages and genders. But one that is associated with the feminine and females, and therefore denigrated as weak and irrational, to be shut down and avoided. Crying is a biological adaptation of our species. Tears come to our eyes to express strong emotion, release stress hormones and rebalance our nervous systems.

We are the only weeping primate. But crying is not uniquely human. This salt-eyed nature of expressing sadness is an ocean dweller's gift. To find our weeping kindred, you have to go down to the seashore. There you will find seals, sea otters and albatrosses that also weep for lost children.

She Cries

The sea seems to facilitate the flow of emotion that brings us back to ourselves. I cannot count the amount of stories I have been told whilst writing this book, of women driving to the sea to scream in their cars, or crying as they walk the sands when their lives overwhelm them. How women swim in the sea (or have a shower or bath) to allow themselves to weep. Something about being immersed in water allows our tears to form rivulets back to source. Something about being in the presence of the Great Mother Ocean allows us to feel held and to let go.

The sea provides a sanctuary for our sorrow, in a way that few spaces on land can or do. In crying we find our way home.

She of the Sea is teaching us, just as she taught our foremothers, how to unfreeze the feeling that has been stuck in our veins. *In order to reach the flow place,* she whispers, *first you must remember how to cry.*

If we see the conscious mind as being expressed through language, then the unconscious is the flow of raw energy before movement, sound, form... It is the fluid medium of deep wisdom. It has to come through the filter of conscious awareness and be shaped before we can witness it.

When we leak out of our skins and touch another out of theirs, this is intimacy: true connection, vulnerable and unarmored. When you become fluid inside, when you are melting down or crying, when you feel all at sea, you are becoming flow, transforming. Let yourself be held, contained as you shapeshift. When your skin can no longer hold you and you are leaking out everywhere, wrap yourself tight swaddled in a blanket or shawl, the arms of a loved one, and know yourself to be in the palm of God(dess). This is the womb space of dissolution and creation where all is uncertain, unknowable, fluid and in flux.

Waves

*It is only when woman can experience
her tears in the moment that she can also
experience her deep feeling values.*

Judith Duerk, *Circle of Stones*

Tears start in my belly. Then my throat. My forehead. My eyes come last.

It is no coincidence that grief is described as coming in waves.

The past few years my autistic meltdowns – what I had previously been taught to understand as panic attacks – have returned…and they have gotten bigger. What started as hyperventilation has become full body rocking and keening. A high-pitched wail of mourning.

I didn't know what I was grieving…

But grieving I was…or rather my body was. My mind couldn't touch the dissolution of my world. It ran in circles trying to find solutions, but was overwhelmed by the magnitude of the storms that had wrecked our family.

It was only in retrospect I realised that this is what I was doing. Mourning for my lost self, my life dissolved in the chaos, mourning for predictability in a world gone mad. It wasn't logical or acceptable. But it was what my body knew how to do on a level deeper than my daily mind went.

When the bottom fell out of my world I would fall to my knees, curl in a ball and rock and wail. Wave upon wave of grief would crash over my head until I could no longer breathe.

It is scary enough when it happens in the privacy of your own bedroom. But when it happens in the doctor's surgery, the supermarket, the car at the side of the road, airport security…then you know you have gone mad.

Except I hadn't.

It was the sanest response my body could muster in a world that no longer worked.

Why, *he asks,* are you crying?
What is wrong
With you?
I don't know
How to answer in words.
I'm crying because
The crying is here,
My sea-wall has ruptured
And I am overcome.
I am a skin taut full of salt water.
There is no more strength in me to hold it in
To stop the deluge.
I am the Caoineadh,[48]
The keener.
I am Weeping Woman,
And I have a world of tears to cry.

Often the tears are not mine.
It is as though the unshed tears of all those around me
Are channelled through me.
At these times of change,
I cry an ocean.
Unlocking the frozen soul
Releasing it into salt water.
I am considered odd
Dramatic, perhaps, for crying so much,
Childish, infantile, immature, out of control, unstable
Hysterical.

Those were the words he used.
And so I try to hide my tears,
Running for cover when the storm threatens.
Until, one day…

Say yes to your dance, *she invites.*
The tears begin to fall,
I pick up my things to leave the class.
But a small voice within
Stops me in my tracks
What if my dance is tears?
They fall faster and faster
In reply.
Yes, yes, yes…
We are your flow.
And I danced through them.

Reflections

How have tears and crying been treated in your life thus far? What did you learn about them as a child growing up? And in adulthood?

Were they considered a sign of weakness, of childishness, of manipulation, of negative femininity?

Do you believe that tears have wisdom? Do you let yourself take that wisdom in?

What in your life remains ungrieved?

What have you done with the tears you wanted to cry but couldn't or didn't? Where did they go? What did they become? Physical or mental illness? Anger or numbness? Or into something more positive – Art? Charity work? Care for others?

What sorrow seeps out of you when you are tired or ill or otherwise unable to contain it anymore?

How might you make safe space for it?

How might you share it: in song, or wailing or chanting or dancing, thrashing in water or on land?

Who do you have in your life that could witness or hold you?

Practice

Weeping Woman

Create an image of the Weeping Woman for yourself out of whatever materials call you. What does she look like? What symbols represent her? What colour and form suit her best?

Paint her, draw her, collage or art journal her. Sculpt her from clay or papier maché and add her to your altar…why not dance her rhythms, sing her song, weep with her?

I have a feeling she might make a powerful doll. Poppets or healing dolls have been used by women for the whole of human history to work magic and act as a cipher for embodied transformation. Perhaps you want to make a Weeping Woman doll…or make a doll to comfort your Weeping Woman.

Shawl Work

Shawls are a piece of clothing associated with the female and Feminine throughout history and cultures – multipurpose, used to keep warm, to comfort, dry tears, provide a dry space to sit or lie, to dance with or carry a baby…

As I was writing this book a dear friend started a project, encouraging us to knit a shawl for ourselves, a gift for our inner wise woman, that would warm the shoulders of our older selves. I began by telling my friend I didn't have the time – or the skills – to knit a shawl. In the end I created several, from which I gain immense comfort. I wear them as I walk the sands. I would highly recommend that you find or make a shawl for yourself and the wise woman that you are becoming.

Crying

How can we release our tears when we have held tight for so long?

You may need space. Or permission. Or a trigger. Or movement. You may need to open your throat and allow your voice to emerge in a scream or a sob or a song. You may need to be alone and get really still and quiet and focus on what you are feeling inside. You may need to sit and talk with a trusted friend or therapist. You may need to dance wildly. You may need to know that you have got to the edge of the world, that there is no further that you can walk, and that to cross over to a new world you must lay your burden down here.

You may want to wrap your shawl round your shoulders and

remember that you are one of the women on the shore, one of millions and millions of weeping women. Allow the warmth to contain you and feel yourself held by something bigger and wiser and stronger than you, whilst the storm within pours out.

She of the Sea is here, the deep Feminine, the oceanic, whose waters will wash away the pain.

9

TRANSFORMATION

*Women remember that once upon a time we sang with
the tongues of seals and flew with the wings of swans.*
Sharon Blackie, *If Women Rose Rooted*

Rebirth

Some days I long to walk fully
clothed into her icy embrace
And just keep walking.
But the waters are shallow here.
The cold would shock me awake.

Each time I longed for an ending,
It was the water that called me home.
And in it I found a new beginning
Through the breath that filled me.

Many times she has guided me
To this liminal place,
Where becoming meets unbecoming,
Freedom meets oblivion.
The crossing place between the
worlds of form and fluidity,
Between surface and depth.

The place of deathbirth.
Or is it birthdeath?
Of dissolution and shapeshifting.

She lures me with the promise of rebirth,
Wrapped in the garb of death.
Come to me,
And let my waters birth you once more.

Bird Woman

Age seventeen, I struggled to move from girl to young woman, and to find a place for my sensitive self in the big world beyond. My grandmother had just died, I had separated from my first love and the meltdowns that were to mark the most stressful periods of my life, were rolling through me. I felt all at sea and rudderless.

Except for one thing: my creativity.

I had fought hard to study both art and drama, rather than the more academic subjects they wanted me to take. During this turbulent time, I found that symbols began flooding through my painting. I had a passion for symbolism and surrealism. My A Level Art portfolio filled with morphing things: tulips turning into glasses; melting faces; bridges being sucked down a plug hole; a woman holding a mirror to her face, her tear turning into a fried egg…and the Bird Woman.

This was the most personal of all my paintings. Set on the cliffs near my home in Ireland, my soul home where I had never been able to live full time. It is a place that calls me **again and again**. A place I have considered jumping. A place I can imagine flying.

The Bird Woman is me. Hands curled into claws like my grandmother's. Standing. Poised. To fall or to fly? To live or to die? Freedom…

When I painted the Bird Woman I did not know of the sirens, mythological birdlike creatures with the heads of women from Ancient Greece, whose voices and beauty could enchant sailors, luring their ships to the rocks. I did not know of the harpies, half-birds, half-women, ugly and terrifying, the personifications of the storm winds, who would steal sailors' food or poison it or fly with them to hell. All I knew was that the Bird Woman was me. I was her. I felt trapped, needing to leap off the cliff and fly, but scared of the consequences, unclear as to whether this was literal or metaphorical.

The Bird Woman comes to me again late one night on a May full moon as I write this book, over twenty years later. I close my eyes and there she is. Her wings folded in. I look again and see that her wings are also a shawl, wrapped around her shoulders, elbows tucked close, she is standing on the cliff looking out to sea. I realise she is connected to Weeping Woman. Weeping Woman is the woman who cannot fly to freedom. Whose voice is silenced by tears.

How many women over the centuries have stood there, back to the world, shawl wrapped tight, no way back, imagining freedom?

I come from a long line of Weeping Women and Bird Women.

I realise, as the image comes through me once again as I finish this book, that the struggle of the Bird Woman is that her soul longs to be free, but her body must remain grounded. The urge to jump is not to crash and die, but to soar and fly.

Shapeshifting

You may have noticed that the theme of shapeshifting runs through this book: selkies, mermaids, bird women, changing moods and tides, human evolution...

The concept of shapeshifting is honoured in most cultures in the oldest forms of shamanism and magic. It is a key feature of most pre-modern tales, allowing a character to slip the bonds of their human form and take on the spiritual or physical powers of a creature from the animal realms: flight, speed, strength, the ability to live underwater... Our fascination with shapeshifting continues today, in novels and superhero movies, as well as in our love of makeover shows and biographies of the rich and famous. We see a dramatic, ritualised expression of shapeshifting by many in the creative sphere – actors, drag artists and rock stars – who, with the application of make up and costume, a new name and a different script, are temporarily transformed into superhumans. They have honed this ability to tap the energy of the psyche and transform almost beyond recognition through their altered physicality.

Conscious, voluntary shapeshifting in order to hide, escape, charm or travel quickly is found in so many classic stories. A character that can shapeshift at will is recognised as having a superpower or gift. Whereas, when a new form is taken involuntarily, through a punishment or curse, and a character is transformed by another person or circumstances, the effect tends to be one of confinement and restraint: the person is *bound* to and by the limitations of the new form. Think of The Little Mermaid swapping her voice for legs, The Children of Lir turned into swans by their stepmother or Medusa turning men to stone with a glance. Like freediving versus being sucked down by riptides it is whether shapeshifting is self-directed and chosen or compelled from without that matters.

Although it seems like big magic, as humans we shapeshift many times in our lives – from baby to child to adolescent to adult to elder – our bodies and personalities shift and change, often dramatically. As women we may well have shapeshifted further, through our menstrual cycles, pregnancy and motherhood. We also change through illness, operations or disabilities, through shifting relationship dynamics and roles, through different forms of creative self-expression, as well as between expressions of gender and sexuality. Our culture has lost its ability to name, mark, and properly acknowledge these rites of passage. We have forgotten how to commune with the power that lies behind these transformations.

oOo

As a creatrix, I am an experienced shapeshifter, consciously moving through worlds of my imagination in waking and dreams. As an autistic woman, I constantly shift between the neurotypical world and my native way of being. As a woman in a man's world, I bend and morph under the male gaze. As a wife and mother, I have learned to shift my breasts and vagina from sexual playthings to vital body parts for my children. As a woman from two cultures, I shapeshift between accents, dialects and customs.

We shift the very essence of ourselves, consciously and unconsciously, every day, in small ways and large, internally and externally, to stay safe, to be seen, to survive. But, for many of us, shapeshifting is something we do unconsciously, because of trauma. It is something scary that happens to us, something shameful and unspoken. Our soul slips from the grasp of the body when it senses peril, when the psyche or body are in a weakened or overwhelmed state, when staying body-bound is too challenging or dangerous. We find ourselves suddenly transformed into something other than our daily selves: dissociating and flying above ourselves looking down, transforming into screaming monsters, wailing banshees, or turned to stone unable to speak or move.

In the past, all this shapeshifting felt like a shameful curse to me: most normal humans do not shapeshift so frequently as I do. They have a fixed persona and way of being in the world. They know who they are…which is just one thing.

The land-world tells us we must choose our form, be one thing or another. We are taught to build a shell, and stay in it. To become it. To forget our soft interior that tastes of salt water and dreams. Some of us are natural shell-dwellers. And some of us come soft-shelled, and have to find ways to survive. And then there are the momentous changes of form…coming out in a new identity, leaving a relationship, claiming a new way of being in the world… So rarely do we find the freedom to match our outer skin to our soulskin – instead we find shells abandoned by others and scuttle into them, passing off these halfway houses of being as our selves.

Most of my work in the last few years has been to find ways to root myself back into my own body on a daily basis, so that I could choose when – and how – I would use my shapeshifting abilities creatively and intentionally, rather than constantly being shapeshifted against my will through trauma response. I found that I intuitively grasped grounding tools (which I have shared with you in this book): picking up and holding pebbles, balancing rocks, making stone spirals and sand labyrinths, connecting my feet to the ground. I have also focused on activities that regulated my nervous system, toning my vagus nerve with rhythmic stimulation, such as swimming, spinning in circles on the beach, dance and listening to calming ocean waves and music, all of which entrained my bodymind into a calm harmony.

Now I see with new eyes the gifts of my natural shapeshifting abilities. This is my creative power, if I can harness it. This is a superpower that many long for. I have the ability to shift and change, to create and recreate myself, to work directly with the energy of soul.

As a fluid medium, water has often been connected to shapeshifting, and the ocean especially, as an environment that is constantly changing – with tides, storms, currents and sun shifting the colour and texture of the water. It is a place where things are immersed and emerge transformed. The sea – She of the Sea – can be a fabulous guide to shapeshifting.

We are learning a more fluid way of being. As individuals. And as a culture. In order to evolve once more – and faster than we've ever had to in our history – we find ourselves having to learn to partner with the process of shapeshifting.

S.he of the Sea

Who is the ocean?

We forget, in all her watery glory, that the ocean is also male.

When we sing praises to the dark lady of creation, beautiful, wild, wise, magical, mysterious, let us remember these are also his qualities and charms.

Who are we harming when we neglect to mention the he of he.r powerful waves, the untamed potency of his storms, his currents, his passions, his gentle breeze, his cleansing embrace, his unseen depths?

Yes, she of the sea. But do not forget he is an entwined aspect of she. Please.

Our boys beg for belonging in nature. They need their gentle inclinations and spirits to be able to perch, to rest at home here on this earth. They need their gentle tides and cleansing waters to be seen in the reflections, the tides and eddies of their souls.

This is more urgent than semantics. This is evolution, and this simple switch just might save us all from another cycle of broken men breaking nature – because when they looked deep into the wild waters, they were unable to see themselves reflected there.

What is the ocean?

Space enough for all the feelings. Depth enough for pain. Waves abundant for joy and splashing, paradox for the summer and the rain.

I love their many faces, their moods, chaos and music. S.he is sound, s.he is peace, s.he is fierce, and always, s.he is wild.

S.he holds it all. S.he is love, as you float suspended between earth and sky. S.he teaches. S.he is home, mother, father, and friend. S.he is the salty smell of important memories, constancy and fate.

S.he reminds me who I am. S.he puts me back together. S.he heals. S.he loves.

S.he is the love from which we came.

Erin Kundrie

The Selkie

*We can live on land but not forever, not without trips
to water and to home. Overly civilised and overly
oppressive cultures try to keep women from returning
home. Too often, she is warned away from the water
until she is thin as a dime and dimmed in light.*
Clarissa Pinkola Estés, *Women Who Run with the Wolves*

There is an old story, along the wild coasts of Scotland and Ireland, of
the selkie. I shall just give the bones of the story here, for those who
are unfamiliar with it. If you are looking for a full version, it is told
in detail in Sharon Blackie's *If Women Rose Rooted,* and Dr Clarissa
Pinkola Estés' *Women Who Run with the Wolves.* There is also a soulful animated Irish film called *Song of the Sea* which you can share
with younger family members.

The selkie is a shapeshifting seal woman whose pelt was taken by a
fisherman, who had fallen in love with her. He promises to return it,
if she will live with him for seven years and start a family. The longer
she lives on dry land, the more she weakens and sickens. Her skin
grows dry, her hair dull. She loses her magic. She knows she must
choose between the family she loves on land...and her own life.

There are many versions of how she eventually gets her sealskin
back. But she does, and slips down to the shoreline on a moonlit
night, back to the waters and her seal sisters. In some versions, she returns occasionally to her children. In one, her daughter develops her
own seal skin and joins her. And in others, she is only ever heard by
her song, seen frolicking in the waves, but never comes back to land.

This idea of the selkie skin is one that resonates on a primal level
with many women, myself included. It is a story we know in our
waters: an archetypal story of what it means to be a wild woman in

the world of men. We of the sea seem to be called to split our time be-tween land and sea – between this world and the Otherworld, inner and outer. Our task is to find healthy ways to shift between the two.

For some of us, our selkie skins were stolen when we were young and innocently sunning ourselves on the shore. For others, it was a willing exchange, for a life we thought we wanted – a partnership, a job, motherhood – when suddenly we found there was no way back to who we knew ourselves to be, and no way forward into what we were becoming. We feel trapped, unable to take off this strange new identity, dying on dry land. To those around us our struggles seem strange. *Didn't we enter this willingly? Isn't dry land where we should live?* But those of us who are born of the sea cannot live on dry land for long. We need to return to the isolation and beauty of the sea, the magic of the Otherworld. We have to immerse ourselves in the depths, with no one clock-watching our return. We must do this or we die. First on the inside, then on the outside.

Once a selkie finds its skin again, neither chains of steel nor chains of love can keep her from the sea.

Tadgh, in *The Secret of Roan Inish*

The selkie represents the soul – the wild Feminine, native of the depths, a magical shapeshifter. She needs immersion in creativity, the sacred, nature, flow consciousness and freedom…but she also needs energetic ties to the bodymind in order to take form and engage with this world. This is her constant struggle, which we recognise intimately. We each find within us this battle between masculine and feminine, land and sea, body, mind and soul played out…the desire for freedom, and the desire for union.

As selkie sisters, we have to learn to ease between forms, to traverse the liminal with less suffering, less resistance…to follow the flow of cyclical transformation.

The sea is a teacher of shapeshifting —
Ever changing, ever the same.
She calls to the shapeshifter within.
The one longing for home.
The selkie, the bird woman
We who must live both on shore and on land
Who breathe air but need the waters.
A half breed,
Never quite at home
Always betwixt, between,
Always having to return to the other place.

Selkie Memories

When I get into the sea, I feel, somehow, I have come full circle. The salty ocean is a place I can own my plump seal skin – this is something that is much harder for me to do on land – putting my juicy flesh fully back on and reclaiming what was always mine...

Like many archetypal tales, I remember seeing mermaid-style stories in Hollywood movies and cartoons and books from when I was young. As I got older, I became fascinated by lands and places which held very old deep tales of the selkies.

I was 22 when I felt called to travel alone to Cornwall. I stood for days on the beach, in what I can only call a huge spiritual calling and awakening... Zennor, on the southwest coast at the tip of Cornwall, and that whole rugged wild coastline feels like a soul home.

The land is steeped in myths of mermaids and selkies, enchantment and magic. In Zennor there is a mermaid chair from around 1400, made with a beautiful carving of a sea goddess. I've experienced similar myths on my travels across Mexico, USA, Iceland and Scotland.

In the last few years, I have felt so called to the Scottish Orkney Islands and the Isle of Lewis, where selkies are as common characters as fishermen. While in these old, old places on the edge, hundreds of images pour out of me in black and white line drawings and vibrant paintings. I have painted hundreds of selkie characters, sea storm witches and goddesses of the land, sea and sky... I turn these images into poetry, sacred dresses, shawls, and prints. They are healing for me and also call deeply to so many others who feel drawn to their stories and messages. I also teach a Fairytale Medicine journey to hundreds of women around the world, and the favourite stories are always ones where selkies are included...they long to hear the myths and really identify with them, even if they have no prior knowledge of the stories.

I love the idea that we may have originally come from a much juicier fluid and freeing ocean landscape than the world we live in now, and that, unlike in many gruesome fairy stories, the selkie woman returns to her true home, the sea, and swims free with her fellow seals... we are not left alone or broken...

Many of us have waited a long time for the selkies to sing us back home...the sea calls to me and so many of us...calls us back into an immense endless consciousness...a kind of bigger version of a womb, a watery Mother Earth womb...one where we feel can feel much more at home in our divine plump salty skins...

Clare Jasmine Beloved

Salt in my Veins

As a teenager I dreamed of escape. I cursed the haar,* rolled my eyes at our white sand beaches and flailed against the wide empty spaces. How could a place be so boring, so quiet, so suffocating? I left and found that I could only breathe when I came home. I lived by hot seas and felt dirty. I cried in a cinema in Israel for the weary fishing boats of *A Perfect Storm*. I fell in love with Boston not knowing that I loved it for its brightly coloured version of home. I lived by the River Thames and scoffed at its pretty greens and puddled floods. I swelled and choked and felt ever more tightly bound.

And then, my belly swelled, and determined that my selkie pup would be born within sight of the sea, I wrapped myself in voluminous layers and flew home, long past the time a pregnant woman should. I had barely glimpsed the shore, before my tiny secret rushed to be born and my heart was washed clean again with the salt rush of joyful tears.

I named her Rhea for the mother of the gods and Iona for the Holy Island. I feel responsible for passing on the salt magic to my daughter, starting with her naming, a suitable name for a carrier of watery secrets. My stories for her are of singing seals and selkies with graves that never dry up. Of drowned Viking princesses and buried Pictish villages.

I do indeed have salt water in my veins.

Donna Booth

---

* A cold sea fog that occurs in coastal areas that border the North Sea, on the eastern coastline of England and Scotland, during late spring and summer.

Freedive

Come with me, slip on your selkie skin, feel yourself ease into it like a homecoming. Let us swim out into the blue, following the call of She of the Sea.

Take a deep breath, fill your lungs.

Fix your eye on the silver line of soul running down into the depths and follow it. Push aside the seaweed, to see the lost worlds beneath the waves.

Under the water everything seems strange. Some noises are swallowed whole and others amplified.

Time moves differently here.

Your body travels slowly, as it pushes through the invisible resistance of water. You are more graceful, weightless and dynamic than on land. Sound is slower. Light too. There is above. And below. Two different worlds. Ruled by different dynamics. Bubbles, like stars, race skywards and burst.

Deeper you go, into the indigo depths, past the shadowy shapes that you may have hidden from in fear all your life, lies perhaps what you most need to encounter now.

Submerged under the water, in the darkness, you begin to remember the most ancient of magics…

Deep Diving

Do you know my favorite secret happy place of all? Immersing myself underneath the deep waters of a lake! With each precise, frog-like stroke, I propel downward, my long hair flying behind me trusting the wind in my lungs to carry me far, far down – down where rays of light are illuminating the dark. Hidden from the upper worlds of humans, this is my introvert's version of heaven. As tensions are left behind in the wake of de-

scent, I remember fluidity in my water born skills: swimming, diving, somersaulting, weightlessness. Only in this sacred company of deep waters are the wild songs coaxed from my belly where rage or grief or joy reverberate in bubbles held safe in a private conversation between the earth and myself.

And then, when it is time to rise, without fear of being too late, of pushing my edges and remembering the strong yet fragile agreement where my life rests between life and death, I break the glassy surface. With that first breath, I roll to my back, throw my arms upward and float, giving thanks for the moon and the sun and the stars and the waters. This, for me, is elation, a kind of ecstasy that is incomparable. And I know as long as I live, I will keep returning, because I am a child born and raised by the sea, fluent in the river's currents, her coursing waterfalls and pathways of wandering small brooks. Truth be told, it is the Lady of the Lake who forever holds my heart and embraces me always in my constant return to her welcoming and mysterious depths.

Alisa Starkweather

Reflections

How have you shapeshifted during your life? Was it chosen or forced? What wisdom does the story of the selkie hold for you?

Practice

Seek out stories of shapeshifting characters that appeal to you – read or listen to them, perhaps take an inner journey with one, or ask for a dream about one, do a movement journey or write creatively about one. You may want to fictionalise your own experiences of shapeshifting, or write your own version of a classic tale.

After doing this, create or find images of shapeshifters to add to your altar space, or items that are symbolic of their powers – a feather for flight, for example.

Symbols

The symbols of the self arise in the depths of the body.

C.G. Jung

Throughout this book, I invite you to begin to identify some of your own magical symbols – objects or ideas that are potent for you: 'potent' meaning that they hold power. You may find them by observing which words, images or symbols feel particularly resonant for you as you read. They may be images that recur regularly in your own art or writing – or that you are drawn to. You might spot them in the clothing or jewellery you choose. Be prepared that they may seem 'weird' or 'uncomfortable' to you, somehow logically inexplicable right now, just as the jellyfish was to me when it kept arising in my art.

Other symbols that have magical meaning for me include: keys, hands, birds, the moon, seaweed, rainbows, water drops, doorways and spirals. They have a magnetic pull for me, and have reappeared again and again through my art since my early teens.

Are your symbols in any way connected to key points of transformation in your journey, as messengers, markers, activators or portals for shapeshifting? Research their history and meaning in myth and story around the world.

10

SHE OF THE SEA

*She was the primeval ocean and she emerged
as herself of herself and all has come forth
through and from her. She is self existent,
and her nature is secret, a mystery to all.*

Egyptian Book of the Dead

She of the Sea Song

Selkie, mermaid, siren, sprite,
Guide this lost soul home tonight.
Surf-tossed, salt-scummed, white horses ride,
Into the depths, where monsters hide.

Becalmed I lie,
No wind, no wave,
No stars to steer by,
No passage safe.

Weed-strewn beaches, storm-tossed stones,
Piles of driftwood, whales' bones.
Mermaid's purse and hag stone round,
Spiral seashells to be found.
Sea glass smooth and starfish bright
Washed up in the dark of night.

Siren's song, beacon's light,
Fog horn calling in the night
Squall emerging, dark and raw,
Pulling ships into its maw.

She is coming, yet unseen.
She is coming, Ocean Queen.
Proceeded by her ancient fame:
She of the Sea, by many names.

Song of the Sea

Does the song of the sea end at the shore,
or in the hearts of those who listen?

Kahlil Gibran

I t is no coincidence that the most common theme of the stories of women and the sea are to do with the voice. So much of the enchantment of the sea is about the freeing of the voice of the Feminine.

A woman's voice has the power to enchant, condemn, or even save her life. This is why one of the greatest successes of patriarchal culture has been the silencing, shaming and dismissing of women's voices.

There are so many stories about the sea and women's voices...

One of the first written stories in Western culture is the ancient Greek tale, *The Odyssey*. It charts Odysseus' long journey home from war, coming across many mythical creatures and much sea magic on the way. In one part of the story, Circe, a banished sea-nymph with magical powers, lures Odysseus' ship to her island. She uses her powers to turn his men into pigs and keep the weather around her island so glorious that he is seduced into remaining there with her. Later she advises him as to how he may keep his ship and men safe as he sails past the sirens, whose voices are said to be so enchanting they make men mad. Odysseus is advised to make his men block their ears with wax. [49] He is determined to hear the song himself, and be the only man to survive having done so, and so he guides his men to lash him to the ship's mast and not release him. This is the power of a woman of the sea's voice. This is her power to seduce...and destroy.

In the tale of *The Little Mermaid,* Ariel is only coming into her maturity when she falls in love with a land-living prince. Unaware of the power of her voice, she willingly trades it for human legs so that she may be with the one she loves. In Louise O'Neill's retelling of the tale, *The Surface Breaks,* the Little Mermaid laments: "How could I have thrown [my voice] away? The only time I was ever happy was when I was singing."

With the selkie, it is her song that first catches her husband's attention. And it is the song of her sister seals that reminds her of her wildness and calls her back to the sea.

We seem to trade our voices before we are fully aware of their power. We learn to plug our ears to our inner voices, when we are taught to keep our thoughts to ourselves. We learn not to cry, to stay dry eyed and quiet in our sadness and our joy. The cost of this is higher than we might realise, as Heather Christle notes in *The Crying Book,* "Perhaps you have noticed that it is almost impossible to sing and cry at the same time. The throat muscles cannot simultaneously obey the command to shape notes and the command to hold themselves open to maximise oxygen intake (a command that crying provokes unconsciously). This leads me to believe that the opposite of crying is not laughter (those two, I would argue, are sisters), but song."

The opposite of crying is not laughter but song. Breathe that in for a moment. Let it land in your body.

We who have reclaimed our right to wail and weep, to grieve and cry, to feel the flow of feelings storm through us and express this, are also reclaiming our natural birthright – our voices, our soul songs.

As you travel through stories of the sea, notice the role of women's voices: their power, their magic…and their silencing. Again and again, we are reminded that powerful magic arises from the salty depths, from the sea, from our tears and our juices, from the wail of grief, the throaty moan of pleasure and our soul songs. The power of woman and sea combined are indomitable.

Morgan le Fay

A little over a year ago, I stood on a grassy clifftop of Tintagel, in Cornwall. The sky is blue and the sun is shining. It's Samhain, and we are singing a song to the sea with a group of priestesses and goddess-loving folk. We can see down onto Tintagel Castle and the beach of Merlin's cave, over the Celtic Sea.

Tintagel is the mythological seat of King Arthur – and as I stood upon this clifftop, I thought of the many stories of Morgan le Fay. In the tales of legend and literature (in twelfth century texts by Geoffrey of Monmouth and Chrétien de Troyes), Morgan le Fay is half-sister to King Arthur and, depending on the telling, Morgan schemes to remove Arthur from his throne and kill him. She is dangerous and mysterious. But she is also the ruler of Avalon, Lady of the Lake, enchantress skilled in the arts of healing and of changing shape.

Morgan le Fay is thought to be connected to, or an incarnation of, the triple goddess – the Morrigan, of Irish and Celtic myth. The Morrigan is a goddess of war, death, and fertility: a goddess of contrasts and layers. Morgan means 'sea born' and she has so many embodiments: sea maiden, siren, mermaid, goddess, fairy, priestess, healer, shapeshifter and witch. Her story is far too old and powerful to be confined to her malevolent 'bit part' in Arthur's legend. Her sea-born name and shapeshifting skills connect her to the very special mirage, where boats and cities appear to float above the water. This phenomenon is still known as the *Fata Morgana* in her honour. The *Fata Morgana* transforms an ocean horizon into an enchanting land of the fae, guiding sailors off course or inspiring joy and longing.

Morgan le Fay embodies illusions, mirages, fairies, myths, legends, the multi-layered and strangely 'other' in a patriarchal world. She is a goddess for every woman who has been held up as Queen and cast down as Harpy (so many of us have experienced both). Oh, how patriarchy loves to control and define women, and when they can't, we are damned as cruel witches, seductive sirens, *and tempestuous tarts. Maybe we seek to bring our heads under the waters of the ocean to drown out that noise and to float in the simple and finite power of knowing, and being with rhythm and wave. To be held in the water womb of Mother Earth.*

Sarah Robinson

Sea Magic

'Witch' is simply a term that men give women who are not afraid of them, women who refuse to do as they are told.

Louise O'Neill, *The Surface Breaks*

Again and again, throughout myth and fairy story, the magical woman's native place was the sea. She is depicted as the mermaid, the selkie, the siren, the dark water witch, the banshee. Her nature fickle, her motivation selfish and malevolent, her sensuality bewitching, her beauty otherworldly: long hair glossy and dripping, breasts buoyant, and what lies beneath, is it legs, or tail or a damp cavern of delights? She is too much temptation to bear. Lust launches bewildered men unthinking into the water, along the cliffs, towards that voice, that body, that promise…towards an embodiment of the Feminine for which they are starving…

Women connected to the sea rarely prosper at the hands of men – above or below water. The price they pay for their visible Feminine gifts is masculine vengeance. They are murdered (Sedna, Dahud and Clíodhna) or domineeringly controlled (Ariel and Circe) by their fathers. A woman who embodies the fullness of Feminine power is considered dangerous. A woman with her own powers, in charge of her own body and soul, cannot be trusted. Her magic must be controlled, or shut down, her voice silenced.

Each of these women swaps a vital part of themselves – a symbol of their soul – in order to obtain freedom and love: Sedna's fingers, Ariel's voice, the selkie's skin. The price for Shes of the Sea has been high in patriarchy: murdered or monstered for their magic, their power, their sensuality. When the Feminine will not submit, she must be controlled or destroyed.

For millennia, women have understood that to stay safe they must submit to the System. In the patriarchal domain the Feminine is always other: strange, misunderstood, lusted after and despised. Those of us who embody the Feminine may try to live by the rules of men, but eventually find we cannot. It is only when our life is in as much danger from the internal incongruence to our soul's nature, as by the threat of breaking patriarchal rules, that we finally act.

Women's magical connection to the sea is not just myth, but history. Tales abound of women using magic to raise storms and capsize boats. The most extreme perhaps was when, in 1590, King James of Scotland started a witch-hunt in his homeland, accusing the jealous local women of causing a storm as he brought home his new wife from Denmark. Over two hundred women were accused of "sailing in sieves" on Halloween night to make the magic, and, as a direct result, many were tried in court, tortured and killed for *their* "crimes."

During the centuries of witch hunts in Europe, water was one of the "trials", used to prove that a person was guilty of witchcraft. "Swimming a witch" consisted of immersing the individual in water. If they sank, they were innocent, if they floated they were a witch… and could then be further tortured before being put to death (a rather handy win-win situation).

Being a woman connected to her body, her sexuality, her creativity, her power, her spirituality, her voice has been a dangerous thing for millennia. And it still is. Just this week it was reported that in Afghanistan – the land of lapis lazuli – new laws have made it illegal for any female over the age of twelve not just to show her hair, but to play music or sing.

The belief in women's power to enchant is still real. Women's power – though denied, dismissed and destroyed for generations – is real. We are remembering.

The tides are turning.
We are reclaiming our magic.

Mermaids

Perhaps the most commonly known of all magical Shes of the Sea is the mermaid, part human, part sea-creature, beloved of little girls and grown dreamers. Mermaids are usually described as enchanting men as they sit combing their long hair on rocks, sing hypnotic songs or tempt men into the depths. Whilst there are references to water-dwelling men, the majority are stories of magical water-women.

The mermaid story that most of us today are familiar with is Hans Christian Andersen's fairy tale of "The Little Mermaid" in one of its many guises, from the original, to the Disney classic, to more recent live action films, to Louise O' Neill's feminist retelling for young adults and her statue in Copenhagen. The story of *The Little Mermaid* has captured the imagination of generations…

Mermaids have an ancient past. The first mermaid stories appeared in Assyria around 1000 BC. They were considered to be the wives of sea dragons, sent as messengers between the rulers of the ocean and human emperors. They appeared in Ancient Greece in Homer's *Odyssey* and Rome, where Pliny the Elder "describes numerous sightings of mermaids off the coast of Gaul, noting that their bodies were covered all over in scales and that their corpses frequently washed up on shore. He comments that the governor of Gaul even wrote a letter to Emperor Augustus to inform him."[50] Strange half-human, half-fish creatures are found in ancient stories in Japan and China. They are regular features of sealore throughout European sea exploration, seen decorating maps, even Christopher Columbus reported sightings on his travels to The New World. In Brittany, there is the tradition of marie-morgans, magical sea women who lure sailors to their death…or alternatively lives of wonder beneath the waves.

But they are not merely a Eurasian phenomenon. Mermaids are known as "*yawkyawks*" to the Aboriginal people of Australia – a name that, again, refers to their mesmerizing songs. In Mexico, freshwater mermaid stories are thought to go back a few thousand years.[51]

Unlike many mythical creatures whose allure has waned, mermaids have a real and prominent place in twenty-first century culture. The hunger for the reality of mermaids is powerful. In 2013-14 US-made fictional documentaries *Mermaids: The Body Found* and *Mermaids: The New Evidence,* purporting to have real evidence of mermaids, were the most viewed programmes in *Animal Planet's* history. Meanwhile, mermaid clothes, toys, colours and hair have been on trend the last few years, as we seek, in the only way we have been taught how by our culture, to reintroduce magic into our lives…through consumerism.

The symbol of the mermaid has been claimed by a UK charity, which supports gender diverse children and their families, mermaids.co.uk. It is a very apt choice, as celebrated trans woman writer and director, Janet Mock, shares in her article for *Allure:* "Like mermaids, trans women are viewed as half-women, half-other. Like mermaids, trans women grapple with people's disturbing curiosity with their genitals. And like mermaids, we are fascinating and beautiful and magical."

Mermaids are alive today for real. The mermaid movement has grown massively in the past decade, with folks donning vibrant tails and taking to the waters in oceans and pools, embodying the magic of She of the Sea in our times.

Mermaid

I'm a mermaid. No, not just in my soul, but in reality.

I know how that sounds, but let me tell you why it's true. Growing up I always wanted to be a mermaid. On my third birthday I wished with all my might to be a mermaid, and it continued every year. I believe if you get one wish a year, it might as well be something spectacular. Specifically, I would petition, "God, please let me be a mermaid. I don't even need to breathe underwater, just the tail would be amazing." Little did I know, this was possible.

You see mermaids in the movies like *Hook* or *Splash*, but I thought it was simply for the films and not something a 'regular human' like me could ever dream of being.

On my 23rd birthday, I ate my cake, made my wish, and curled up with my mermaid book, finishing it early. Longing for another under the sea adventure story, I went online, and an article about Hannah Mermaid, a professional mermaid, came up in my search. The whole world froze with the question: You can be a mermaid and get paid for it? Even more exhilarating: becoming a mermaid is possible? This revelation ignited a deep dive into all things mermaid, and I found a community of mermaid hobbyists, professionals, and tail makers and started my journey to becoming one.

Today, eight years later, I perform as Mermaid Harmony, one of the hundreds of professional merfolk. Similar to being a clown, but with better makeup, less terrifying, and I won't scar your children for life. I have a tail made of silicone I wear to swim in both the ocean and pools, and I 'tail up' for parties or just for fun. I have shell bras, more biodegradable glitter than my husband is okay with, and a treasure chest filled with mermaid crystals.

For me, the world has always been brimming with possibilities. I was a theatre major, and taught children in after school programs, helping them learn new ways of seeing the world by playing games, or storytelling. Being a mermaid is a continuation of that, allowing me to bring wonder back to people. The world can be loud, and the idea of magical creatures is tossed over the shoulder as ridiculous, but when I show up, people dream again. They whisper their hearts' desires of what they once thought was impossible: going back to school, traveling the world, painting... These are simple, wondrous things we keep locked up, awaiting someone to grant us permission to dream out loud again. This was the first magic I discovered in being a mermaid.

After swimming in the ocean in my tail, I realised another magnificent reality: the magic of the sea is also real. This magic comes to you during the quiet moments of aware- ness in the water. It happens when performing for a party or swimming with friends. You feel the water pressing against your fins as you gently sway back and forth, your fluke slicing through the water, as effortless as breathing. Slip- ping under the water, you look down and see your tail shimmering in golds, and hues of purple and orange. The waves echo in your ears as the sea's thrum washes over your whole body. With- in this moment, everything else ceases to exist. You are one with the sea. You are a mermaid, fierce, strong, bold, beautiful, and present. Fully. Here.

This is the magic I always dreamed of being a part of. This is the reality I knew existed when I wished each year on my birthday. This is the wonder I extend at parties and in my con- versations with people. We tune out joy and dreams because we think being human means not believing in fairytales, but our life is part of creating a larger tapestry of possibilities that we all are a part of.

Being a mermaid is a pathway to remembering how the world was created: with a breath and a wave of possibilities.

Aj Smit

The Thousand Names of She of the Sea

We call on you, She of the Sea,
She of a thousand names.
Gaia, our Earth mother,
Mother of all life.
You, Thalassa, Danu, Tiamat…
Mother goddesses of the primeval waters.
You, Mare, Marie, Mary,
Star of the Sea,
Mother of God,
Hold us in your blue robe,
As we weep.

We call your names.
You, Sedna, Inuit Seal Mother of the deep cold seas
And your stormy counterpart,
Arnapkapfaaluk, withholder and destroyer,
Show your righteous fury at your treatment.
You, Tsovinar, daughter of the seas.
You, Yemoja, mother of fish children, river goddess of Nigeria,
Whose waters broke to create us.
You, who travelled with your stolen
people, shapeshifting to become
Yemanja, Queen of the Ocean in your new lands.
You, Mami Wata, African mermaid mama.
You, Rán, Norse goddess, mother of the nine waves.

You, Nehalennia, goddess of the North Sea,
You, Sara La Kali, Romany saint, Queen of the Outsiders,

Adorned with flowers, floating on the waters.
We feel your wisdom flow through us,
We see you rise.

In Greece your names are as many as your islands.
Isis Pelagia, mistress of the sea, guide of boats.
Aphrodite, goddess of dawn, beauty and love.
Galene, goddess of calm seas.
Leucothea, helper of sailors in distress.
Amphitrite, goddess of the sea.
Circe, daughter of Oceanus, exiled magic-maker,
Who turned the beauteous Scylla into a man-eating monster.
You snake-haired Gorgons – Medusa, Euryale and Stheno –
Protectresses of oracles, who turn men to stone with a glance.
You, daughters of Ceto, granddaughters of Gaia.
You, three thousand Oceanids,
Arise!

You, goddesses of the great Pacific,
Pele, she of volcanoes, taught by the shark god to surf,
You, little sister goddess Hi'iaka,
And you, shapeshifting Mamala,
Hear our call.

You, sacred Shes from the Celtic shores:
Morgan le Fay, priestess and mist-caster.
Domnu, Queen of the depths.
Dahud, daughter of king and banshee,
Who lives between Earth and Sea.
Lí Ban, water goddess and seabird shapeshifter.
And Clíodhna… Clíodhna…
Your wave is coming in.

We see you.
We hear you.
We name you.
We know you,
Beloved,
Shes of the Sea.

She is Real

In my work, I deal with archetypes and symbols, elemental energy blueprints found in the collective consciousness, story, art and metaphor, through many cultures. But never have I discovered these so embodied in one mytho-historical woman…let alone two!

I was so excited to discover these Celtic goddesses of the sea – Clíodhna and Dahud – 'out of the blue,' just as I finished writing the book. It seems they have been with me all this time.

These two, women whose stories and symbols had been the heart and soul of *She of the Sea.* I didn't know their names, their reality, until after I had written my own knowing in my own hand, seen their reality in the world with my own eyes.

This is often the way with the Feminine, I have found. Some part of us just knows. But the rest of us resists. And so begins our quest to gather evidence, names, stories…to learn a new language to be able to express this instinctive knowing and our lived experience which our current culture has neither the words for nor the interest in. And as our proof and courage grow, we begin to see that She, the sacred Feminine, has been around us all the time, hiding in plain sight, putting down breadcrumbs for us to follow until we see her with our own eyes, know her by name.

Dahud

Dahud-Ahes (or Dahut) is a Celtic goddess who belongs to the wild land and seascape where the waves meet the shore at the tip of the peninsula of French Brittany. Her name, Dahud, means "good witch," and Ahès, "key holder."

The legend starts with the King Gradlon of Cornwall falling in love with a banshee, a woman of the fairy-mounds, called Malgven. Together they had a daughter named Dahud, who was born at sea. She was raised in the ways of the Goddess by her mother before Malgven died, or mysteriously returned to the Otherworld.

Dahud is a child of Earth and Sea: born "in between" as the child of a banshee and a Christian Father. This existence at the edge of two worlds re-appears often throughout her myth. Dahud teaches us to live firmly rooted in our bodies, in the Earth, as well as caring for our soul journey and spiritual origins: she teaches us balance.

The Celtic tradition being mostly matriarchal, Dahud inherited the Pagan ways of her mother and always fought to keep them alive. As it was getting increasingly difficult to practise the ancient ways in Brittany, Dahud asked her father to build a city where she could reign and live as she pleased. The city was named Ker-Ys (*Ker* meaning 'city' and *Ys* meaning 'below' in Breton). It was founded on the magical, liminal space between the Earth and the Sea, to which Dahud belonged, one foot in each world. It was so close to the ocean, almost merging with it, that it had to be surrounded by a giant wall to protect it from the waves.

Ker-Ys became a city of abundance, pleasure, and celebration, with the best of every continent brought there: food, jewels, textiles, musicians. The wilder she got, the angrier the Christian monks grew. They accused her of worshipping the Devil and tried to convince her father, the King, that the princess should be removed, or God would punish them all.

It is an interesting detail in the story that Dahud is not actually the one carrying the keys of the city. She never is, in any version. The keys represent sovereignty over the city that she rules, and yet they are in the possession of her father. This is where Dahud's initiation is triggered, as she chooses to steal the keys from her father while he is asleep, and to give them to the Devil, disguised as a seductive stranger. She puts her own healthy masculine to sleep, and gives her power away to the trickster.

The tale ends with Dahud's punishment for her naiveté, which will also lead to her transformation: the Devil takes hold of the keys, opens the gates of the city, and lets the wild ocean engulf Ys. As the whole city is sinking, King Gradlon rides the waves on his late wife's magical seahorse, Morvarc'h. He gets Dahud to ride with him, trying to save both of them, but the weight pulls the seahorse down. Saint Guenolé, the monk representing the Church in this legend, presses the King to let his daughter drown with the city, as she is the cause for its demise. With a heavy heart, the King lets go of his daughter's hand. The Church has won, and the Ruler of the land has let the Ancient Goddess sink into oblivion. Alongside Dahud, the Old World disappears.

But the ultimate teaching of Dahud's myth is yet to come.

In the end, all threads are gathered back together. Dahud – as the Ancient Goddess, with her wild ways and full sovereign power – does drown, and therefore reintegrates the Otherworld of her mother. She returns to the mysterious Underworld from which she came, and to which she was always destined. There, she transforms into a marie-morgan – a Breton mermaid. In her imagery post-drowning, she is often represented with the key around her neck, as if the journey – as painful as it may be – had allowed her to take her power back. In the Underworld – the soul world – she can finally become Queen.

The legend says that Dahud and Ys never died, but only returned to the Underworld temporarily, waiting for the time when the earthly world would be ready to welcome the Goddess again.

> When someone on the shores of Brittany hears the bells of Ys ringing from below the sea, Ys – and the Goddess – will rise again from the depths.[52]
>
> **Julie Collet, priestess of Dahud**

Clíodhna

Clíodhna, daughter of the god of the sea, Manannán Mac Lir. Ruler of the Celtic Otherworld, goddess of love and beauty, Queen of the Banshees and a shapeshifter who takes the form of a sea bird. I am dizzy with the coincidences. I knew her, without knowing that I did.

Clíodhna came to form here in Cork, the county of my birth, the home of my soul. She of the waves, who comes accompanied by birds. Sometimes depicted as an old woman wrapped in a shawl, crouched on the shore. She is the weeping woman, the banshee and guardian of the Celtic Sea. But she is also the most beautiful woman to have ever existed, a seductress who used her beauty to lure men to their deaths on the seashore.

She advised the Lord of Blarney Castle in a dream to kiss the first stone he saw in the morning on his way to court, to give him "the gift of the gab" – self-expression through his voice. I visited Blarney Castle for the first time during the writing of this book with a good friend, seeking out the ancient Feminine in this place of tourists…the ancient witches' yew, the standing stones, the cave, the poison garden. Not knowing, not knowing! *Were you the robin that fluttered and hovered before me in the fern garden, landing on my hand? Were you trying to tell me?*

And then there is the final piece…her foretelling that a great wave will one day flood the whole of this area: Clíodhna's Wave. Read on, dear reader, read on. For magic is afoot when the sacred Feminine reveals herself.

I am She

I am she who dives deep.
I am she who sings the world into being,
And dances between air and water.
I am she who lies on the rocks sunning her soulskin.
And sees the reflections of other worlds in the rock pools.

I am she who flies with the tides,
And darkens with the moon.
I am she who is the mother of us all.

I am liquid love…
Sacred flow…
The depths from whence we all swam.
I am the ancient mother,
Who loved you into life.
She who softens the sharp edges of broken glass
Into frosted beauty.
She who turns cliffs to sand.

I am the ecstasy of surrender,
The ocean of delight washing you clean.
I am the wave and the spiral.
I the ascension and the deep dive.
I am the plunge into pleasure,
The wetness of wanting, the danger of desire.
I am she who drips
Salty life into your mouth,

Who floods your mind
With love.

I am abandon.

Breathe me in,
Breathe in my salt kiss through your skin.
Feel me inside you deeper than you have ever dared go.
To a place beyond breath,
Beyond vision.

I am she who surrenders herself to the flow.
I am she who is free in the sea.
The breeze steers me,
There is nothing left to cling to
And so I let go.

I am she who glides
Who trusts her body to the waters.
I see by the light of the jellyfish moon,
By the flight of the seagull.
I row into the cavern of mystery,
where all perspective is shifted.
I am a lone traveller of dark places.
I am the eye of the world.
I am the voice of the waves.
I am she.
I am She of the Sea.

Reflections

Have you ever heard/witnessed/expressed the voice of the Feminine before?

What have you learned – consciously and unconsciously about the voice of the Feminine?

What special powers do you consider it to have? Are these positive or negative?

What do you fear might happen if you express the voice of the Feminine?

Practice

Gather Her Images

Do a Google search and seek out images of She of the Sea from different cultures and times – goddesses, mermaids, selkies, sea witches, sirens… Which depictions draw you in most? Which scare you? Which enthral you?

Print them off the internet, cut them out of magazines, buy the work of artists who represent her or create an image of She of the Sea for yourself out of whatever materials call you. Paint her, draw her, collage or art journal her. Sculpt her from clay or papier maché, needle-felt or knit her…why not dance her rhythms, sing her song? What does she look like? What symbols represent her? What colour and form suits her best?

Adorn your altar or desk or bedside table with some of these images of She of the Sea.

Play music as you add these to your altar and sing over your altar – "Kai – the Song of the Mermaid" by Lisa Dancing Light on the *She of the Sea* Spotify playlist is an excellent choice as it is simple and repetitive, a deeply sacred unleashing of the power of the Feminine voice.

11

RITUALS AND CEREMONIES

Performing ceremonies helps us navigate the
turbulent waves and builds up the spiritual strength
to ride the challenging waves of any crisis.
Sandra Ingerman, *The Book of Ceremony*

Initiation

The beginning of any new way of being requires an initiation. This is the first time that can never be repeated: losing our virginity, giving birth, publishing a book, swimming in the cold wild water. Each of them requires our full courage to show up in our bodies and step into our souls. They can be, if we choose to mark them as such, ceremonies of commitment to a new way of being, both worldly and spiritual, a way of marking a rite of passage. They challenge the bodymind to leave its everyday comfort zone and break through an invisible barrier to meet the soul where she longs to be. An initiation often requires us to risk pain, shame, loss, rejection or failure in order to more fully embody the soul. It requires that we step through fear and ego to meet ourselves. There is no halfway, no rehearsal – you have to turn up and risk stepping out of your old skin and into your destiny.

Each of the sacred sea crafts from weaving sea silk to diving for shellfish, from water witchery and sea priestessing has been passed down from older to younger practitioners in uninterrupted traditions. But as the tides have turned, and the modern world encroaches upon the natural and the sacred, we are finding ourselves having to reclaim, recapture, reimagine and reanimate practices, initiating ourselves and each other intuitively. We are having to get the wisdom from source once more, learning to hear the song of the sea for ourselves and finding new stories to explain it, new rituals to connect to it, new ceremonies to honour it.

These ceremonies are not *just* for us as individuals. They make energetic impressions on the ground and in the water they are performed on, in the people who share them. As Rowena Pattee Kryder says in her book, *Sacred Ground to Sacred Space,* "By learning nature's scripture and applying her pattern language through art and ritual, we can draw the healing subtle energy into the environment."

My dearest hope is that if we can begin to re-find the sacred in the expanses of the ocean and ourselves, perhaps we can then learn how to apply this knowing to our land lives and imbue them with sacredness.

Ceremony

I am offering ideas for several sea ceremonies here, combining many ritual elements from the exercises I have shared in this book. There are a couple for if you have access to a beach, and one to do from home. You might choose to do one to mark an important point in your personal journey, a full moon, a point on the wheel of the year, such as summer or winter solstice or the equinoxes…or just because!

All of my ceremonies are intuitively created and usually quite spontaneous. Please know there is no 'doing it wrong' – what I am sharing is how I did them. If you are new to ceremony, these guidelines may be useful to follow closely, or you may want to have someone more experienced lead you.

The main elements are:

Creating a sacred space or container for the ritual.
Creating an intention for the ritual.
Preparing and connecting to your bodymind.
Your ceremonial activity – connecting to the spiritual dimension.
And finally, an activity to ground the energy.

I did the home-based ceremony alone and shared the beach one with a group of women (my circle of stones) on winter solstice. The first hour's songs on the Spotify *She of the Sea* playlist are all suitable for the indoor ceremony, the final songs on it are good chants to use for the outdoor ceremony.

Shore Ceremony

We gather on the darkening shore, moon rising. I take a stalk of sea kelp in hand and begin to draw the seed of the labyrinth pattern.

Then its arcing lines.

The others collect pebbles and lay them in the centre of the labyrinth and light the lanterns. We gather around, beginning to sing and move in a circle, an improvised dance.

We are a circle, within a circle,
With no beginning and never ending.

Then one after the other we walk the labyrinth of sand.

The lines of the labyrinth ruffle the smooth, beige sand, cool and damp beneath my feet. Circling inwards, eyes down, the sweeping lines of the labyrinth guide me. My feet follow the spiral path that will lead me to the centre. Though my mind wants to make sense of it and plan ahead, I quieten it down. All I need is trust: follow the pattern, go with the flow.

I rest in the centre, lantern flickering. Breathing deep into my belly, I feel myself fully rooted in the present moment, connected to the flow of life. For the first time all day my thoughts slow down to near stillness. In my mind's eye I lay down the burdens I do not want to carry any further with me.

The gentle breeze caresses my cheeks as if in thanks. Looking out on the vast ocean, wave upon wave into infinity, I enjoy the sense of my own smallness.

I am here.

I choose a pebble and on it place a wish for myself, holding it in one hand as I walk out. I place the lantern on the sand before leaving the labyrinth. Each woman does the same, until everyone has walked the spiral and it is illuminated in flickering candlelight.

This is winter solstice, the longest night of the year. The indigo waves lapping the shore, the bright stars emerging in the chill night air. We share secrets and make plans over mugs of steaming mulled juice, warming our hands, stamping our feet, hearts and cheeks glowing.

On spring equinox we walk the sands together to see the sunset and reflect on the journey of the last three months. Come summer solstice we plan to swim together, wading out into the waters, blessing our bodies, drying off on the sands as the moon and stars come out.

Labyrinths of Sand

My love of drawing labyrinths in the sand with my magic red walking pole is a result of having carried that uniform shape in my memory since I was a child. I am still exploring why the drawing of this symbol means so much to me. As I draw it in the soft Cornish sand as the tide recedes, it takes me back to the Rocky Valley seven-circuit labyrinth near Tintagel, carved into the rock face.

I was four years old and we were on a family holiday in North Cornwall. The footpath led us to a farmyard with several huge white hissing geese on guard. I was so frightened. These creatures were bigger than me and their open orange beaks jabbed at the air as they came closer and closer. I was shaking with fear. My six-foot dad scooped me up into his arms and like the hero he was strode through the yard.

The next thing I remember is being in a wooded area and looking down Rocky Valley to the sea. Ivy was hanging in great swathes from the rock face beside us. Daddy swept aside the ivy curtain to reveal a small carving in the rock. I stared at it, mesmerised, and put my tiny finger onto the carving and traced its path to the middle. This was the most magical and unforgettable moment of my childhood.

I have been drawing labyrinths for well over twenty years now. Tiny ones to finger trace. Large ones in the sand to walk. These last three years my interest and curiosity has taken me *to many beaches in South West England to draw them. It is not just the location – next to the sea – but the colour, texture and moisture level of the sand. It's how near the receding sea, the objects already on the beach become part of the magic. The strangers' footprints, rocks, seaweed, stones and shells become part of the ritual. It's the drawing of it with my magic stick.*

Then it's how to walk it? What intentions do I carry with me? What do I leave in the centre? To whom do I dedicate it?

With the wind in my hair and the sound of waves breaking, I begin to walk the path.

I make a wish, that one day I would come across a labyrinth drawn by someone at low tide and I walk it. Just as maybe someone came across one of mine drawn in the sand and walked it, before the sea washed it away.

This summer my wish came true.

Francesca Prior

Immersion

I had written a book about the sea, but still I was holding back. A year of many lockdowns had meant only intermittent opportunities to swim in pools, and I was feeling the lack of it. My health had been bad for months. My energy was flatlining. I was fed up of being housebound, bedbound. My body and soul were longing for freedom and flow.

The book was finished, but I knew I still needed to do one more thing to keep my side of the deal. In *Burning Woman,* I marked the end of the book with a Burning Woman ceremony, dancing naked around a bonfire with two other women, the thing I had been too scared to do. Six months later, my unofficial wise woman mentor,

ALisa Starkweather, who appears as if by magic at each part of my initiation journey, invited me to visit her to celebrate the launch of the book. Over fifty of us spontaneously danced naked around a massive bonfire under the stars to the rhythm of drums.

For *She of the Sea* I knew I needed to answer the call I had been avoiding, to do what ALisa had recommended seven years earlier, when my soul was shocked out of my body during my baptism of fire: immerse myself in the cold, wild sea.

It was Easter Sunday, early April, the sun was shining, the children were sugared up and bickering, so we headed down to the shore for a walk. My youngest suggested we paddle in the sea. We stuck a toe in and screamed. At 9°C (48 F) and just a degree warmer on land, it wasn't exactly what you would call balmy. We went in again, up to our ankles, it was so cold I couldn't feel my feet as I walked back up to the others on the rocks.

"Can I go home and get my swimming stuff?" she asked.

"Sure," I said.

"Are you serious?"

"Yes. I'll get mine too."

"Really?"

No one would believe me.

But I meant it. As I made my commitment to full body immersion, I looked down and spotted a piece of my favourite bright blue sea glass, very rare on this beach, the same colour as the cover of this book, its message was clear: it was time.

We headed home and I placed the sea glass on my altar with a smile. We put on our swimsuits, grabbed towels and loose warm clothes and drove down to our village beach.

Ignoring the dogwalkers bundled up in coats and scarves and hats, we threw our clothes off and ran down into the water, laughing and shrieking. Up to our knees, 3,2,1 and in I plunged. It was so cold my heart nearly exploded out of my chest. But I felt more alive than I had in months.

The wind had picked up and the clouds drawn over. That was it for the day. But as I walked back to shore, to warmth and safety, I knew

I would be doing that again and again. I had overcome my inner resistance and plunged fully into life again…daring to dive beyond safety. My whole body tingled and felt warm from the inside. On this day of rebirth, I had been reborn too.

As I stood wrapped in my towel on the shore, I looked up and saw two crows pecking in the shingle. The guardians of my next book were right there with a message: *it is time, for you, and She of the Sea, to go out into the world. It is our time now.* It was what I needed, the prompt to finally let go of this book that I had finished again and again but not been able to birth.

I offer this experience to you, to show how simple and everyday ritual and ceremony can be. No fancy clothes or words, no candles or incense, little preparation, just us showing up with intention, taking action with purpose, finding the magical in the mundane, making meaning as we go.

Once home, I wrote this down, created a completion altar with the sliver of bright blue sea glass at the centre, as well as some freshly picked rosemary. I pulled some cards and sat with the knowing that the book was complete, as the *She of the Sea* soundtrack played once more. And I promised that this was the first of many cold swims.

The next day I had a migraine, but the day after that I was back down to the sea, this time alone. As I left the house two crows flew over. As I parked the car clouds blocked the sun and the wind got up. I was determined to keep my side of the deal. Clothes off, towel on sand. This time I walked in slowly, reverently, reaching down to wash my hands and face in the icy water. I waded slowly out, up to my thighs, looked up and made a deal: *I will immerse myself when you show me the sun.* I waited for a minute, then the clouds shifted away, illuminating a pathway of light from me to the light-house island. I walked into it, submerging myself once more.

My Beloved Teacher

My experience with the Ocean is spiritual. She's a fierce and loving teacher. My resting place, and where I've done some of my hardest work. Time and time again, I have felt called to her shores, where I seek and find clarity. To answer her call, is an opportunity to look within, and face unwanted fears. I remember challenging myself while living in the Florida Keys. Whenever I went swimming, I would encounter a barracuda. Eventually this made me so uneasy that I stopped going into the water. To make a long story short, SHE made it quite clear that I could not allow fear to rule me. I needed to get back in the water. So I did. 30 seconds in, I saw one, then another, and another! More and more barracuda appeared. 50, 60, 70... I was swimming through a den of barracuda! I could hear HER coaching me to regulate my breath, put my arms at my side, slow down, and be present to the moment. Honestly, it felt like an eternity. At one point I remember looking squarely in the eye of one of those big bad denizens of the sea. He looked at me so curiously. Indeed, I must have been a sight to see. Eventually, I passed through the pack and proceeded to have the most magnificent snorkeling adventure that I have ever had. When I started to head for shore, I suddenly realised that I had to go back the same way that I came. Yes, I snorkeled through that den of barracuda, twice!

Deeply transformational and profoundly liberating, that experience strengthened both my mind and spirit, and put an end to my fear of barracuda. That's the kind of relationship that I have with the sea, my beloved teacher. She frees me.

Marsia S. Harris

She of the Sea Ceremony

This is an elaborate ceremony, which allows you to connect to the sea and the sacred Feminine wherever you are in the world. It can be done in your bedroom (which is where I do most of my ceremonies), or in a living room, garden or a larger space like a community hall if you are sharing it with others. The instructions below are very detailed for those who need more guidance. If you already have a movement or ritual practice, then of course follow your own intuition.

You will need...

For your altar

> A small table top, shelf area or temporary space on the floor, somewhere it is safe to light candles.

> Candles – either white- or sea-coloured nightlights – and matches or a lighter.

> Pebbles, fossils, sea shells, sea glass, blue/green/white crystals…

> A small vessel to hold water.

> Pictures or figurines that represent She of the Sea or the sacred Feminine to you: selkies, mermaids, goddesses…

For your movement

> A way to access and play the *She of the Sea* Spotify playlist (it can be downloaded) or other sea-themed music of your choice.

> Flowing blue/turquoise clothing that feels sensual – a loose long skirt or wide legged trousers, or something tight fitting and stretchy so you can feel the free movement of your body.

> Enough space to move in. If the flooring is cold, have a mat, towel or blanket laid out ready to lie on, as well as cushions for body support, as needed.

> Beside this area lay any shade of sea blue/green silk or a thin cotton scarf.

For your ceremony

> Herbs, incense, a spray bottle or an essential oil that feels connected to the sea – for me it is rosemary or lavender.

> A small jug of water.

> Tarot, goddess or picture cards.

> Your journal, a pen and/or coloured pastels or pencils.

> A pot of salt.

Gathering and cleansing

First gather the items you will be using above, and have them to hand. Then read through the next couple of pages.

The first part of ceremony is clearing space. First you create temporal space, by communicating to others that you are not to be disturbed until you reappear (this is likely to be an hour.)

Then it is closing the door to the space you will be using.

Next we begin physically cleansing and clearing space. This might look like organising the items that you will be using, clearing off the surface that you will be building your altar on, as we did at the end of Chapter 1. It might be soaking your body in a seaweed bath, having a bracing cold shower, washing your hands and face (perhaps with cold salt water) and then putting on the clothing you will be wearing for the ceremony. It might mean burning herbs or putting on an essential oil diffuser. Or perhaps you would like to spritz the air with a water spray containing salt water (perhaps infused with moon-charged crystals, herbs or essential oils). It might mean making a protective circle of salt around the area you will be working in. All the while hold in mind your intention to create sacred space and a meaningful ceremony for yourself.

Altar building

When you and your space feel ready, press play on the playlist – the first track is waves. Begin to place the items on your altar space, in a way that looks and feels right to you. Stay with your breath and place the items with reverence and intention.

In the very centre, place a small bowl or other vessel with a pinch of salt at the bottom. You may then choose to place the unlit candles in the centre. Or you might place the other items and then the candles around the outside. Trust yourself. Allow an intention or prayer for this time to arise for yourself. Something simple and easeful. Do not light the candles yet.

Movement

Connecting to flow

As the waves turn fully into music, move into the centre of your space. Closing your eyes, allow your body to gently move to the music, this is much slower and subtler than what many of us would know as dancing. Imagining you are a piece of seaweed being gently swayed by the flowing water. Allow a feeling of joyous looseness in your whole body.

In time, settle down on the floor. Let your body fully relax, letting your breath follow the tempo of the music, softening and releasing any tension that you experience as your mind gently scans over your body. Imagining your breath is a wave on the beach, allow the in-breath to be like a gentle wave lapping up the shore. Your out-breath is the wave travelling back down. Imagine that with each breath the sea is covering more and more of your body.

Your body remains relaxed as you find that you are now lying on the bottom of the seabed, looking up. The sound of the sea is much quieter here, the movement is less. Your perceptions are deeper. You may choose to lightly place the scarf over your face so that you can begin to open your eyes and experience this altered perception of being underwater – but only if it feels safe and comfortable to do so.

Stay here, allowing your breathing to remain slow, and your body to be deeply relaxed.

Allow a change in the music to move you gently to sitting, and then keeping the peace within you, gently raising your arms, allowing them to stretch up and out, rolling your shoulders.

Altar work

Bringing your flow energy and inner tranquility with you, approach your altar space once more, noticing how your energy has shifted.

Take the jug of water and pour it into the bowl. Hold it for a few moments and watch the salt dissolve. Take a drop on your finger and anoint your forehead, and maybe your heart and womb space too, with a dab of water, asking for the qualities of water in your own life – flow, depth, clarity. Then take some on your fingertips and scatter it on the ground, sharing prayers for the waters of the world.

Using your essential oil, put a drop on each candle, away from the wick. Then light each candle. I tend to have three and light one with a prayer of blessing for myself, one for my family and friends and one for the Womancraft or earth community.

You may now choose to draw a card or two from your deck, reflect on what you have drawn and lay them on the altar.

The Final Part

Where you go now depends on your needs. You may want to sit for a few moments in silence and then blow out the candles, put on a piece of jewellery from the altar space and go back to your daily life. You may choose to allow your voice to emerge, making sounds/singing, humming or chanting along to the music – this is excellent for toning your vagus nerve, calming your nervous system. This may also be an excellent time to allow yourself to let go and weep, wail, scream and sob, releasing any pent-up sadness or grief. You may desire more movement, allowing yourself to shapeshift through movement and imagination, allowing your body to move like different animals of the sea – a fish, a diving bird, a dolphin… You may go back to meditation and the breath, following it down into the depths of your consciousness. Or you may be called to draw or write in the journal you have beside you – to capture the experience you have had, a symbol or words that came to you, or perhaps to create an image of She of the Sea that has emerged for you.

What is calling you? Read your own bodymind's signs. Now, it is time for you to respond.

Grounding and Closing

When you are finished, take a couple of moments to give thanks for the process, and to do something that helps you to feel grounded, such as taking a deep breath, pressing your hands or feet firmly into the ground, and blowing out the candle with a final prayer or intention.

Meeting Her

I didn't meet the ocean till later in life.
Till desperation and despair flung me into a car to blindly cross
the continent without any sense of what would be on the other side.
But when we met
I had no place to put her vastness.
She overwhelmed me.

Ohio is land locked.
The Ohio river offers some elemental water magic.
Just enough current to keep things moving.
I was born on those riverbanks an alien outsider,
I watched as the humans seemed to understand how to make life
work while I had to be medicated to not fear everything or feel like
I wasn't falling down a black hole.
I did not know I was a titan trying to make home in a shoe box.

A moment came when I knew my soul was breaking.
When I knew the damage would be permanent.
Spirit conspired in my favor and I offered to help a friend drive to
San Francisco.
Two girls running, seeking, and desperate for something different.

When the ocean finally met me,
I unconsciously recognised that she was the only thing big, deep,
and wide enough to hold
my grief, anger, and madness.

My heart thrilled at her power and bigness.
Now I realised it was because it mirrored my own.
I could not go back to my river home.
I had to expand into my greatness.

Which I did.

For ten years I lived with the smell of the ocean in the air.
We made friends.
We made love.
I never stopped fearing her,
But I learned her as a master teacher.

On the week I decided I needed to return to Ohio
to take care of my mother,
a giant elephant seal beached itself at my feet.

Beautiful like me.
I wept.
I thanked the ocean,
and this harbinger of change, who
reminded me that I had grown so big because the ocean and the
stars had given me the room to.

Khara Scott-Bey

Reflections

What has your experience been with ritual and ceremony up to now?

How do you feel about integrating more ritual and ceremony in your life?

Are you comfortable with leading your own rituals or do you prefer someone else to take the lead? Why do you think this is?

What initiatory processes have you experienced in your life? Were they marked and celebrated? If so, how? If not, why?

12

SEA CHANGE

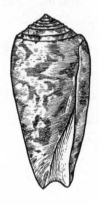

*One of the most calming and powerful actions you
can do to intervene in a stormy world is to stand
up and show your soul... To display the lantern of
soul in shadowy times like these – to be fierce and to
show mercy toward others; both are acts of immense
bravery and greatest necessity. Struggling souls catch
light from other souls who are fully lit and willing
to show it. If you would help to calm the tumult,
this is one of the strongest things you can do.*

Clarissa Pinkola Estés

Soft*

The mist is rolling in,
Softening the edges.
The spirit of the sea is rising.
First the lighthouse disappears,
Then the shoreline, the hills,
Erased by ghosts
Creeping landwards once more.
Time dissolves.
The wind-bent trees become shadowy figures,
Old men hunkered in the mist,
Clinging to solid ground.
Our world disappears,
Another world opens up
Right here.

Lost Lands

The largest ship in history (at that time) set off from very close to where I live on the Cork coast on its fated journey across the Atlantic. When the Titanic hit an iceberg and was sinking it sent out its distress call…SOS…

Save Our Souls.

---

*   "Soft" is a folk term in Ireland for weather that is halfway between mist and light rain.

Save
Our
Souls.

Today, this call is heard once again.
We send a flare up, illuminating the night sky.
Hope in the darkness.
Save our souls.

This area of the coast where I live has been called "the graveyard of the south coast"[53] due to its treacherous rocky headlands. It has known many SOS calls and been the site of many courageous rescues, from generations of brave and selfless volunteers. Many a night I have seen the flare go up, the lifeboat men pour from the pubs, their dinners and their beds to save a stranger's soul, in danger on the dark seas, launching their boat into the unknown. As I write this, the search and rescue helicopter buzzes overhead, a modern addition to the team of heroes.

Sometimes the sea saves us…and sometimes we need saving from the sea.

There are numerous written accounts of shipwrecks here, as well as many more passed on by tradition. Wrecks fascinate us, divers explore them looking for treasure, for clues to lost worlds, for reasons why.

As I was writing this book, a shipwreck from the ancient Greek era, contemporary with the Odyssey, was found in Bulgarian waters, two kilometres down. With it, resurfaced once more the possibility of the historical roots of the mythical story of the return of the Greek hero to his homeland.

Closer to home, a ghost ship – a freighter that had sailed halfway around the world by itself with no captain or crew[54] – ended up on our rocky shore. We are drawn to it in our thousands – old folks, the middle-aged and children alike – clambering along the treacherously muddy cliffs for a glimpse, despite the warnings on the news to stay clear. We are fascinated by this vessel and its story. It is symbolic of something deeper, I feel, a metaphor for our times: a ship abandoned by its crew, floating aimlessly, washing up on the rocks.

But it's not just sea-going vessels that the sea devours. It encroaches on the land, too.

My favourite place on the beach as a child was the sharp black rockpools on our strand, with my shrimp net in hand. It was only as an adult I heard my father-in-law tell that at the far end of these rocks lie foundations. There were houses here, not centuries ago, but within the living memory of the older people in the village. A village called Seamount, swallowed by the sea.

Around the headland, a whole road was subsumed by the waves. Today, parts of the shore are lined with massive boulders trying to keep back the sea. During the most severe storms we can lose several metres of shoreline in one night. We go down to the beach and find the life buoys lying on their sides, their concrete roots exposed. The Council moves them back. Until the next storm.

At my father's house, which backs onto the bog, the wind whips the trees, salt stains the windows. On the most severe spring tides the bog floods and the sea reaches the bottom of the garden. On stormy nights you feel that you are actually at sea.

Sea level rising isn't just theoretical for us here. It is real. Geography departments around the country come on field trips: we are a case study for coastal erosion. Beauty comes at a price. Many envy our proximity to the beach. But we are vulnerable here. Exposed. According to maps just released by Climate Central, by 2050 half of our village will be under flood level. Large parts of many of our towns and cities here in Ireland, in the UK, in Holland and Bangladesh, whole Pacific islands...gone.[55]

This land where I live was formed 400 million years ago of two types of sandstone, old red and yellow. The old red formed the solid headlands and the yellow the soft parts, which are being eaten into by the sea. They were formed during desert conditions in Ireland, something almost impossible to imagine now with the constant rain. They remind us that our land has known many climates. After the dry times, the floods. Our island was invaded by warm sea, and only the mountains remained unsubmerged. The sea-life from this time created the limestone deposits which are plentiful in the area. The remains of their bodies made the rock which now provides the literal building blocks for our towns, cities and field walls. The granite here was transported from Scotland by a massive ice sheet, which pushed down from Scandinavia, bringing flint from the North.[56]

This is not just ancient history. This place we call home is in flux still, being reclaimed by the sea. She is nibbling away at the land. Softening the edges. Asking us to think again, build anew. Asking us to live with her in a different way. So that we will not be another of the countless places lost to the sea.

Throughout history we have been both haunted and held in thrall by the idea of worlds subsumed by the sea and the treasures they may hide. The myth of Atlantis has been one that has captured imaginations since the ancient Greeks. A technologically, culturally, and some say spiritually advanced place, Atlantis is said to have been destroyed about 9,000 years ago in an unknown catastrophe. It has been claimed to have been discovered in places as far apart as Antarctica, Bolivia, Malta, Turkey, various places in the Caribbean and most recently off the southern Atlantic coast of Spain.[57] Ker Ys in Brittany, home of Dahud, is another lost land that lies between myth and history. Nineteenth century folklorists claim it could be seen at extreme low tides, and its bells could be heard tolling beneath the waves.[58]

We have definitive proof, however, of Doggerland, a rich boggy land-bridge, which connected southeastern Britain to mainland Europe, in what is now the North Sea. Evidence of its sudden loss, only 8,000 years ago, is being regularly found and pieced together by many university departments.

And more recently still, Dunwich, known as "the British Atlantis" was first damaged in storm surge flooding in 1286. By 1362, most houses and many churches had been taken by the sea. Not a backwater village like our Seamount, Dunwich was "a thriving port, second only to London in terms of trade and importance [...] the capital of the Kingdom of the East Angles and boasted a rich and growing population."[59] It now lies "50 feet below the surface and up to a mile out from the beach along which visitors walk today. In its watery tomb lie eight churches, five houses of religious orders, two hospitals and three chapels."[60]

There are many eerie stories and poems about the church bells that can be heard from the lost churches of Dunwich. I studied one, "Sea Tongue" by Kevin Crossley Holland, whilst at Cambridge, not far from Dunwich. The tolling of the ghostly sea bells stayed with me. And then, as I was writing this book, I experienced them on my own shoreline.

We walk the beach,
The bells are tolling,
Calling the faithful back to land, to church,
to the worship of the Sky God
But we are here, visiting Mama Ocean –
The wind whips around
Now it sounds as though the bells are ringing in the sea,
Warning us of their fate
Warning us, perhaps, too late.
We are not the first, not the first, not the first...

Meltdown

The message in a bottle arrived on the Donegal shore in the north of Ireland.[61] It had been left at the North Pole, just two years before, by passengers onboard an icebreaker. It was thought it would be found in decades, if not centuries, left as it was in the centre of the ice. Instead, after a year of record ice-melt, the bottle found its way 2,300 kilometres to the nearest shore. Reminding us that the waters connect us all. Though we cannot see the ice of the frozen poles, their melting impacts everyone.

There is another sort of meltdown, one which I am intimately familiar with, which I feel has a lot to teach us about the process both of resetting our own systems, and the process of climate change, its internal wisdom and how best to respond. A meltdown happens when a brain and nervous system are so stressed and overwhelmed that they stop functioning in their normal way. This happens far more frequently for autistic people than neurotypicals. The logical prefrontal cortex becomes foggy and goes offline. The ancient limbic system kicks in. And what you see on the outside is often interpreted as being over-emotional or bad behaviour: crying, screaming, rocking, kicking, curling in a ball, or sometimes silent shutting down. The brain is resetting itself in the only way it knows how.

It can be unsettling to watch, but believe me, it is much, much more frightening to experience. Especially surrounded by people who do not understand, in the busy sensory harshness of the modern world. Before a meltdown there are warning signs. An inner agitation. Background sounds get louder, speech becomes distorted and hard to follow, objects lose their solidity. Complex actions, thoughts, speech, coordination, movement become blurred. You lose the ability to sense where you are in space. You can no longer feel your extremities. Arms and legs feel like they are no longer under your control. Everything is both sped up and slowed down, like being underwater...except no one else around you is experiencing this. They are expecting you to act normally. But the harder you try, the faster the invisible water level rises. Then suddenly it takes you down, gasping for breath, body flailing, tears flowing, down, down...it feels like your soul is being sucked from you.

If we see meltdowns as pathological, we try to stop them mid flow. This is what our culture teaches us and so the default position of many people is to feel embarrassed, judge, freak out, punish or turn away when they see someone in distress. Whereas if we see meltdowns as nature's way of resetting the nervous system, we respond with compassion during and after, and later take time to reflect on what happened and change the environment around us so that such extreme resets will not be required in the future.

Can you see the connection with climate change? Ignoring it won't work. Judging it won't work. Shame doesn't help. Punishment is pointless. It is real. We have to accept it as our living Earth's natural response to immense stress. We have to trust the wisdom of it as a reset mechanism. We must do what we can to mitigate the worst, for sure, so that as few of us get hurt as possible. But there is innate intelligence to what She is doing. It is well past time that we learn to work with Gaia, as She processes the stress that we were largely responsible for, and then figure out how not to stress Her to that degree again.

Climate change is an energetic feedback loop. It is a process, which, however much we would like to, we cannot just stop in its tracks. The triggers have been building up over decades, centuries… We have ignored them, rather than reducing the pressure on Her, we have intensified it. We have not treated our planet as an infinitely intelligent and complex being, but rather as a dumb rock.

She is showing us her intelligence. It is up to us how we respond.

Do we learn to listen and work with Her? Or do we continue to ignore Her, because we have become too lazy or arrogant or 'advanced' to understand Her way of communicating?

The neurotypical world, modern Western culture, the masculine, the patriarchal, capitalism are presented to us as normal, inevitable. They are not. They are neither the only, nor are they the best, way for humans to live.

Revelation

*Sometimes the sea swallows secrets, sometimes it spits
them out. Things that are lost can often be found.*

Jan Carson, "Sea Border"[62]

The sea gives, the sea takes away…

We worry about what we are losing, what is being submerged…

But there is another side of the sea's story.

Of what is being revealed, what is emerging from the depths, that
has been hidden for much of our history: fossils and memories from
times and places previously submerged are coming to light.

As I wrote this book, I read the story of Mary Anning, another
woman scientist of the Victorian era, first belittled, then taken advantage of in a world of men.

A coastal dweller in the small town of Lyme Regis in Dorset, very
close to where I lived with my mother, Mary Anning
spent her childhood gathering small ammonite
fossils from the beach to sell to tourists. As
her finds grew larger, including some of
the best-preserved dinosaur skeletons
ever found in the UK, she forced a
different narrative, one which ran counter
to the biblical tale of the perfection and
dominance of the singular creation of the Father God. Her discoveries
became vital pieces of evidence for extinction. Something only
previously hypothesised by George Couvier in 1790. Until then it
was believed that every living thing was created by God, and He
would never have created a species only to destroy it.

The fossil record tells us how things were, how they have changed,
and how life has evolved.

But this is not just history.

Life is still evolving. Ecosystems are changing, and faster than ever before.

Because of us.

Karmic Ripples

We must be willing to let go of the life we have
planned, so as to have the life that is waiting for us.

Joseph Campbell

Change is coming.

These last two years, no one can deny it. The evidence is everywhere: social, biological, climate upheaval, on land...at sea. We have seen the plague ships – cruise ships full of infected elders, looking for somewhere to dock; a hospital ship in New York harbour to treat the sick from this modern plague. They are a warning to us.

The cry of the sea is getting stronger. The Pacific Ocean gyre, a whirlpool of plastic waste three times the size of France, is growing. The bleaching of coral in unprecedented quantities. Sea levels rising. Ice melting. Governments inactive as school children strike.

We freeze in the face of such loss.
Inundations the size of legend foretold,
In our lifetime.
In our lifetime.

We find ourselves
Out of our depth...

And this is only the beginning.

We are living through the fastest environmental change of our short history. Change that we started unconsciously, through how we have lived. A process that we are no longer in control of, as repeated small actions produce karmic ripples of ever-expanding proportions. We have ignored the interconnected magnificence of earth's systems at our peril.

The year just gone, 2020, was the warmest on record in the world's oceans. They are heating faster than at any other time in the last 2,000 years. Whilst the thought of a warmer ocean here in Ireland is a nice one for us swimmers, warmer oceans mean more severe storms, typhoons, hurricanes, flooding incidences and warmer atmospheric temperatures, leading to heatwaves and forest fires on land.[63] We can see these effects already. This winter there have been more storms in the Atlantic than ever before.[64] On the south coast of Ireland this meant yellow weather warning, orange warning, red warning, day after day, week after week, month after month, for storm winds, rainfall and flooding. In the Caribbean and South East of the US, it meant hurricane after hurricane, damage, destruction and death. Along the coasts of Europe, the sea is weeping people fleeing war and oppression: immigrants stowed away in refrigerated lorries, refugees packed into tiny inflatable dinghies crossing the Mediterranean.

We are already becoming numb to it.

In 2019, 16-year-old Greta Thunberg sailed across the Atlantic in storm season to attend the United Nations' Climate Action Summit, focusing the world's attention on taking action. This celebrated teenage climate change activist, and youngest ever Time magazine Person of the Year, as well as a fellow autistic woman, is right that our leaders and we as communities need to treat the rising sea levels and climate change as an emergency, a priority, bigger than any other. Which it is.

Her 2021 address to the World Economic Forum was stark:

"The climate and ecological crisis can no longer be solved within today's systems... The longer we avoid this uncomfortable truth and pretend that we can solve [it] without treating it as an emergency, the more precious time we will lose. And this is time we do not have."

She is right that we need urgency. But the term "emergency" triggers trauma and fear. What we need is emergence, from this cultural paradigm.

Old Foundations

It is coming.
The tide has turned,
We cannot hold it back.
It is rushing in,
Higher and higher.

The waters are rising.
We have been here before...
In those days the people were fewer.
An ark was built,
The giraffes and antelopes were saved,
But not the unicorns and selkies.
Magic was washed away,
Into the seas,
Whilst the Sky God jealously ruled his land,
And people claimed every part of it for their own.

The tides have turned
She is returning,
Can you hear Her?

Sea Change

*I am trying to heal this world, this beautiful, dying
world. I think on some level we all are. Either we are
trying to heal or we are trying to forget. Because we
know the hour is now. Because we know this is real and
it's come this far. And the work is healing, remembering,
restoring, transforming. Listening. Taking responsibility.
Moving aside. Lifting up. Trying. Going back, going
forward, holding still. The work is to try and to fail and
to try again. The work is to love in the face of despair.*

Clementine Morrigan, *Fucking Magic #1*

One night, when I am feeling stressed and overwhelmed, I dream of
a hyper-modern skyscraper. There is an old-fashioned boat incongru-
ously sticking out of the side of it. *Where is the sea?* I wonder.

The boat is packed with people bending, over-loaded, suspended
high in the air. Suddenly it snaps in half.

I am in the tall tower with many others, watching on horrified and
helpless. On my mind at this time is the pandemic, the quarantined
coronavirus ships circling the globe, looking for safe harbour.

This is just one of my anxiety dreams. We all seem to be flooded
with them, as things get more and more out of our rational control,
more uncertain and unsettled. Our inner seas are rising in concert
with the sea levels. Our unconscious minds spilling out into our daily
lives. Meanwhile, our logical minds are stuck in loops of helplessness
and powerlessness, unable to bridge the gap between what is…and
what must happen.

Sea change is coming. We can smell the salt in our nostrils, the tides
are rising. We must shift and change with it. The outer sea is calling
our inner seas to action.

My children can see it. They range from fifteen to ten. They go on school strikes, make posters, give their money to homeless and reforestation and ocean charities. They pick up litter and know that climate change is real. My ten-year-old informs me her sister has told her they will die from it in ten years.

My heart aches.

What is this disconnect? Between a generation that is living into a future more unknown than any in human history, and older ones that are unwilling (or is it unable?) to see beyond their stories and their experiences of the past – that everything is getting better, growth must continue.

Humans, on the whole, are naturally change averse. We like to do what we have done; it feels safer that way. But we have entered transition times, as a direct consequence of our actions, and the actions of our parents and grandparents and great-grandparents. We cannot do what we have always done. The world we know – both manmade and natural – has changed, is changing. But we do not know what to do now. And so, we double down, working harder and faster, distracting ourselves. Or we numb out.

This is an imminent death, on a scale far larger than any of us have ever had to deal with. There is no one here who has done this before who can lead us through.

Traditional factions are becoming even more violently entrenched between conservatives wanting to revert to the old and known, to revive the glorious past…and liberals and progressives knowing that change must happen for the thriving of all. We believe two very different stories about what is happening and why, and how we should respond. We are in opposition about what needs defending. And so, we fight each other, rather than face the unknown together.

As I have learned through my adult years, when you are driven by unprocessed trauma or unconscious narratives, you are doomed to either keep recreating them, or to keep hiding from what might trigger them. This is where we are now as individuals and a species: perpetuating trauma on a global scale, on all beings. As Sigmund Freud warned, "Unexpressed emotions will never die. They are buried alive and will come forth later in uglier ways."

Humanity stands in the sinking sands, collectively unable to take action, unable to find the wisdom of these times. Unwilling to learn from this influx of fluidity.

The severity of the climate emergency we find ourselves facing into, is a direct result of traumatised humans freezing in the face of loss, fighting in the face of imminent destruction and most sickeningly, actively profiting from suffering. In the Bible, God sent floods and plagues to punish the world, destroy the sinners and start afresh. There are many who – consciously or unconsciously – take what is currently happening as punishment for the errant ways of humanity, rather than a natural consequence. But to take a moralistic stance on climate change and its role as punishment is to trigger shame and defensiveness, which makes us retract our energy to stay safe...or attack and blame others. Neither is useful to us right now.

As Deb Dana notes in *The Polyvagal Theory in Therapy*, "A working principal of the autonomic nervous system is 'every response is an action in service to survival.' No matter how incongruous an action may look from the outside [...] it is always an adaptive survival response. The nervous system doesn't make a judgement about good or bad: it simply acts to manage risk and seek safety."[65]

The traumatised self clings to the past like a limpet on the rocks. When we are scared or sense danger, we act instinctively to protect our self. Singular. Or our immediate family. We are now at a time where to survive we have to act to protect ourselves. Plural. We are going to have to remember how to join our nervous systems up to work collectively, as a species level organism.

The globe is littered with the remains of cultures past that couldn't do this. Reminders of peoples who couldn't navigate cultural division or heed the changing climate. The people of Seamount, Atlantis and Dunwich learned the most basic lesson of life on earth: when our cultural narratives are at odds with reality, reality always wins. If we do not adapt to the cycles and patterns of nature, we do not survive.

What we need to hold close is that whilst this is a death, it does not have to be Death. This does not have to be the apocalyptic disaster movie that Hollywood churns out to give us adrenaline thrills. It does not have to be The End of Days, foretold by Christianity, Hollywood and death cults alike. This is the end…of patriarchy as we have known it, of a linear-growth economy…but it doesn't have to be The End of the World.

Other narratives are possible. But to access them we have to look beyond our current story of who we are and what life is about and for. We must move beyond our narrow patriarchal mindsets, beyond perfectionism and into a more expansive and interconnected way of being and knowing ourselves, as a species and individuals. We are going to have to risk taking creative action and making mistakes, rather than putting our energy into criticising others. We are going to have to get more comfortable at trying new things…together. Taking brave risks…together.

"We're being summoned by the world itself," states Bill Plotkin in *Wild Mind,* "to make many urgent changes to the human project, but most central is a fundamental revisioning and reshaping of ourselves, a shift in human consciousness."

Death can lead to rebirth, rather than oblivion, this is what the Feminine teaches us.

Crisis is both danger and opportunity.

Can we imagine another culture, another way of being?

Can we begin to tell another story?

A New Story

We need a story that will educate us, a story
that will heal, guide and discipline us. We need
something that will supply in our times what was
supplied formerly by traditional religious story.
Thomas Berry, *The Dream of the Earth*

This is a time of transition, of cultural and ecological shapeshifting on an unprecedented scale. As we have learned, at times of transition it is powerful and supportive to gather together as a community and mark this rite of passage together: to acknowledge what is falling away, and focus our energy on where we are going to.

We are in need of a new, uniting narrative that can carry us over stormy seas to a destination we do not know. We need a story about who we are as humans to help us navigate the changes ahead. We need a narrative of ourselves as resilient and creative, capable of meeting challenges, a species that has always adapted and grown in a mystical unseen dance with the cycles of life on this planet. Of our bodyminds as having been shaped by the oceans for millions of years. Of the unconscious as an available and precious shared repository of wisdom that is the basis of all cultures. Of the vitality and sanctity of wild places. Of ritual and prayer as technologies of communication with a universe that is not indifferent but intelligent. Of the natural world being an intimate part of us and in direct communication with us...

I believe that the sea can be central to this process of transition. It shifts us naturally into a state of consciousness where our thinking brains slow down, our bodies relax and our ability to listen and observe more deeply come online. This is the first step of conscious creative action: becoming aware whilst feeling safe in our bodies.

We are neither powerless as we fear,
Nor omnipotent as we might wish.
We have the power of imagination, will,
creativity, embodied action and cooperation.
And when we partner with the dynamics
around us, the unseen forces at play,
We are capable of the in-credible.
This is [how] magic [happens].

We have forgotten what the sea is to us. We have forgotten its power. We must remember the sea as our place of origin – physical and psychological. We will take little action based on logic or reason alone, any action taken by force will be short lived. We will not save what we do not love, what we do not feel protective of, what we do not feel belonging to. Whereas, when the soul is engaged, when we feel connected to each other and the world, when we feel something emotionally, we engage every part of ourselves. As Wallace J. Nichols notes in *Blue Mind*, "When humans think of water – or hear water, or see water, or get in water, even taste or smell water – they *feel* something. [...] These emotional responses to our environment arise from the oldest parts of our brain, and in fact can occur before any cognitive response arises."

Our instinctive passions – for nature, for each other, for the sacred – have always been the enemy of the patriarchy. They may yet be the saving grace of humanity. If we dare to face down shame and judgement and express them.

This gives me hope. And hope – plus creative action – is what we need.

Indeed, this year marks the start of the United Nations' Decade of Ocean Science for Sustainable Development (2021–30). Collective vision and leadership *are* there, at the very top of *some* of our major organisations. It is also there in tens of thousands of grassroots projects. And hundreds of millions of individuals.

A study carried out at the end of 2020 by the UN, of over a million people of all ages, from fifty high-, middle- and low-income countries, representing more than half the world's population gives me hope. It makes clear that though there is division and disagreement, which we witness flaring on social media, in government chambers and at community meetings, still a majority of people – two-thirds – agree that climate change is a "global emergency," and back major actions to tackle it.[66]

The coronavirus pandemic has been good training for us as a species. Instead of being able to wish it away, pay it away, legislate it away, we are having to learn fast how to observe its patterns, be informed by data, keep updating our understanding rapidly, and communicating effectively. We are having to learn to work collectively as local and global communities, adapting our behaviours through social distancing and lockdowns, changing learning, working and social practices, which had previously seemed set in stone. But frustratingly, even here there is disagreement and resistance from many who want the old story to continue, from those who do not trust these changes or the evidence and those who would prefer to deny their reality. And governments have shown two worrying precedents, which we can see played out in climate change responses too: one is wilful, strong-man arrogance and denial, the other is a 'Project Fear' approach, scaring and threatening people into action, whilst pushing through draconian measures. Both are dangerous ways of harnessing power and the basest of human responses.

I believe another way is both possible and necessary. "Active hope," as Joanna Macy terms it. We must believe that change is possible. That we have within us the power to make it. Despair and depression are rooted in isolation and a feeling of being alone. Trauma keeps us trapped in this state. Our current System perpetuates it with stress, overload, anxiety and disconnection. But when we are able to work through and move beyond overwhelm and trauma, post-traumatic growth is possible. Defined by one of the researchers who identified it as "the positive changes that occur in the aftermath of a trauma as a result of the process of a struggle with these traumatic events," it looks like, "Increased personal strength; increased connection with and compassion towards others; greater appreciation and gratitude for their life, especially the small things; they might find a new mission in life; and they undergo an existential change, engaging with questions about the purpose, meaning and value of their life."[67]

Our past and present struggles do not have to define us negatively. When we have the belief that we are not powerless and alone, but rather that what we do matters, that we are loved and helped and connected, we are able to tap into so many more resources: we are able to be creative, to consider new solutions. When we work together with each other, with the forces of nature, the patterns of the mystery, we are capable of miraculous things.

"Magic," as Starhawk says, "is when the impossible becomes the inevitable."

Sea Powered Change

It is vital that the sea is front and centre of our vision as we address climate change, as it absorbs 90% of the excess heat in the atmosphere[68] and provides 50- 80% of the oxygen we breathe.[69]

The ocean has so much to offer us, as we transform our culture and turn around environmental degradation. Seaweed, it seems, could be front and centre of our future. It is being explored for alternatives for plastics for packaging, as a wearable fabric for clothing,[70] environmentally friendly laundry detergent,[71] and biofuels.[72] Meanwhile, several recent studies have shown that feeding both dairy and beef cattle with a diet supplemented with seaweed reduces their methane production (one of the greatest contributors to climate change) by a staggering 82%.[73]

Whilst we worry about deforestation on land, where, according to UN figures, 10 million acres are cleared each year,[74] a staggering 3.9 billion acres of sea floor are deforested each year through trawling with dragnets.[75] The effects of this can be clearly seen in satellite imagery from space. Industrial-scale dragnet fishing is an extremely new phenomenon. It can be legislated out of existence, allowing for more traditional and sustainable local fishing methods.

Most of the conversation around carbon capture centres around forests, but 93% of the world's carbon is actually stored in the oceans.[76] A study from the World Wildlife Foundation in Wales discovered that seagrass "absorbs carbon dioxide 35 times faster than tropical rainforest, stores 10% of the annual ocean carbon and locks up that carbon in sediments that can stay out of harm's way for millennia."[77] It also provides a much-needed habitat for breeding fish and protects coastlines from erosion. Seagrass has almost disappeared over the last century, as have kelp forests, but they, alongside other seaweeds, offer a way of trapping carbon in far greater amounts than tree planting on land can do, where humans are often in conflict over land usage. Bearing in mind our planet is over 70% ocean, seaweed is a much better – and faster growing – bet for turning around our climate crisis.

Planting and preserving these ecosystems is something that absolutely lies within our power. The largest volunteer-led project yet is currently underway on the south coast of England, where they are replanting 8 hectares of seagrass.[78]

Seaweed forests regenerate much more quickly than land forests. A small-scale study in Scotland paves the way for this on a larger scale: "In 2008, Arran's Lamlash Bay 'no-take-zone' became the first community-led marine reserve in Scotland, with a 50% improvement in biodiversity noted in the first decade."[79]

Currently only 7.5% of the sea is designated as Marine Protected Areas,[80] (a figure that the UN was hoping would be 10% by 2020). Incredibly, though, the majority of protected areas still allow fishing and, mind-bogglingly, drilling for oil and natural gas.[81] Experts suggest that we need to have 30% protected in order to avert disaster. Leaving large areas of sea free from human interference is surely well within our capacities.

With collective action, working with rather than against nature, we can turn things round. Where there is a will to do things differently, where creative minds work together, we will find a way…and the sea holds so many possibilities.

Creating the Ocean

From a young age I've found solace in the mystery of the ocean and all the unknowns that lurk in its depths. I love to float in the ocean and allow the rhythmic movements of the waves to push and pull my body, like a slow dance to a soothing love song, it generates a sensation of bliss and serenity.

Scuba diving has given me the opportunity to experience the ocean in another way. From the intricately embellished patchwork of the corals themselves to the countless multi-colored creatures that reside in the crevices of the reefs and the glistening schools of fish that appear to travel as one, every cubic inch of a prosperous coral habitat appears to be thriving and teeming with complexity.

However, the once buzzing and lush coral reefs are quickly transforming into an algae field encrusting dead coral skeletons. Large areas, once covered with vast piles of delicate branching stag-horn corals, are now piles of eroding rubble. Absent are the multitude of fishes and invertebrates that once dwelled in the crevices of the reefs. Nevertheless, we seem to continue about our daily routines, unaware of the wondrous treasure that is vanishing. Our lack of connection with our seas has led to a sense of apathy regarding their decline. Through art, I aim to create a connection that will enact a positive change. Working in clay, I explore the intricacies of these diverse underwater ecosystems, moulding and sculpting each coral type in a way that brings this underwater world to the surface. Celebrating their beauty while highlighting the threats they face.

Anna-K Cuffe

Creative Action

We must shape ourselves into visionaries
with the artistry to revitalise our
enchanted and endangered world.

Bill Plotkin, *Wild Mind*

It is time to dream a new dream. To apply a different narrative to the place we now find ourselves.

It is time to move away from destructiveness and fear-based action, which have defined Western patriarchal capitalism thus far, and towards conscious co-creation. To shapeshift from me to we. From force to flow. From linear to circular. From death cult to life loving. It requires a simplification of our 'needs.' A slowing down. A reconnection to the natural world and the innate sacredness of it. It requires a reimagining of what it means to be human, and an application of both our feeling and our intelligence in creative collaboration with the forces of nature. As Clementine Morrigan says, "Capitalism requires disenchantment. To remember enchantment, to reconnect with a pulsing, living world, is to resist capitalism and environmental destruction."

We need to be guided by both soul and science, evidence and intuition, courage and collective will. There is a place for us all in this project: for scientists, engineers, biologists, farmers, politicians, ecologists, teachers, tech folk, visionaries, artists, writers, magic makers and everyday folk of every age. We who mourn the human cost, the destruction of cultures, the loss of life…but see the bigger picture… of how things might be.

A Circular Economy

Ellen MacArthur is an English sailor best-known for her many world-record breaking solo sailing expeditions. She is a woman of incredible courage and resilience. In 2000 she was the fastest solo woman to cross the Atlantic east to west, as well as the youngest and the fastest woman to singlehandedly circumnavigate the globe (in 2001 in a single hulled boat and in a trimaran in 2005.)[82]

She is now using her global platform to draw attention to new way of living, inspired by her experience of having to be self-sufficient and sustainable on her long ocean voyages, where every resource was limited and precious. Her foundation promotes the potential and benefits of building a circular (as opposed to our current linear model) economy "based on the principles of designing out waste and pollution, keeping products and materials in use, and regenerating natural systems. [...]Only then can we create a thriving economy that can benefit everyone within the limits of our planet."[83]

If we return to the idea of the sea as a metaphor for consciousness, the depths – as yet undiscovered – of the unconscious may hold what we need: untapped, unactualised energy, resources, intelligence and abilities. To access these, we must first become aware of, rather than resistant to, them and then learn how to engage with them. The sea teaches us the transformation of consciousness to a flow state: that calm, engaged, creative frame of mind which allows us to fully harness all the strengths of our bodyminds. She teaches us the wisdom of cycles. She teaches us interconnectedness. She speaks directly to the inner voice of intuition, which is easily drowned out by the voices of others, the inner critic and our fears. But the more time we spend in attendance to her, we strengthen our ability to hear this voice, until it is louder, and easier to hear most of the time, rather than just occasionally.

The time has come
To shapeshift
To create
To make magic
To call on a power greater than ourselves,
The power that harnesses the tides and the storms.

Our ancestors knew this was within our capabilities.
But we,
Who have lost the faith of our fathers,
And the magic of our mothers.
Can we answer the call?

Taking Action

What can we do? is the cry that arises again and again, when faced with climate change.

The first step, I believe, is individual: Focusing on the inner sea – healing our own trauma so that we can step into our power, share our voices and take action, rather than hiding and denying and being triggered into panic. Using all the aspects of the sea: from colour to sound, seaweed to swimming to heal your bodymind. Find ways each week that you can practice moving out of your comfort zone whilst keeping your nervous system regulated. Make it a practice to challenge yourself to move from the easy and habitual to the courageous.

In terms of the outer sea, we can each be responsible for our own contribution to the ocean's health by making informed personal decisions:

> Taking our rubbish home and picking up litter when we walk.

> Not letting dogs foul on beaches or run unsupervised in bird wildlife sanctuaries.

> Following laws on gathering from the seashore.

> Using sea-safe sunscreen (14,000 tonnes of this end up on coral reefs every year).[84]

> Eating seafood that has been sustainably caught by local fisher people.

The second is to act locally: Adopt a piece of beach or a body of water and dedicate ourselves to it: knowing it, speaking on its behalf, representing it within our community, in local and national government decision-making. Become intimately familiar with the wildlife and plant life there throughout the seasons. Monitor and bring awareness to:

> Water quality (effluent pollution, oil spills…).

> Littering and dumping.

> Noise and traffic levels.

> Changes in behaviour, migration and population numbers of species, including the beaching or mass deaths of seabirds or creatures and coral bleaching.

> Habitat destruction.

> Coastal erosion.

> Excess or illegal development.

The third is to join together: We are more powerful together. Support charities and businesses that are cleaning our oceans, educating the public on marine biology and developing sustainable fuel sources. Be sure that governments implement and enforce legislation against unsustainable and damaging practices.

These include:

> Industrial fishing, where massive trawlers and their drag- and driftnets not only kill far more sea creatures than are eaten, and wreck ecosystems but also release carbon from the seabed.

> Ignoring of fishing quotas.

> Illegal hunting of whales, seals and dolphins.

> Nuclear testing at sea.

> Dumping of waste at sea.

> The impact of massive cruise ships on the ocean and the communities where they dock.

> The need to move from oil drilling to sustainable forms of energy.

And finally, be creative and support the creativity of others, as a way to raise awareness of the vital richness that the oceans bring us on every level: make art with beach waste, sand, salt, stones...; sculpt sea forms; make ceremonies; draw sea birds; paint whales; write articles; dance; cook with seaweed; compose sea songs; photograph the ocean's beauty...as so many of the contributors to this book do beautifully.

When we treasure what we have and share this with others, through art, teaching, ritual celebration, advocacy and community projects, we awaken our soul connection, motivating us to protect what we love and know. Engaging our creativity also engages the problem-solving part of the brain that we need right now, and helps us embody reflective action. As Rowena Pattee Kryder says in her book, *Sacred Ground to Sacred Space*, "In a time when traditional societies are breaking down, the issue of the role of sacred art in culture becomes critical...We need to see our relationship to the creative process of the cosmos." See pinterest.ie/dreamingaloudnt/seaart to get inspired.

The Power to Heal

Water captivated me from a young age. Years later, She mesmerised my sister. As children, we pretended to be mermaids as we swam in the sea, dreaming of diving deeper beneath Her surface someday as marine biologists. My sister passed away at the age of nine from AML leukemia. I was left alone to swim against the current of societal perceptions and stereotypes as an African American woman from the South daring to have such dreams. With my audacity and a deep breath, I dove in, never looking back at the shore.

The sea's importance in my life is as strong as Her tides.

I feel most connected to my sister's spirit through the sea. The sea speaks to me and has guided me through every milestone. Through my grief She reminded me that no matter how dark the deepest depths may seem, you are never alone and there is light if you reach for it. Within Her I found the hope I needed to continue living.

I found the strength I needed to follow our dreams of becoming a marine biologist. I had the privilege of living on O'ahu for a few years as I attended university. Throughout my studies, I had the privilege to learn first-hand within Her realm. My heart is still overflowing between the giddiness of seeing a flying fish soar out of the water, the awe of a manta ray dancing before me, the indescribable feeling of a whale's song resonating through my bones, the hope in seeing a reef thrive again, and the wonder I have felt in witnessing bioluminescence on an evening dive. I had the opportunity to volunteer with the local Marine Mammal Response Team, and to care for some truly remarkable creatures—including endangered species – to learn from them, and to teach others about them. I was able to highlight the challenges they face, and how

244

we can better care for them and the sea we share. Seeing people light up when they realise they can create a wave of change through their intentional actions is why I do what I do. I learned enough of the language to be conversational and help identify some of my favorite sea creatures to Hawaiian-language immersion groups that would visit the aquarium. When sharing my passion with a kind man, he said "Mai ke kai mai ke ola, e malama I ke kai" which loosely translates to "From the sea comes life, protect the sea."

I also embraced the seemingly impossible childhood dream of transforming into a mermaid to continue to share the light and joy of my sister. My tails are orange and gold for leukemia and childhood cancer awareness. I swim with other mermaids, creating unforgettable memories for those who walk by and are surprised to see merfolk splashing about in the shallows. I also swim with the children at an oncology camp in the summer each year. As a mermaid, I feel whole because it represents my connection between my purpose, my soul, and the sea. Mermaiding allows me to engage curious humans with interactive education to learn about the extraordinary life within Her waters.

From the sea comes life, and I owe mine to Her. Her ever-changing tides hold much power. Her power to inspire curiosity imbued me with a desire for exploration. Her healing waters blessed my sister with a little more time—a gift I will be forever grateful for. Her raging moods hold centuries of wisdom, reminding me that I can hold it all. Her grace and elegant beauty shimmer in the moonlight as She dances along the shore. Through it all, She holds the power to wash away everything—all the chaos, destruction, unknowing, grief, and despair—and hold me as I am, all that I was created to be: She is home.

Ayesha Sosa

Rising Tide

The sea has always been a medium of change. She holds within her life and hidden mysteries…as well as death and destruction.

She was here long before us.
She will be here long after us.

The streaming presence of water causes life to spring forth. The flooding and storming of water causes the dissolution of structures, breaking them down to their most essential parts. It washes them away and repurposes them…as flotsam, beach treasures, sea glass, sand and salt.

Our culture is beginning to be broken down, dissolved. But we have forgotten that these cycles of lifedeath are an obligatory condition of life on this planet. They keep the game of life going. Keep it fluid and interesting and scary and unpredictable. They add chance and fate and change to the dance. They add an unseen rhythm, that we ignore at the cost of our own suffering.

We have forgotten that our thoughts are not the main program of life, our heartbeats not its central tempo. The cycles of nature are. They always have been, and always will be. We have lost our ability to hear them. To feel them. To know them. To move with them.

Our ancestors were flexible – they moved with the seasons, taking their homes with them. In the past we would not have built on floodplains or boglands. We knew that these were the spaces betwixt and between, these were the places of shifting. We would leave space for the wild unknown.

But we have forgotten, with our concrete and steel and arrogance and greed, the ways of the water. We have become dried out husks of humans – living in one place, doing one thing for our work, following our minds. We have lost our ability to hear the song of the sea.

This world, *this* culture will not survive that. What we are experiencing now is the death of this way of being.

But it does not have to be the end of humanity.

The sea promises lifedeath. We will have to regain our fluidity once more in how and where we live, the energy we run our lives on, how we focus our communities, our connection and respect for the nature of the sea and the earth.

We have to reconnect with the bigger picture, the greater intelligence at work. We are not, nor ever have been, autonomous beings. There has always been the oceanic at work – influencing us, shaping us, shaping our culture, speaking through it, guiding us.

> *The waters are rising…*
>
> *The song of the sea is calling…*
>
> *Reminding us of lost worlds subsumed, cultures which*
>
> *held tight to their temples of stone too long,*
>
> *Until the bodies within them were reclaimed by the sea.*
>
> *This is not a new story. Just a new chapter.*
>
> *We are both the dying and the living.*
>
> *We are both the midwives…and those being born.*

We who have lived the life of the creatrix know how to swim in shifting waters. As we leave the confines of the riverbanks, we enter open ocean and come back – at last, at last – to our true natures: tidal and wet. We who have given birth with our bodies know the process. We who have travelled through the darkness of illness and dissolution know the way. We who have shapeshifted know how it works.

Memories come flooding back. The Feminine is emerging. We have been here before, known this before, done this before. Underwater, like in a dream, we cannot quite focus our eyes. And yet we can see – not details but outlines. Our hearing is muffled, but our more ancient senses come back online underwater. We are flooded with the knowing of what was submerged in our waters before we could talk, it buzzes wordless under the surface of ourselves, before, behind, between language – that we know is there but could never quite reach.

Until now.

It is there, we just have to acclimatise to this new way of being – to begin to build and then inhabit the lost lands they said never existed. To remember that magic is in all things. It simply needs to be released.

What if all we need to do is to forget what we have been taught and remember what we know?

What if we can stop resisting and fighting and shaping nature...and allow her to change us?

What if we trusted ourselves to the flow?

What if it was easier than we believed?

What if it is the most natural thing in the world to us?

What if we heeded the call?

What if?

The bells under the waves are tolling.
As the waters rise,
We rise too.
This flood of the Feminine will not be assuaged.
The wild ways are taking us back,
Enough,
Enough
Of hard and dry and fast,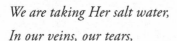
The waters are rising…
And so are we.

We are taking Her salt water,
In our veins, our tears,
Landwards.
We are the flood
Of Feminine consciousness.
We speak for the sea.
For life.
For the sacred.

We are we of the sea.
Our time has come.

Reflections

Do you consider this earth your home? In what ways does your behaviour reflect this belief?

How can you personally respond to climate change in a way that is not panicked or complacent?

What practical actions can we take as individuals?

How can you expand these out to share them with your community?

What psychological shifting needs to happen in order for a new culture to arise within you? Within your community?

What is dying? How can we grieve what is happening – both alone... and even more importantly together?

How can you be a voice for the sea?

What commitment will you take to act on behalf of the sea and her communities?

What acts of healing are you taking for your own trauma?

Do you see – and feel – the connection between your personal creativity and your ability to co-create "the more beautiful world our hearts know is possible"[85]?

CLOSING

The sea does not reward those who are too anxious,
too greedy, or too impatient. To dig for treasures shows
not only impatience and greed, but lack of faith.
Patience, patience, patience, is what the sea teaches.
Patience and faith. One should lie empty, open,
choiceless as a beach—waiting for a gift from the sea.

Anne Morrow Lindbergh, *Gift from the Sea*

The Road Home

I see the birds approaching as I drive down the Bog Road. Clouds and flocks and murmurations of birds coming towards me. I follow them. Down along the winding boreen where this book started, its hedges now bare and brown. I park in the empty beach car park, waiting for the icy rain to stop.

It slows to a soft mist, then the sun breaks through, and what was previously grey and overcast sparkles in the low white rays of the midwinter sun. Raindrops hang from the brittle grasses like diamonds.

Flock after flock of birds keep flying over: a graceful group of grey collared doves; black rooks coming from their winter roost; the graceful white arcing of gulls; and higher up the honking Vs of migrating geese.

They are coming to the bird sanctuary.

Sanctuary: a place of both sacredness and safety.

This is what the beach has always been for me.

This is what it is for so many of us that live here. A place of sanctuary. We are so blessed to have it. Especially in these ever-more turbulent times. We have a protected space for the birds. But, I believe, they are also holding space for us.

I walk down to the sand and pick up some of the storm-tossed seaweed to put on our garden, to help us grow our vegetables for next year. Even in this midwinter cold and gloom, in the dark days and bleakness – whether of soul or season – that which has been tossed up by the storm will help new life to grow. Birthdeath keeps cycling. May it keep cycling still. May we learn to live more wisely with these cycles.

This book has chronicled the process of meeting and providing a grounded body for your soul to pour through: a sanctuary to welcome your soul home. It is a continual and deepening practice. My hope is that it will be a treasured companion to the process of birthdeath that we experience many times in our individual lives, and which we are now experiencing collectively too.

I have a sense that this book marks the end of a cycle. A decade of coming to peace with motherhood, discovering my neurodivergence, reclaiming my sexuality, embracing my creativity and spirituality, finding my place in community…embracing all my parts, and in a very public way. The end of one cycle is the beginning of a new one. Who knows where it will take me, what forms will emerge. If you had told me on my thirtieth birthday that I would birth one book, let alone ten in the next decade, I would never have believed you.

These books have helped me find myself…and I know they have helped many others. They were my lifeline when I couldn't stay alive. The medication I am now on has turned down the intensity of the birthdeath urge in my own body. It has made my mind foggier, but living easier. Writing in long form with the complex weaving and structure that these books require is much harder for me. The burn-outs and breakdown and middle age have left me with far less energy, which I need to use more wisely. We shall see. All I know is that by applying what I have learned from the whispers of my soul and the ideas I have discovered along the way, I have been freed from the tight circles I had been walking, and see that it is, it always was, a labyrinth in shifting sands.

The final year of writing this book was the first year of the Covid-19 pandemic. A year of death and deep change. And yet what was most wonderful during the strangeness of lockdowns (three and counting) was that the previously plane-trailed skies were pure blue, the beaches and lanes were full of walkers and the soundtrack to our days was not the engines of cars but the birds, their waking and roosting marking time.

The birds are our teachers in these changing times. Those that fly over our lives and those that come and nest and settle. They remind me that there are seasons of settling, seasons of flying, seasons of swimming in warm blue waters and seasons of longing to throw yourself from the cliffs.

Death is ever-present. I, like so many of us, have lost loved ones these past months. The darkness has been lurking in my mind again during the last weeks of writing. But as I sit here, I reflect that, perhaps, it is not what I think. Perhaps rather than death with a capital D, it is the death of a part of me that is looking to die with the old year. After weeks of resisting, I allow it. The relief to feel that old part of me float away on the wind is palpable. I feel lighter. And wonder why I always cling so hard.

As the wind blows and the birds fly, I'm reminded how small and insignificant I am. And how very, very much I belong here. To this piece of coast, these sharp black rocks, these round grey pebbles, these ever-changing waves, these birds. However hard I struggle with belonging to the people here – people anywhere – *this* is what I do belong to.

I seem to forget this so easily. I need to take time to remember it everyday and support myself to be able to access it, to be able to step outside of my bubble of safety and screens in my small house and busy life and remember the expansiveness of being which doesn't require social skills. It simply requires showing up and being buffeted by the wind. Allowing for the possibility of transformation. Allowing the reality of simply being without agenda. Allowing the wind and waves and stones to remake me again and again.

I pick up the seaweed and walk along the sandy path back to the car. I look up and see a rainbow – the sign of hope – arcing across my path, reminding me that the sacred is always close at hand, listening, whispering, nudging.

It is there for a minute, maybe two, as I scramble for my phone to take a photograph to remember this magical moment, which in fiction would seem contrived: the sacred covenant, that the world never again will be flooded. Yet here it is, real.

And then, just as quickly as it appeared, it disappears. Where do the colours come from? Where does the rainbow go? This ephemeral symbol of hope and beauty that can only be carried in our hearts, photographs and memories. Real but intangible.

This is the reminder I need that magic is here. Now.

The sun has gone behind a cloud. The wind is whipping wildly.

The birds are settled somewhere out of sight. A single crow sits, watching.

And I am here, standing by the sea, colours in my heart, knowing how blessed I am.

May yours be the sparkle of light on the ocean,
The whisper of foam on the sea,
The warm sand guiding your feet safely home,
A pebble in your pocket from me.

Some sea glass, a starfish, some driftwood, a whelk,
Treasures washed up on the shore.
A flower, a feather, an urchin, a pearl,
Keep your eyes open for more.

May you know yourself held in the palm of Her hand,
Blessed by the waves wild and free,
Blown by the wind, anointed with salt,
Beloved of She of the Sea.

A Note on Terms

If you are new to my work, you will find yourself coming across these terms quite a lot, and perhaps wondering what I mean by them. I want to explain my reasoning for them briefly here. Think of these concepts and words as the main characters of the book, and this is where you get to meet them.

Archetype

To me, She of the Sea is an archetype, a universal energetic blueprint, which though it may differ subtly from culture to culture, is common to all humans, just like the idea of a Mother, Teacher or Queen would be. The focus of my work is on reclaiming lost archetypes of the feminine – energies which have been forgotten, side-lined, ignored or buried during patriarchal times, but which hold great power for us in these transition times as we imagine new ways forward. Different people approach archetypes in different ways. For some it may help to imagine an archetype as real, a living, breathing otherworldly inhabitant, a spirit or aspect of the Goddess. For others, it is an energy force that can be tapped into and released into our world when we embody its qualities. For others it is merely a metaphor, an idea which can inspire us. When terms, like Feminine, are capitalised they refer to the archetypal understanding of a concept (following the style of *Burning Woman*). When I refer to a human individual who is embodying an archetype, the term is not capitalised.

Bodymind

The term bodymind is used throughout this book and may be new to you. Popularised by Ken Dychtwald in his book, *Bodymind,* it seeks to linguistically close the artificial schism between body and mind within Western culture and instead approach the human being holistically.

God(dess)

This is the term I am coming to use to refer to my understanding of the Mystery, the source of the sacred, the divine. For me it embraces, literally with its beautiful embracing brackets, both Masculine and Feminine qualities that we have ascribed to the divine, whilst allowing for the sacred to move beyond previous limitations of gender. My own personal journey the last ten years has leaned deeply into the Feminine aspects, whereas the first thirty years would have been almost fully in the Masculine.

Psyche/Soul

The term soul is often only used in religious or spiritual contexts. The way that it is used in this book is as an acknowledgement of ourselves beyond the physical body. It is an attempt to express in a single word the innate *beingness* of each of us that cannot be touched or photographed but which is the true expression and experience of ourselves.

The etymology of psyche is "animating spirit," from the Latin *psyche* and from Greek *psykhe* "the soul, mind, spirit; breath; life, one's life, the invisible animating principle or entity which occupies and directs the physical body."[86]

The Feminine

The feminine/Feminine, can be one that many find challenging. I get it: I used to too. And still do when it's used in the pink, fluffy way. Please refer to my words from *Burning Woman* just in case it is a term you struggle with too.

Whatever gender we were assigned at birth, we all have both "masculine" and "feminine" energies and drives within us. And we're all born into a patriarchal culture which sees and shapes us differently into stunted, restricted versions of the full people we could be.

"The feminine" as it is currently used in our culture is usually shorthand for: beautiful, gentle, slim, restrained, non-confrontational, carefully cultivated, domesticated, emotional, girlish and weak. It is often a term of disparagement...because the feminine has

been blacklisted. Most qualities deemed not masculine, or in any way pertaining to women, have been slighted, shamed or silenced. Both genders in our culture have learned to suppress signs of the feminine in order to survive and be accepted, which has led to a hyper-masculinised culture of men…and women. As women in Western culture, we have been taught to value more masculine traits and denigrate, disregard or trivialise more typically feminine ways of being.

So, let's differentiate now by using a capital F. The Feminine is your deepest life force which is expressed through your female body. It is that which feels most true to you as a woman: uncultivated and raw.

Defining the Feminine is immediately problematic – it sets up a dichotomy with the Masculine. And in this world, we have a habit of making dichotomies into good and bad.

The reality we are currently inhabiting is the shadowlands where immature masculine and feminine are waiting transformation into a creative partnership of their fully mature selves.

The masculinity we see running rampant in the patriarchal system is not the developed Masculine, but the defensive toxic masculine, the immature, ego-based masculine trying to defend a man-made hierarchical order against chaos, nature and the Feminine.

The Patriarchy

We inhabit a system that has been constructed, ruled over and policed for millennia by men, prioritising the needs, perspectives, bodies and minds of men. The System (often referred to as patriarchy in feminist thought) has forcibly separated humanity down gendered and sexed divides. It has violently enforced the primacy of what it recognises as the male and the masculine whilst devaluing, destroying and suppressing that which it defines as female and feminine. We must of course be clear that the term patriarchy does not mean that men as individuals are bad or wrong or inherently guilty. After all men suffer at the hands of patriarchy too. And many women claim to not even experience it at all.

Whether we consciously acknowledge it or not, patriarchy is the paradigm in which our bodies have grown, our lives have been shaped, our health managed and our minds bound for tens of generations. It has controlled, ordered and interpreted our lives across religious, political and cultural fields in consciously gendered ways that have systemically and historically discriminated against women. Our current System is informed by three main strands of patriarchy: the patriarchy of the mind – law, the patriarchy of the body – medical science, and the patriarchy of the soul – the Church.

REFERENCES

Nature and Reflection

Enchantment – Sharon Blackie

Muddy Mysticism: The Sacred Tethers of Body, Earth, and Everyday – Natalie Bryant Rizzieri

Swims – Elizabeth-Jane Burnett

The Grassling – Elizabeth-Jane Burnett

Sea Garden – H.D.

The Other Side of the River: Stories of Women, Water and the World – Eila Kundrie Carrico

Susceptible to Light – Chelan Harkin

To the River – Olivia Laing

The Outrun – Amy Liptrot

Arctic Dreams – Barry Lopez

The Wild Places – Robert MacFarlane

Underland – Robert MacFarlane

The Electricity of Every Living Thing: A Woman's Walk in the Wild to Find Her Way Home – Katherine May

Wintering – Katherine May

Dream Work – Mary Oliver

House of Light – Mary Oliver

Upstream – Mary Oliver

Salt on Your Tongue: Women and the Sea – Charlotte Runcie

The Blue of Distance – Rebecca Solnit

Wanderlust – Rebecca Solnit

Strands: A Year of Discoveries on the Beach – Jean Sprackland

When Women Were Birds – Terry Tempest Williams

fatbirder.com/world-birding/europe/irish-republic/county-cork/

birdwatchireland.ie

nature.com/articles/s41598-019-44097-3

God(dess), Magic, Ritual and Ceremony

The Holy Wild – Danielle Dulsky

Jailbreaking the Goddess: A Radical Revisioning of Feminist Spirituality – LaSara FireFox

The Sea Priestess – Dion Fortune

The Prophet – Kahlil Gibran

The Book of Ceremony: Shamanic Wisdom for Invoking the Sacred in Everyday Life – Sandra Ingerman

Seasons of the Witch – Patricia Monaghan

Fucking Magic #1 – Clementine Morrigan

The Untraining of a Sea Priestess – Stephanie Leon Neal

Burning Woman – Lucy H. Pearce

Walking with Persephone: A Journey of Midlife Descent and Renewal – Molly Remer

Yin Magic: How to be Still – Sarah Robinson

Yoga for Witches – Sarah Robinson

Queering Your Craft: Witchcraft from the Margins – Cassandra Snow

A Spell in the Wild – Alice Tarbuck

The Way of the Sea Priestess – Louise Tarrier

Six Ways – Aidan Wachter

Restoring the Goddess: Equal Rites for Modern Women – Barbara G. Walker

Weave the Liminal – Laura Tempest Zakroff

witchcraftandwitches.com/witchcraft/witches-circe/

patheos.com/blogs/keepingherkeys/2018/07/kirke-the-original-witch-her-story-themes-correspondences-and-more/

en.wikipedia.org/wiki/Sea_witch

nationalgeographic.com/history/magazine/2019/09-10/scotland-witch-hunts/

hakaimagazine.com/article-short/ceremonies-sea/

bbc.co.uk/newsround/56021940

Fiction

The Scent Keeper's Daughter – Erica Bauermeister

Remarkable Creatures – Tracy Chevalier

Rebecca – Daphne du Maurier

The Hours – Michael Cunningham

The Child from the Sea – Elizabeth Goudge

The Starless Sea – Erin Morgenstern

The Sea, The Sea – Iris Murdoch

The Surface Breaks – Louise O'Neill

The Essex Serpent – Sarah Perry

Lighthousekeeping – Jeanette Winterson

The Complete Works of Virginia Woolf

To the Lighthouse – Virginia Woolf

Mythology

Water Witchcraft: Magic and Lore from the Celtic Tradition
– Annwyn Avalon

If Women Rose Rooted: The Power of the Celtic Woman – Sharon Blackie

Isis Pelagia: Images, Names and Cults of a Goddess of the Seas
– Laurent Bricault

Fairy Queens: Meeting the Queens of the Otherworld – Morgan Daimler

Waters of Life – Eileen Dunlop

The Odyssey – Homer

Old Ways, Old Secrets: Pagan Ireland, Myth, Landscape, Tradition
– Jo Kerrigan

Thirty-Two Words for Field: Lost Words of the Irish Landscape
– Manchán Magan

Circe – Madeline Miller

The Red Haired Girl from the Bog – Patricia Monaghan

The Way of the Seabhean: An Irish Shamanic Path
– Amantha Murphy with Orla O'Connell

Anam Cara – John O'Donohue

Benedictus – John O'Donohue

herstory.ie/mythicwomen/2019/6/19/Clíodhna

feminismandreligion.com/2015/10/28/chliodhna-celtic-goddess-of-beauty-the-sea-and-the-afterlife-by-judith-shaw/

ancient.eu/Medusa/

en.wikipedia.org/wiki/Medusa

ancient.eu/Siren/

en.wikipedia.org/wiki/Siren_(mythology)

britannica.com/topic/Amphitrite-Greek-mythology

en.wikipedia.org/wiki/List_of_water_deities

letthemflourish.com/blog/2016/blackmermaidsarereal

goddessconference.com/dahud/

en.wikipedia.org/wiki/Saint_Sarah

Neurobiology and Psychology

The Crying Book – Heather Christle

Flow – Mihaly Csikszentmihalyi

The Polyvagal Theory in Therapy: Engaging the Rhythm of Regulation
– Deb Dana

The Hidden Messages in Water – Masaru Emoto

Civilization and Its Discontents – Sigmund Freud

The Origin of Consciousness in the Breakdown of the Bicameral Mind
– Julian Jaynes

Memories, Dreams, Reflections – C.G. Jung

The Natural Medicine Guide to Schizophrenia – Stephanie Marohn

Blue Mind: The Surprising Science That Shows How Being Near, In, On, or Under Water Can Make You Happier, Healthier, More Connected, and Better at What You Do – Wallace J. Nichols

The Book of Human Emotions – Tiffany Watt Smith

Women's Psychology and Inner Development

Circle of Stones: Woman's Journey to Herself – Judith Duerk

Women who Run with the Wolves: Contacting the Power of the Wild Woman – Clarissa Pinkola Estés

The Dance – Oriah Mountain Dreamer

Gift from the Sea – Anne Morrow Lindbergh

Burning Woman – Lucy H. Pearce

Full Circle Health: Integrated Health Charting for Women – Lucy H. Pearce

Medicine Woman: Reclaiming the Soul of Healing – Lucy H. Pearce

Moon Time – Lucy H. Pearce

Why Women Need Chocolate – Debra Waterhouse

Pregnant Darkness: Alchemy and the Rebirth of Consciousness – Monika Wikman

You Have the Right to Remain Fat – Virgie Tovar

The Bower Monologues – Issue 2 Escape and Retreat

deconstructingyourself.com/nonduality-freud-and-the-oceanic-feeling.html

Your Authentic Voice – Lucy H. Pearce (e-course)

Ecology, Economy and Politics

The Dream of the Earth – Thomas Berry

The Great Work – Thomas Berry

Cradle to Cradle: Remaking the Way We Make Things – Michael Braungart and William McDonough

The More Beautiful World Our Hearts Know is Possible – Charles Eisenstein

The Shock Doctrine – Naomi Klein

This Changes Everything: Capitalism vs the Climate – Naomi Klein

Sacred Ground to Sacred Space: Visionary Ecology, Perennial Wisdom, Environmental Ritual and Art – Rowena Pattee Kryder

Active Hope – Joanna Macy and Chris Johnstone

Zugunruhe: The Inner Migration to Profound Environmental Change
– Jason F. McLennan

An Inconvenient Truth – Al Gore

theoceancleanup.com

yourstory.com/herstory/2019/09/women-activists-climate-change

greenpeace.org

theguardian.com/environment/2021/jan/13/
climate-crisis-record-ocean-heat-in-2020-supercharged-extreme-weather

ellenmacarthurfoundation.org/circular-economy/
what-is-the-circular-economy

bbc.com/travel/story/20200805-denmarks-300-year-old-homes-of-the-future

theguardian.com/environment/2021/feb/04/
cacophony-human-noise-hurting-marine-life-scientists-warn

theguardian.com/environment/2021/mar/18/
cows-seaweed-methane-emissions-scientists

theguardian.com/environment/2021/mar/26/
marine-biological-association-young-writers-ocean-decade-challenge

The Story Between Stories – Charles Eisenstein (e-course)

Shipwrecks and Lost Worlds

The Book of Cloyne – Cloyne Historical Society

"Sea Tongue" – Kevin Crossley Holland

theguardian.com/commentisfree/2018/
oct/27/i-can-see-odysseus-lashed-to-the-mast-of-this-ship-sirens-song

en.wikipedia.org/wiki/Doggerland

livescience.com/23217-lost-city-of-atlantis.html

Atlantis Rising (Disney+)

"How time and tide put paid to Dunwich" –
Stephen Moss theguardian.com/news/2017/jan/09/
how-time-tide-put-paid-dunwich-suffolk-weatherwatch

"After the Flood" bbc.co.uk/programmes/b015pb04

East Anglian Daily Times eadt.co.uk/news/
weird-suffolk-the-lost-port-of-dunwich-1-5418226

Seashore

Forgotten Skills – Darina Allen

Edible Seaweeds of the World – Leonel Pereira

Wild Food: A Complete Guide for Foragers – Roger Phillips

Prannie Rhatigan's Irish Seaweed Kitchen – Prannie Rhatigan

Collins Complete Guide to Irish Wildlife – Paul Sterry

The Book of Pebbles – Christopher Stocks and Angie Lewin

Edible Seashore: River Cottage Handbook No. 5 – John Wright

seaweed.ie

theguardian.com/science/2020/sep/15/welsh-seagrass-meadow-global-restoration-pembrokeshire-climate-plant-project

theguardian.com/environment/2020/oct/27/what-victorian-era-seaweed-pressings-reveal-about-our-changing-seas

ryandrum.com

en.wikipedia.org/wiki/Rosemary

naturespiritherbs.com/seaweed-health-benefits

theherbalacademy.com/seaweed-101

connemaraseaweedbaths.com/health-benefits-of-seaweed-baths

solasnamara.ie/seaweed-baths

irishtimes.com/news/health/is-there-any-science-behind-benefits-of-seawater-therapy-1.472923

bbc.com/travel/story/20170906-the-last-surviving-sea-silk-seamstress

westlabsalts.co.uk

maldonsalt.co.uk

healthline.com/health/himalayan-salt-bath

betteryou.com/health-hub/magnesium-flakes-vs-dead-sea-salts-whats-the-difference

betteryou.com/health-hub/constantly-craving-chocolate-magnesium-deficiency-could-be-the-reason/

ncbi.nlm.nih.gov/pmc/articles/PMC6163803

oceanservice.noaa.gov/facts/whysalty.html

en.wikipedia.org/wiki/Mary_Anning

mysticalraven.com/history/14558/
what-is-a-hag-stone-and-why-are-they-so-special

puffinsandpies.com/2019/08/01/hagstones

Aquatic Ape

The Aquatic Ape – Elaine Morgan

The Descent of Woman – Elaine Morgan

"The Waterside Ape" – David Attenborough (two-part series) 2016

Part 1: bbc.co.uk/sounds/play/b07v0hhm

Part 2: bbc.co.uk/sounds/play/b07v2ysg

en.wikipedia.org/wiki/Aquatic_ape_hypothesis

africanrockart.britishmuseum.org/country/egypt/cave-of-swimmer

Crystals

The Encyclopedia of Crystals – Judy Hall

Crystals for Beginners – Karen Frazier

HausMagick: Transform Your Home with Witchcraft – Erica Feldmann

crystalspoint.com/blue-crystals

happyglastonbury.co.uk/product-category/crystals/crystal-a-z

beadage.net/gemstones/colors/blue

realgems.org/list_of_gemstones

crystaladdictcloset.com

thecrystalcouncil.com

gemstagram.com

charmsoflight.com

Creativity

SoulCollage Evolving: An Intuitive Collage Process for Self-Discovery and Community – Seena B. Frost

Star, Branch, Spiral, Fan – Yellena James

Creatrix: She Who Makes – Lucy H. Pearce

The Rainbow Way: Cultivating Creativity in the Midst of Motherhood – Lucy H. Pearce

Sun Gardens: The Cyanotypes of Anna Atkins – Larry J. Schaaf

Skill Share – creative e-courses

Domestika – creative e-courses

Modern Watercolour Techniques e-course on Domestika, Ana Maria Calderon

Sunprint Notecards: The Cyanotypes of Anna Atkins

See many of Atkin's cyanotypes here publicdomainreview.org/collection/cyanotypes-of-british-algae-by-anna-atkins-1843

medium.com/exposure-magazine/anna-atkinss-ghost-and-the-conception-of-the-combination-cyanotype-c080a57ba10d

Salt art – buzzworthy.com/salt-art

My Pinterest board of sea art pinterest.ie/dreamingaloudnt/seaart

Shapeshifting

Travelling the Fairy Path – Morgan Daimler

Shape Shifters: Shaman Women in Contemporary Society – Michele Jamal

Jaguar in the Body, Butterfly in the Heart: The Real Life Initiation of an Everyday Shaman – Ya'acov Darling Khan

Fairy Tale Medicine – Clarejasminebeloved.com (e-course)

en.wikipedia.org/wiki/Harpy

en.wikipedia.org/wiki/selkie

travelpirates.com/captains-log/fact-or-fiction-mermaids-sirens-and-harpies_11260#

about-mythical-creatures.weebly.com/harpies-and-sirens.html

audubon.org/news/sirens-greek-myth-were-bird-women-not-mermaids

en.wikipedia.org/wiki/Mermaid

oceanservice.noaa.gov/facts/mermaids.html

Blue

The Virgin Blue – Tracy Chevalier

Colour – Victoria Finlay

The Little Book of Colour: How to Use the Psychology of Colour to Transform Your Life – Karen Haller

Underland – Robert MacFarlane

Bluets – Maggie Nelson

The Essex Serpent – Sarah Perry

The Secret Lives of Colour – Kassia St Clair

en.wikipedia.org/wiki/Blue_and_white_pottery

bourncreative.com

empower-yourself-with-color-psychology.com

colorpsychology.org

Symbology

Sacred Symbols: Peoples, Religions, Mysteries – Robert Adkinson

The Book of Symbols – ARAS

Womb Awakening: Initiatory Wisdom from the Creatrix of all Life – Azra Bertrand and Seren Bertrand

The Complete Language of Flowers – S. Theresa Dietz

The Signature of All Things – Elizabeth Gilbert

Word & Image – C.G. Jung

10,000 Dreams Interpreted – Gustavus Hindman Miller

Designa: Technical Secrets of the Traditional Visual Arts – Adam Tetlow

Li: Dynamic Form in Nature – David Wade

The Woman's Dictionary of Symbols and Sacred Objects – Barbara G. Walker

WORD+image – Lucy H. Pearce (e-course)

almanac.com/content/flower-meanings-language-flowers

Women of the Sea

The Island of Sea Women – Lisa See

roadsandkingdoms.com/2017/the-female-free-divers-of-jeju

welshhat.wordpress.com/types-of-costume/working-dress/cockle-women/

en.wikipedia.org/wiki/Ama_(diving)

nytimes.com/2014/03/30/world/asia/hardy-divers-in-korea-strait-sea-women-are-dwindling.html

nps.gov/safr/learn/historyculture/maritimewomenhistory.htm

maritimemuseum.co.nz/collections/stories-and-blogs/top-20-sailing-superstitions

Sue Perkins – *Japan*, Episode 2 (BBC)
kcet.org/shows/japan-with-sue-perkins/episodes/episode-two

theguardian.com/sport/2015/aug/04/free-diver-natalia-molchanova-feared-dead

youtu.be/MPsv5z67PrQ

bbc.com/news/av/world-44537158/100-women-you-are-truly-free-while-freediving

magicseaweed.com/news/abundant-roots-of-women-surfing-a-legacy-of-hawaiian-medicine-women-royalty/12306

rnli.org/about-us/our-history/timeline/1838-grace-darling

She of the Sea in Film

Alice Through the Looking Glass (2016). Alice as ship's captain, navigating the prejudice of patriarchal society.

Ama (2018). A short film by Julie Gautier, expressive dance underwater on a held breath. youtube.com/watch?v=bdBuDg7mrT8

Ama-San (2016). Documentary film about the Japanese Ama divers. vimeo.com/ondemand/amasan

Ammonite (2020). A fictionalised account of the life of British fossil collector Mary Anning.

Birth as We Know It (2009). Documentary about water birth around the world. vimeo.com/105050501

BlueHue (2016). Short, award-winning documentary about a woman who cold water swims naked daily in Snowdonia. vimeo.com/134002940

Freedive Against All Odds (2017). Documentary about freediver Ashleigh Baird. youtu.be/vfCrBob3N-c

Giving Birth in the Ocean, 'AQUADURAL', Birth Undisturbed Episode 6 (2018). Short documentary about water birth around the world. youtu.be/x27UOIiqkn4

Goop Labs: Wim Hof (Netflix, 2020). An interview with "Ice Man" Wim Hof, sharing his practice of cold water swimming and ice baths.

Hydrotherapy (2020). An award-winning short documentary on overcoming a life-changing illness through wild swimming.

Moana (Disney, 2016). Animated film set in the Pacific featuring Moana, the strong-willed daughter of a chief of a Polynesian village, is chosen by the ocean to reunite an ancient relic with the Goddess.

My Octopus Teacher (Netflix, 2020). Oscar-winning documentary about a man healing through his relationship with an octopus in a South African kelp forest.

Ondine (2009). An Irish romance about the selkie.

One Breath Around the World (2019). Short documentary film following freediver Guillaume Néry. youtu.be/OnvQggy3Ezw

Seaspiracy (Netflix, 2021). A hard-hitting documentary on the state of the oceans and destructive fishing practices.

She is the Ocean (2018). Documentary about nine women who live and work in the sea.

Sofia Rocks the Cenotes (2019). Short film of Colombian world record-holding freediver, Sofía Gómez Uribe, running back up from a 60-foot freedive clutching a rock. youtu.be/SrZRMoi-yO4

Song of the Sea (2014). Magical animated Irish tale of the selkie, with a beautiful soundtrack.

The Big Blue (1988). Captivating movie by Luc Besson, based on the real-life friendship of two freedivers.

The Little Mermaid (Netflix, 2018) and (Disney, 1989). Two versions of the classic tale.

The Secret of Roan Inish (1994). Another Irish selkie movie!

Cards

The Starseed Oracle – Rebecca Campbell and Danielle Noel

The Witches' Wisdom Tarot – Phyllis Curott and Danielle Barlow

The Japaridze Tarot – Nino Japaridze

Ocean Dreams – A Mystic Oracle – Danielle Noel

Sea Whispers Oracle – Lyn Thurman

Music

This is a selection of the songs that I listened to on loop as I created the material for this book, most of these and many more are on the *She of the Sea* Spotify playlist, which you can access at tinyurl.com/SheoftheSea

"Mama Ocean," *Dreamwalker* – Kai Altair

"Fisherman" – Lewis Barfoot

"To the Water," *Whisper to the Wild Water* – Maire Brennan

"The Sea," *Spirals* – Eleanor Brown (via Bandcamp)

"Selkies," *All in the End is Harvest* – Eleanor Brown (via Bandcamp)

"Medhel an Gwyns," "How the Tide Rushes in," *Poldark* – Anne Dudley

"Kai – The Song of the Mermaid," *Sophia Songs* – Lisa Dancing-Light

"An Ocean and a Rock," *Sea Sew* – Lisa Hannigan

"Song of the Sea," *Song of the Sea* – Lisa Hannigan

"We, the Drowned," "Prayer for the Dying," *At Swim* – Lisa Hannigan

"May it Be" – Voces 8

"Cry for the Sea" – Mother Turtle

Chants

"We are a Circle," "Sacred Waters," *Sacred Chants and Invocations* – Jehan

"The River is Flowing," "Born of Water," *Return of the Goddess* – Lila

Movement

"Rain, in Your Black Eyes," *...and the things that remain* – Ezio Bosso

Meditation/Relaxation

"The Blessing," *As I Return* – Essie Jain

"Le Onde," *Seven Days Walking* – Ludovico Einaudi

"De Profundis," *Out of the Depths* – Terry Oldfield

"Calm Waves," *The Beautiful Sounds of the Ocean*

GRATITUDES

My gratitude goes out to all those who supported and were involved in the creation of this book.

My circle of stones women who have travelled with me through dark places and joyous togetherness, on many beautiful beach walks. Many of these women helped to create the first stone spiral over a decade ago and who I was honoured to share such a magical winter solstice ceremony with.

All of the contributors who responded so enthusiastically to my invitation, dived into their depths and shared their voices and experiences so courageously and authentically. Thank you for trusting me with your words.

All the brave people who have shared with me the magic of cold water swimming and showers in their lives. You inspire me! Thank you for your gentle patience as I resisted for so long.

The greater Womancraft community for cheering me on via social media as I wrote, longing this book into being. A book is not much without a readership. And a special shout out to Rosie Slosek (@ themoneyhaven) who fuelled me with exquisite packages of chocolate, heart-felt cards and cheerleading messages to get me through the hard times, and who explored the grounds of Blarney Castle with me.

To the musicians for the music that I gathered on the Spotify playlist, which carried me through, as well as the artists whose work I have collated on my Pinterest boards. Thank you for the beauty.

My trusted early readers, Mary Tighe and Paula Youmell, for reading yet another of my raw books.

My dear Patrick for listening to me both give up – and finish – this book dozens of times over a couple of years, without judgement. And my children for understanding more and more each time what writing means for me, for tolerating with great humour my latest special interest, and not teasing me too much as more and more blue crystals arrived in the post.

To my mother who passed on her love of the sea and of labyrinths, my step-father who taught me to sail and row, and my father who took me out to walk the rocks barefoot as a child.

And to She of the Sea, my greatest teacher and healer.

CONTRIBUTORS

D o take time to seek out the powerful creative work and soulful offerings of the folks who contributed to this book. They are people who give me hope, and who make the world a richer and more beautiful place.

Adeola Sheehy-Adekale (p.13) is a mother, writer and women's circle facilitator who leads courses in creativity and all aspects of the feminine experience. The written word has been her expression, safe haven and dearest love for as long as she can remember. Be it fiction, poems, essays or musings on life, her pen is almost always attached to paper. She lives in the UK. www: adeolasheehyaworldinwords.com

Aj Smit (p.190) is a weaver of joy and a professional Mermaid currently based in Texas. She writes and leads Red Tents and offers coaching, as well as ritual and adornment services to help you live an embodied life of joy. FB/IG: @TheJoyWeaver www: thejoyweaver.com

Alice Gray (pp.26, 121) is inspired by nature, mythology, fairy tales and ancient artefacts. She hand-makes sacred objects out of porcelain clay that explore the Sacred feminine and celebrate Mother Nature. She makes Yonis, Goddesses and Selkies to be worn, held and for special places. She lives in the small coastal town of Saltburn on the North East Coast of Britain. www: selkiearts.co.uk

ALisa Starkweather (p.178) is the founder of many powerful women's initiatives: the Red Tent Temple Movement; Daughters of the

Earth Gatherings; the Women's Belly and Womb Conferences; the women's mystery school; Priestess Path Apprenticeship and co-founder of the international women's initiation, Women in Power: Initiating Ourselves to the Predator Within. She is a Shadow Work and breathwork facilitator as well as a keynote speaker and life coach. Thirty-five years of dedication to women's empowerment gave her a reputation where she is known for her passionate archetypal work that focuses on transformation, healing, community, ritual and the rebalancing of the sacred Feminine. www: alisastarkweather.com

Anna-K Cuffe (p.238) is a ceramic artist, a diver and an ocean activist, born and based in Kingston, Jamaica. She completed a Bachelor of Fine Arts in 2017 at the Edna Manley College of the Visual and Performing Arts, receiving a Cecil Baugh Award for Excellence in Ceramics. Initially, her sculptures often took a formalistic approach to art, focusing exclusively on the form of the pieces rather than the content. However, she soon ventured away from solely creating art for art's sake and aimed instead to contribute to the conversation about our dying coral reefs. www: theartisticmermaid.com

Ayesha Sosa (p.244) is an ambitious dreamer with a passion for animals and conservation education. She holds a Bachelor of Science degree in Marine Biology with a minor in Psychology from Hawai'i Pacific University as well as her NAUI Advanced, Rescue, and Nitrox Scuba Diver certifications. She lives with her soldier that lured her from the sea and their two feline furbabies. She enjoys mermaiding and practicing aerial arts, and aspires to continue living life fully. IG: @MermaidAyesha

Chelan Harkin (pp.112, 155) is a published poet. Her first book is *Susceptible to Light.* Her dream-turned-plan is to write mystical (heart opening) poetry her whole life long because that's her thing and it's important to try and do our thing when we can here on this sweet earth…that's what generates the good stuff. She lives with her husband and two small guru-munchkins (kids) in Washington state, US. IG: @chelanharkin

Claire Robinson (p.23) lives on the West Sussex coast where she longs for a room of her own, while working for a disability charity and tending to young children. She also facilitates discussion and writing groups for Mothers Uncovered, whose anthology *The Secret Life of Mothers* features a number of her pieces on motherhood. www: allgristtothemill.wordpress.com

Clare Jasmine Beloved (p.175) carries art, poetry, hope, circle work, creativity and art to new audiences: from prisons to housing estates, government conferences to dole queues…reawakening lost dreams and inspiring a bigger vision of what is possible. A highly experienced facilitator, she has worked with thousands of people at workshops and retreats, as well as speaking at conferences around the world. She is based in Liverpool, UK. www: clarebeloved.com

Donna Booth (p.177) is a wellbeing coach, retreat host and writer based in Caithness, the land beyond the Highlands. She writes a self-care column for Holistic Therapist magazine and is working on a non-fiction book, *The Practical Goddess* and a novel about drug dealing selkies. She loves wild gardens, stormy seas and anything with a touch of the mystical. www: thepracticalgoddess.com

Eleanor Brown (p.144) is a songwriter and music maker who connects deeply with the natural world and the changing times, creating from both the descent and the rising. Her albums including All in the End is Harvest, Spirals, Meet You There and The Caravan Sessions. She lives in the UK. www: eleanorbrownmusic.com

Eila Carrico/Erin Kundrie (p.172) is a weaver and wordsmith who delights in the mystery and magic of landscapes and memory. Her first book, *The Other Side of the River,* was published by Womancraft Publishing. www: EilaCarrico.com

Francesca Prior (p.205) has passion for labyrinths and ginkgo biloba trees. Mother and grandmother working in and with the community and the world. A bringer of light especially into mental health. She loves nothing more than drawing seven-circuit Cretan labyrinths in the sand, snow, paper, paint or textiles. She lives in Dorset, UK.

Gia Daprano (p.67) is a homeopath, a PhD student, a nomad, a proud 'nonna', plant lover and teacher of academic English. Gia is a trainee counsellor with a deep interest in using tarot and dreams as counselling tools. Being of Italian/Irish traveller descent, she still considers herself a nomad, although these days she is settled in Plymouth, UK. Contact via Forage Plymouth Facebook page

Heidi Wyldewood (p.76) is a priestess, wayshower, sacred activist and pilgrim: exploring and teaching spiritual wellbeing and soul crafting via the concepts of living myth, ritual, shadow work, sovereignty, and indigeneity. She lives in the New Forest, England. www: barefoot-heartsong.com

Helen Cuddigan (p.69) was born in England, lived in France and now lives with her two children and partner in the picturesque fishing village of Ballycotton, Co. Cork, Ireland. Working as a freelance Marketing Consultant, she has been benefiting from year-round sea swimming for two years and throughout treatment for breast cancer.

Julie Collet (p.195) is a French photographer, painter, soul healer, weaver and Priestess of the Breton Goddess Dahud. Her roots are in Brittany, France, and it is this ancient Celtic landscape that inspires most of her work. www: juliecolletgoddess.wixsite.com

Khara Scott-Bey (p.215) is an artist, activist, therapist, and priestess whose work is rooted in community-based healing practices, embodied leadership, and pleasure activism. She is a practitioner of Generative Somatics and the Be Present Empowerment Model and Ifá. Currently she's located in New Orleans, Louisiana but also calls Yellow Springs, Ohio home. www: livetobecome.com

Laura Lewis (p.141) is a single home educating mother of three beautifully wild children. The moments she manages to steal away for herself are usually spent reading and writing, most often focused on unpicking and reweaving the meaning of life into something that feels closer to truth. She is also the co creator of Roots + Wings, a platform for women who are walking the path home to themselves. Their offerings, including a twelve-week guided journey and an oracle deck, are designed to support women in traversing the inner terrain of the self: mind, body and soul. IG: @re_weaving

Lina Garvardt (p8) was born in Kazakhstan with Russian, Tatar, German, and Ukrainian roots. In 1996 her family moved to Northern Germany after the collapse of the Soviet Union. She studied Slavic languages and literature (M.A.) in Hamburg, and completed a drama training. Now she is working as a freelance artist. IG: @lina.garvardt

Marsia Shuron Harris, aka **Mother Turtle,** (p.209) is a singer, songwriter, photographer, and fluid art painter. She is also a personal development coach and the creator of "Healing the Stories We Tell Ourselves with Mother Turtle," a workshop she designed to address limiting beliefs. Marsia enjoys rural life in Massachusetts, US and lives on a hilltop where she continues to be inspired by the natural beauty that surrounds her. WWW: motherturtle.com

Melanie Clark Pullen (p.65) is an actress, writer, artist and coach who is passionate about seeing women flourish. She is based in Northern Ireland. WWW: strutandbellow.com

Molly Remer (p.47) is a priestess, creatrix, and teacher. She and her husband Mark co-create original goddess sculptures at Brigid's Grove in rural Missouri, US. Molly is the Womancraft author of *Walking with Persephone* as well as *Womanrunes, Earthprayer,* the *Goddess Devotional, She Lives Her Poems, Sunlight on Cedar, Whole and Holy.* She writes about thealogy, nature, practical priestessing, and the goddess for *Feminism and Religion* and *Sage Woman* magazine. WWW: brigidsgrove.etsy.com

Natalie Bryant Rizzieri (p.96) is a poet, writer, activist, mother, mystic and Womancraft author of *Muddy Mysticism: The Sacred Tethers of Body, Earth, and Everyday.* Her poetry is published in journals such as *Denver Quarterly, Pleaides, Terrain.org,* and *Crab Orchard Review.* She is the founder and director of *Friends of Warm Hearth,* a movement of forever homes for abandoned Armenians with special needs. She lives in Flagstaff, Arizona with her family. WWW: nataliebryantrizzieri.com

Sarah Robinson (p.185) is a yoga teacher, goddess guide and Womancraft author of *Yoga for Witches* and *Yin Magic,* based in in Bath, UK. Her background is in science; she holds an MSc Psychology and Neuroscience and has studied at Bath, Exeter and Harvard Universities. Through work with yoga, meditation and the Goddess temples of Glastonbury and Bristol, she has found a love of combining science, spirit and sparkle both on and off the mat! www. sentiayoga.com

Sharyn Ginyard (p.62) is a professional R & B oldies singer and producer living in Philadelphia, Pennsylvania, as well as a mother, grandmother who still works. A student of kundalini yoga she is presently mentoring in the Emergence Priestess Program with Elisha Halpin and the Heroine's Mystical Journey as an assistant with Megan Moore in state college, Pennsylvania.

Shanta Lee Gander (p.130) is an artist and multi-faceted professional with work that has been featured in *PRISM, ITERANT Literary Magazine, Palette Poetry, BLAVITY, DAME Magazine, The Crisis Magazine, Rebelle Society,* on the Ms. Magazine Blog. The 2020 recipient of the Arthur Williams Award for Meritorious Service to the Arts and 2020, Shanta was named as Diode Editions winner for her debut poetry compilation, *GHETTOCLAUSTROPHOBIA: Dreamin of Mama While Trying to Speak in Woke Tongues.*
   Based in Vermont, US, she offers virtual creativepreneurship workshops. www. shantaleegander.com

Valerie Moran-Clark (p.25) is a writer, artist, and peer support advocate focused on erasing the remaining vestiges of sanism and ableism in the otherwise wonderfully weird worlds of modern witchcraft, social justice, and creative spaces. They live in Massachusetts, US. www. vmoranclark.medium.com

Vanessa Oliver-Lloyd (pp.110, 154) is an archaeologist and an artist. She believes in the healing power of art and ritual and loves to combine the two. She teaches you how to play with your Shadow through art journaling classes at Art Witch Academy (which she co-runs with two other art witches) and on other platforms. Vanessa is a French Canadian currently living in Shanghai. www. artwitchacademy.com

INDEX

ABOUT THE AUTHOR AND ARTIST

Lucy H. Pearce is the author of multiple life-changing non-fiction books, including Nautilus Award silver medal winners *Creatrix: she who makes, Medicine Woman, Burning Woman,* and Amazon number-one bestsellers (in Menstruation), *Moon Time* and (in Art and Hobbies) *The Rainbow Way.* Her writing focuses on women's healing through archetypal psychology, embodiment, historical awareness and creativity.

Her words have been featured internationally online, in print media and books including: *Divergent Mind; If Women Rose Rooted; Goddess: when she rules; Tiny Buddha's Guide to Loving Yourself* and many editions of the *Earth Pathways* and *WeMoon* diaries.

An award-winning graduate in History of Ideas with English Literature from Kingston University and PGCE from Cambridge University, Lucy founded Womancraft Publishing, publishing paradigm-shifting books by women for women, in 2014. She is a multi-faceted creative whose work spans the expressive arts, exploring the lost archetypes of the Feminine. The cover art is her work.

The mother of three children, she lives in a small village by the Celtic Sea in East Cork, Ireland.

lucyhpearce.com
womancraftpublishing.com

ENDNOTES

1. *Le Testament d'Orphee*

2. manchan.com/sea-tamagotchi

3. youtu.be/UkNUu3ZKY9E

4. *Fucking Magic #1* – Clementine Morrigan

5. *Gift from the Sea* – Anne Morrow Lindbergh

6. wakingtimes.com/2014/08/22/shaman-sees-mental-hospital

7. seaweed.ie/qanda

8. manchan.com/sea-tamagotchi

9. bbc.com/travel/
    story/20200805-denmarks-300-year-old-homes-of-the-future

10. *Edible Seaweeds of the World* – Leonel Pereira

11. imj.ie/2743-2/

12. scielo.br/scielo.php?script=sci_arttext&pid=S2359-39972019000600306

13. theguardian.com/environment/2020/oct/27/
    what-victorian-era-seaweed-pressings-reveal-about-our-changing-seas

14. theguardian.com/environment/2020/oct/27/
    what-victorian-era-seaweed-pressings-reveal-about-our-changing-seas

15. ryandrum.com/seaweeds.htm

16. *Blue Mind* – Wallace J. Nichols

17. *Blue Mind* – Wallace J. Nichols

18. Spending at least 120 minutes a week in nature is associated with good
    health and wellbeing. nature.com/articles/s41598-019-44097-3

19. *Blue Mind* – Wallace J. Nichols

20. history.com/news/where-did-the-expression-worth-ones-salt-come-from

21. catholicsacramentals.org/blessed-salt

22. healthline.com/health/halotherapy

23. *Why Women Need Chocolate* – Debra Waterhouse

24. ncbi.nlm.nih.gov/pmc/articles/PMC4455825/

25. *See Colour* – Victoria Finlay and
The Secret Lives of Colour – Kassia St Clair

26. *Underland* – Robert MacFarlane

27. medium.com/exposure-magazine/anna-atkinss-ghost-and-the-conception-of-the-combination-cyanotype-c080a57ba10d

28. Many artists teach classes on them, and the chemicals needed are easily available. The simplest way to start is by purchasing a Sun Print Paper kit. The paper is already coated with the chemicals, and all you need to do is add water, sun and whatever you are wanting to print. This paper is available from some art shops, and Amazon. It is quick and fun for all ages. If you are needing a dose of simple, soothing creativity, contact with the natural world and a big splash of blue, I highly recommend trying this technique.

29. *Fucking Magic #1* – Clementine Morrigan

30. *Thirty-Two Words for Field* – Manchán Magan

31. From *Womb Awakening* – Azra and Seren Bertrand – which in turn is referencing the film *Aluna* by Alan Ereira.

32. cliffsnotes.com/literature/m/mythology/summary-and-analysis-greek-mythology/the-beginnings-8212-creation

33. cs.williams.edu/~lindsey/myths/myths_17.html

34. *A Spell in the Wild* – Alice Tarbuck

35. *Flow* – Mihaly Csikszentmihalyi

36. *Blue Mind* – Wallace J. Nichols

37. maritimemuseum.co.nz/collections/stories-and-blogs/top-20-sailing-superstitions

38. from-ireland.net/fishermen-craftsmen-customs-folk/

39. manchan.com/sea-tamagotchi---teelin--donegal

40. magicseaweed.com/news/abundant-roots-of-women-surfing-a-legacy-of-hawaiian-medicine-women-royalty/12306

41. theguardian.com/sport/2015/aug/04/free-diver-natalia-molchanova-feared-dead

42. bbc.com/news/av/world-44537158/100-women-you-are-truly-free-while-freediving

43. bbc.com/news/av/world-44537158/100-women-you-are-truly-free-while-freediving

44. David Attenborough. "The Waterside Ape"

45. en.wikipedia.org/wiki/Anaximander

46. bbc.com/news/science-environment-56017967

47. *Birth into Being*

48. In Ireland and parts of Scotland, a traditional part of mourning is the keening woman (*Caoineadh* in Irish, pronounced 'kee-na') from *caoin* meaning "to weep or wail". Those who expressed grief best would often be paid to attend funerals and to share their keening songs.

49. See *The Odyssey* and *Circe*.

50. Wikipedia – Mermaids

51. mexicounexplained.com/la-tlanchana-mexican-mermaid-legends

52. *The Book of Cloyne*

53. corkbeo.ie/news/local-news/ballycotton-ghost-ship-still-popular-18747414

54. Coastal.climatecentral.org

55. From "The Physical Setting" by Nollaig O'Shea in *The Book of Cloyne*

56. livescience.com/64176-lost-city-atlantis-spain.html

57. theguardian.com/news/2017/jan/09/how-time-tide-put-paid-dunwich-suffolk-weatherwatch

58. eadt.co.uk/news/weird-suffolk-the-lost-port-of-dunwich-2433298

59. theguardian.com/world/2020/nov/05/arctic-time-capsule-from-2018-washes-up-in-ireland-as-polar-ice-melts

60. theguardian.com/environment/2021/jan/13/climate-crisis-record-ocean-heat-in-2020-supercharged-extreme-weather

61. bbc.co.uk/sounds/play/m0003cm6

62. yaleclimateconnections.org/2020/12/a-look-back-at-the-horrific-2020-atlantic-hurricane-center/

63. yaleclimateconnections.org/2020/12/a-look-back-at-the-horrific-2020-atlantic-hurricane-center/

64. *The Polyvagal Theory in Therapy* – Deb Dana

65. theguardian.com/environment/2021/jan/27/
un-global-climate-poll-peoples-voice-is-clear-they-want-action

66. theguardian.com/lifeandstyle/2021/may/11/post-traumatic-growth-the-
woman-who-learned-to-live-a-profoundly-good-life-after-loss

67. ecoworldonline.com/what-is-seaweed-fabric-fabric-from-the-ocean/

68. breakingnews.ie/world/seaweed-study-helps-make-washing-clothes-
environmentally-friendly-1016237.html

69. bellona.org

70. theguardian.com/environment/2021/mar/18/
cows-seaweed-methane-emissions-scientists

71. fao.org/state-of-forests

72. *Seaspiracy*

73. waterencyclopedia.com/Bi-Ca/Carbon-Dioxide-in-the-Ocean-and-
Atmosphere.html

74. theguardian.com/science/2020/sep/15/welsh-seagrass-meadow-global-
restoration-pembrokeshire-climate-plant-project

75. bbc.com/news/uk-england-devon-56819082

76. theguardian.com/environment/2021/mar/26/
marine-biological-association-young-writers-ocean-decade-challenge

77. protectedplanet.net/en/thematic-areas/marine-protected-areas

78. *Seaspiracy*

79. en.wikipedia.org/wiki/Ellen_MacArthur

80. ellenmacarthurfoundation.org/circular-economy/
what-is-the-circular-economy

81. travelandleisure.com/style/beauty/reef-safe-sunscreen

82. *The More Beautiful World Our Hearts Know is Possible*
– Charles Eisenstein

83. etymonline.com/word/psyche

ABOUT WOMANCRAFT

Womancraft Publishing was founded on the revolutionary vision that women and words can change the world. We act as midwife to transformational women's words that have the power to challenge, inspire, heal and speak to the silenced aspects of ourselves.

We believe that:

› books are a fabulous way of transmitting powerful transformation,

› values should be juicy actions, lived out,

› ethical business is a key way to contribute to conscious change.

At the heart of our Womancraft philosophy is fairness and integrity. Creatives and women have always been underpaid. Not on our watch! We split royalties 50:50 with our authors. We work on a full circle model of giving and receiving: reaching backwards, supporting TreeSisters' reforestation projects, and forwards via Worldreader, providing books at no cost to education projects for girls and women.

We are proud that Womancraft is walking its talk and engaging so many women each year via our books and online. Join the revolution! Sign up to the mailing list at womancraftpublishing.com and find us on social media for exclusive offers:

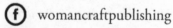 womancraftpublishing

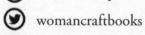 womancraftbooks

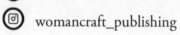 womancraft_publishing

Signed copies of all titles available from
shop.womancraftpublishing.com

Burning Woman

Lucy H. Pearce

2017 Nautilus Award Winner in the program's 'Women' category of books for and about Women's journey. A breath-taking and controversial woman's journey through history – personal and cultural – on a quest to find and free her own power.

Uncompromising and all-encompassing, Pearce uncovers the archetype of the Burning Women of days gone by – Joan of Arc and the witch trials, through to the way women are burned today in cyber bullying, acid attacks, shaming and burnout, fearlessly examining the roots of Feminine power – what it is, how it has been controlled, and why it needs to be unleashed on the world in our modern Burning Times.

A must-read for all women! A life-changing book that fills the reader with a burning passion and desire for change.
Glennie Kindred, author of *Earth Wisdom*

Creatrix: She Who Makes

Lucy H. Pearce

2019 Nautilus Award Winner in the program's 'Women' category of books.

*Creatrix is more than just a fancy name for a female artist. She is artist **plus**…artist plus priestess, artist plus healer, artist plus activist: her work has both sacred and worldly dimensions. She is an energy worker first and foremost, weaving energy into form, colour, words and sound, in order to transform herself and those her creations touch.*

What does it mean to live a life in service to your creativity, and in direct connection to the creative source?

With Creative Inquiries and Practices, this interactive book is written for all those that must create in order to live: for the Highly Creative, the Highly Sensitive, the multi-passionate, for those that shake when they share… Soulful, serious-minded, irreverent and authentic, let Creatrix take you on a journey to the heart of your creative soul.

Muddy Mysticism:
The Sacred Tethers of Body, Earth and Everyday

Natalie Bryant Rizzieri

Muddy Mysticism is a spiritual memoir, a lyrical articulation of an emergent feminist mysticism and a heartfelt response to the lack of mystical literature by women who have chosen a life of family, love, work and the world. Like many women she found the faith of her childhood no longer fitted…yet still there is a longing for the sacred. Through poetry, reflection and experience she moves into the possibility of direct experience with the divine…beyond a belief system. Exploring the possibility of daily life in the modern world not as something to be transcended or escaped…but as a mystical path in its own right.

The Way of the Seabhean:
An Irish Shamanic Path

Amantha Murphy

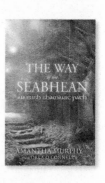

"The seabhean ('sha-van') is the Irish female shaman, healer and seer, the woman who walks between the worlds."
What if we didn't have to look to other traditions for our spiritual practice?
What if we could connect to the roots of our own ancestors' rituals?

Amantha Murphy was schooled in the ancient and hidden lore of wise women and healers, rooted in the Irish landscape and guarded over the years by her female forebears. In *The Way of the Seabhean,* she brings to life shamanic practices from the Irish tradition, combining story, ritual, energy teaching and the insights gathered from her own shamanic journeying.

At its core lies the pre-Celtic understanding of the Tree of Life and the Wheel of the Year, containing the seasonal turning points such as Samhain and Imbolc, their attendant festivals and the role and powers of long-suppressed Irish goddesses. Along with the better-known goddesses, Medb, Brigid, Áine and the Cailleach, we also meet a pantheon that includes Tailtiú, Boann, Macha, Tlachtga. These goddesses are archetypes, aspects of ourselves, which can help us to understand and embrace our many facets.

The Other Side of the River:
Stories of Women, Water and the World

Eila Carrico

A deep searching into the ways we become dammed and how we recover fluidity. A journey through memory and time, personal and shared landscapes to discover the source, the flow and the deltas of women and water.

Rooted in rivers, inspired by wetlands, sources and tributaries, this book weaves its path between the banks of memory and story, from Florida to Kyoto, storm-ravaged New Orleans to London, via San Francisco and Ghana. We navigate through flood and drought to confront the place of wildness in the age of technology.

Part memoir, part manifesto, part travelogue and part love letter to myth and ecology, The Other Side of the River is an intricately woven tale of finding your flow…and your roots.

Walking with Persephone

Molly Remer

Midlife can be a time of great change – inner and outer: a time of letting go of the old, burnout and disillusionment. But how do we journey through this? And what can we learn in the process? Molly Remer is our personal guide to the unraveling and reweaving required in midlife. She invites you to take a walk with the goddess Persephone, whose story of descent into the underworld has much to teach us.

Walking with Persephone is a story of devotion and renewal that weaves together personal experiences, insights, observations, and reflections with experiences in practical priestessing, family life, and explorations of the natural world. It advocates opening our eyes to the wonder around us, encouraging the reader to both look within themselves for truths about living, but also to the earth, the air, the sky, the animals, and plants.

Part memoir, part poetry, part soul guide, Molly's evocative voice is in the great American tradition of sacred nature writing.

Made in the USA
Monee, IL
02 January 2022